VOCABULARY CONTROL
FOR
INFORMATION RETRIEVAL

Vocabulary Control FOR INFORMATION RETRIEVAL

Second Edition

F. W. LANCASTER

Professor
Graduate School of Library Science
University of Illinois

INFORMATION RESOURCES PRESS
Arlington, Virginia
1986

Available from
Information Resources Press
1700 North Moore Street
Suite 700
Arlington, Virginia 22209

Z
695
L25
1986

Library of Congress Catalog Card Number 84-082260

ISBN 0-87815-053-6

The Author

Frederick Wilfrid Lancaster is a professor in the Graduate School of Library and Information Science, University of Illinois, where he teaches courses in information storage and retrieval, evaluation of information services, and bibliometrics.

Professor Lancaster is the author of more than 30 papers and reports in his fields of specialization. One of his papers, "MEDLARS: Report on the Evaluation of Its Operating Efficiency," was judged the Best American Documentation Paper for 1969. He is also the author of numerous books, including *Information Retrieval Systems: Characteristics, Testing, and Evaluation*, 2nd Edition (Wiley, 1979), for which he received the American Society for Information Science Best Information Sciences Book Award in 1970 (1st Edition); *Vocabulary Control for Information Retrieval* (Information Resources Press, 1972); *Information Retrieval On-Line* (Melville, 1973), for which he received the 1975 American Society for Information Science Best Information Sciences Book Award; *The Measurement and Evaluation of Library Services* (Information Resources Press, 1977), for which he received the 1978 ALA Ralph R. Shaw Award for Outstanding Contribution to Library Literature and which was selected in 1985 by the ALA Reference and Adult Services Division as one of the 25 most distinguished reference titles published during the past 25 years; *Toward Paperless Information Systems* (Academic Press, 1978), for which he received the 1979 American Society for Information Science Best Information Sciences Book Award; and *Libraries and Librarians in an Age of Electronics* (Information Resources Press, 1982). He is co-author with John Martyn of *Investigative Methods in Library and Information Science: an Introduction* (Information Resources Press, 1981).

In 1980, Professor Lancaster received the first Outstanding Information Science Teacher Award from the American Society for Information Science.

Preface

The earlier edition of this book, which was published in 1972, was perhaps the first monograph devoted exclusively to all aspects of vocabulary control in information retrieval applications. Although this subject ages more slowly than many other branches of information science, it is by no means static, and a new edition has been needed for some time. Therefore, I hope that this second edition proves useful to those making decisions regarding vocabulary control for data bases of various types, for those involved in the construction of thesauri, and for teachers and students of information retrieval.

In the first edition, a deliberate attempt was made to comprehensively review the relevant literature. This approach seemed appropriate then, but it no longer seems necessary. In this edition, I have chosen to cite only those sources most directly related to the points I want to make. A slight change has also been made in the scope of the book. The second edition, unlike the first, is devoted almost exclusively to the thesaurus or to thesaurus-like aids to natural-language searching.

I would like to thank Derek Austin, who offered a number of helpful suggestions for Chapter 5, and Jean Aitchison and Amy Warner, who reviewed the entire text. I also would like to thank Kathy Painter, who did her usual superb job in typing the manuscript.

Contents

Exhibits

1 *Why Vocabulary Control?*

In information retrieval systems, it is usually necessary to control the vocabulary used to describe the subject matter being dealt with. *Vocabulary Control for Information Retrieval,* as the title indicates, discusses various aspects of vocabulary control within the information retrieval context. In particular, it focuses on the *thesaurus,* since this is the vocabulary control device that has been used most in information retrieval applications during the past 20 years. Nevertheless, other approaches also are considered, including the operation of information retrieval systems without vocabulary control.

The major components of a typical information retrieval system are presented in Exhibit 1. The input consists of documents (this term is used in its broadest sense to encompass printed and other records of all types) acquired by the information center that implements the system. This implies the existence of selection criteria and policies, which, in turn, implies a detailed and accurate knowledge of the information needs of the community to be served. Once the documents are acquired, they need to be "organized and controlled"

1

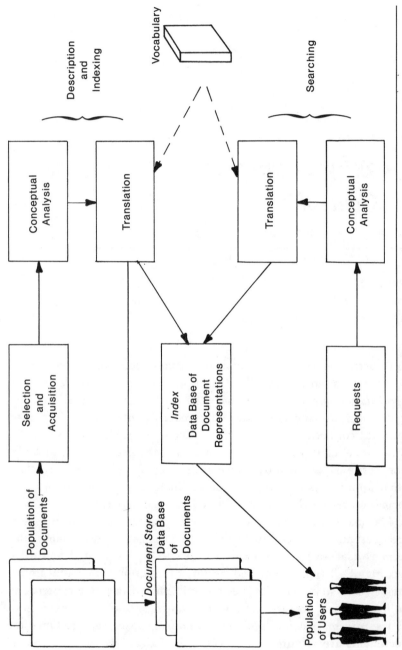

Exhibit 1   The major components of an information retrieval system.

so that they can be identified and located in response to various types of user demand. Organization and control activities include classification, cataloging, subject indexing, and abstracting. Two important elements are the physical description of the document (*descriptive cataloging*) and the choice of access points (e.g., authors, titles) to make the description findable in catalogs and bibliographies.

As depicted in Exhibit 1, the subject indexing process involves two quite distinct intellectual steps: the "conceptual analysis" of a document and the "translation" of the conceptual analysis into a particular vocabulary. For efficient conceptual analysis, the indexer needs both an understanding of the document's subject matter and a good knowledge of the needs of the system's users.

The second step in the indexing process is the translation of the conceptual analysis into a particular vocabulary. In most systems, this involves a "controlled vocabulary," that is, a limited set of terms that must be used to represent the subject matter of documents. Such a vocabulary might be a list of subject headings, a classification scheme, a thesaurus, or simply a list of "approved" keywords or phrases.

Once indexing has been completed, the documents are entered into some form of document store (document data base) and the indexing records into a second data base, where they are organized in such a way that they can be conveniently searched in response to various types of subject (and other) requests. The data base of indexing records, or "document representations," may be as simple as a card file or an index in printed form. In a modern setting, however, this data base is more likely to be a machine-readable file on magnetic tape or disk; it can be regarded as the "index" to the document store. The index depicted in Exhibit 1 consists of a bibliographic description of each document in the collection, along with various access points to make this representation retrievable not only by terms describing its subject matter but also by such characteristics as author and title.

A bibliographic (document) data base is assumed in the diagram. The steps will not change significantly if a different type of data base is involved (e.g., a numerical file or what tends to be referred to in Europe as a *data bank*). The contents must still be indexed to make them accessible, but the "document store" could be replaced by machine-readable tables of data (physical, chemical, numerical, statistical).

The steps involved at the output side of the service are very similar to those involved at input. The user population to be served submits various requests to the information center, and members of the center's staff prepare search strategies for the requests. It is convenient to consider the preparation of search strategies as also involving the two steps of conceptual analysis and translation. The first step involves an analysis of the request to determine what the user is really looking for, and the second involves the translation of the conceptual analysis into the vocabulary of the system. The conceptual analysis of the request, translated into the language of the system, is the *search strategy*, which can be regarded as a request representation in the same way that an indexing record can be regarded as a document representation. The only real difference between the two is that the former usually contains "logic" (i.e., a certain set of logical relationships among the terms is specified), whereas, in the latter, the logical relationships among terms are more likely to be implicit than explicit.

Once the search strategy has been prepared, it is "matched" in some way against the data base of document representations. This can involve a search of card files, printed indexes, microfilm, or magnetic tape or disk. In a contemporary setting, the search might be performed from an on-line terminal at some library although the data base being searched is loaded on a computer hundreds or thousands of miles from the searcher. Document representations that match the search strategy—that is, satisfy the logical requirements of the search—are retrieved from the data base and delivered to the requester, either printed out or displayed at a terminal. The process is completed when the requester is satisfied with the results of the search. (In some cases, this may mean that he is persuaded that nothing in the data base exactly meets his needs.)

Exhibit 1 clearly indicates the central role played by the vocabulary in a typical retrieval system. Indexers are required to use terms from this vocabulary to describe the subject matter of documents. The same terms must also be used in the search strategies through which the data base is interrogated. One can get some idea of what might occur if the system operated without vocabulary control by examining the list of terms in Exhibit 2. All these terms (and the list is certainly far from complete) could conceivably have something to do with the process of "joining" (i.e., of materials such as metals and plastics). The list contains a wide variety of types of terms: Some (such as bonding, brazing, gluing, and welding) represent joining processes; some (such as plates and sheets) represent things that can

Adhesion	Inert gases
Adhesives	Mechanical joints
Alloys	Nailed joints
Arc welding	Nails
Bonded joints	Oxidation
Bonding	Panels
Bonds	Plates
Brazed joints	Rupture
Brazing	Screwed joints
Brazing alloys	Screws
Brittleness	Sheets
Cements	Shielded arc welding
Corrosion	Shielding gases
Cracking	Soldering
Deterioration	Soldering irons
Failure	Solders
Fatigue	Stiffened joints
Fracture	Strength
Gas welding	Stress
Gases	Submerged arc welding
Glued joints	Tensile strength
Glues	Weldability
Gluing	Welding
Gums	Welding rods
Hinged joints	Welding torches

Exhibit 2   Select list of terms dealing with joining of materials.

be joined; others represent types of joints (bonded, nailed, welded); and yet others refer to substances (glues, solders) or tools (soldering irons, welding rods) used in joining, to properties of materials or joints (brittleness, strength), or to processes that may affect joints (corrosion, deterioration, and so on).

These terms might appear in an alphabetic subject catalog or an alphabetic subject index (e.g., of an encyclopedia or an abstracting service), where they would be interspersed with many other terms that relate to other topics. In such a case, various problems arise for the person looking for information on joining. First, some of the terms listed mean virtually the same thing; that is, they are synonyms or near synonyms. An example is "panels" and "plates"; at a more technical level, "shielded arc welding" might be considered synonymous with "submerged arc welding." If such terminological distinctions are not worth making within the context of a particular field, it would certainly seem desirable to merge the nearly synonymous terms by choosing one and referring from the other, as in the following example:

Panels → Plates

Another problem arises because some words are ambiguous if taken out of context. Thus, "bonds" could refer to a type of security (investment) rather than to joints, and "nails" could refer to fasteners or to parts of the body. It would be desirable to reduce such ambiguity—for instance, by using a parenthetical qualifier:

Nails (fasteners)

Perhaps the most serious problem, however, is that terms with related meanings are widely separated alphabetically. Although it is unlikely that anyone would want to perform a search on every aspect of joining, it is certainly possible that someone would want to retrieve all information dealing with one form of joining, say, adhesive bonding. The alphabetic sequence, unfortunately, separates many terms bearing on this topic: adhesives, bonded joints, cements, glues, gums, and so on. Again, it would be useful to the seeker of the information if all the terms whose meanings were related were linked in some way, as in the following example:

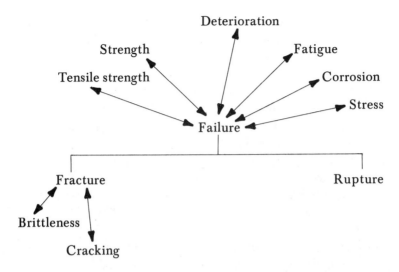

Note that two kinds of relationships are depicted in this diagram. First, there is the permanent relationship between a thing and kinds of that thing (i.e., between a genus and its species): Fracture and rupture are always kinds of failure. Second, there is a more transient relationship; for example, the *process* of failure may be induced by other processes such as corrosion and fatigue, and it may be influenced by such material properties as strength and brittleness. The permanent generic relationship is sometimes referred to as a paradigmatic relationship or an a priori relationship, whereas the more transient relationship (failure may be due to corrosion but is not always due to corrosion, and corrosion does not always lead to failure) is sometimes referred to as a syntagmatic or an a posteriori relationship.

These examples, based on the terms illustrated in Exhibit 2, clearly demonstrate the objectives of vocabulary control within an information retrieval system. These objectives can be summarized as follows

1. To promote the consistent representation of subject matter by indexers and searchers, thereby avoiding the dispersion of related materials. This is achieved through the control (merging) of synonymous and nearly synonymous expressions and by distinguishing among homographs.

2. To facilitate the conduct of a comprehensive search on some topic by linking together terms whose meanings are related paradigmatically or syntagmatically.

Indexing tends to be more consistent when the vocabulary used is controlled. Indexers are more likely to agree on the terms needed to describe a particular topic if they are selected from a pre-established list than when given a free hand to use any terms they wish. The same is true for the process of searching: It is easier to identify the terms appropriate to some information need if these terms must be selected from a definitive list. The controlled vocabulary, then, tends to bring the language of indexers and of searchers into coincidence.

A controlled vocabulary need be nothing more than a limited set of terms that must be used by both the indexer and the searcher. More commonly, however, some structure will be imposed on the terms so that those whose meanings are related are brought together or linked in some way. This helps both the indexer and the searcher select the best terms to represent a particular topic. Perhaps more important, it helps the user identify all the terms needed to perform a comprehensive search on some subject.

2 *Pre-coordinate and Post-coordinate Systems*

Classification pervades information retrieval activities. Indexing is obviously a classification process. When an indexer determines that a particular document deals with the effect of television on the reading abilities of preschool children and assigns to the document the terms PRESCHOOL CHILDREN, TELEVISION, and READING ABILITY, he is, in effect, assigning the document to three classes identified by these terms; that is, the indexer groups the document with others that have previously been placed in one or another of these classes. The terms used by the indexer to represent subject matter can be considered labels that identify various classes. They can legitimately be called *class labels*, although they are more commonly referred to as *index terms* or *descriptors*. The complete set of terms used to describe subject matter within a particular data base is sometimes known as an *index language*. Clearly, a *controlled vocabulary* is a type of index language in which the terminology is controlled.

Classification also is evident in the way a data base is searched. Search strategy involves deciding which classes, represented in some data base, are likely to contain items relevant to a particular information need and then interrogating the system in such a way that the members of these classes are retrieved. This implies the ability to combine classes so that the only items retrieved are those that satisfy a particular logical requirement. If one wants information on the reading abilities of preschoolers, only items that appear in *both* the class PRE-SCHOOL CHILDREN and the class READING ABILITY should be retrieved.

For effective information retrieval, complete flexibility in combining classes is essential. Consider, for example, a document indexed under the following terms: LAKES, WATER POLLUTION, MERCURY COMPOUNDS, and FISH. Presumably, this document deals with the effect on fish of lake pollution caused by mercury compounds. Not only should this document be retrievable in response to a search for the precise topic, represented by the interrelationship of the four classes, but it should also be retrievable in response to a search involving *any level of relationship* among the four classes (e.g., FISH and MERCURY COMPOUNDS; WATER POLLUTION and LAKES; MERCURY COMPOUNDS and WATER POLLUTION and FISH), since it can be considered relevant to any of these relationships. Herein lies the fundamental difference between pre-coordinate and post-coordinate retrieval systems. (Soergel, 1974, uses "pre-combination" and "post-combination" to distinguish the two types of systems.)

The distinction is depicted in Exhibit 3. A document has been indexed under four terms (i.e., assigned to four classes). In a post-coordinate system, the multidimensionality of the relationship among the four classes can be retained: No sequence of classes is needed, so all carry equal weight, and the document can be retrieved regardless of which combination of the four terms the searcher uses. This is true for all computer-based systems (off-line and on-line), for microfilm retrieval systems, and for various predecessors of modern systems (peek-a-boo cards, punched cards, edge-notched cards). When a subject index is implemented by means of printed pages or in the form of a conventional card catalog, however, true multidimensionality is sacrificed. It is possible to build an entry in which all index terms are retained, but, clearly, the terms must be arranged in a linear sequence, and access to the document can be made only through the first term in the

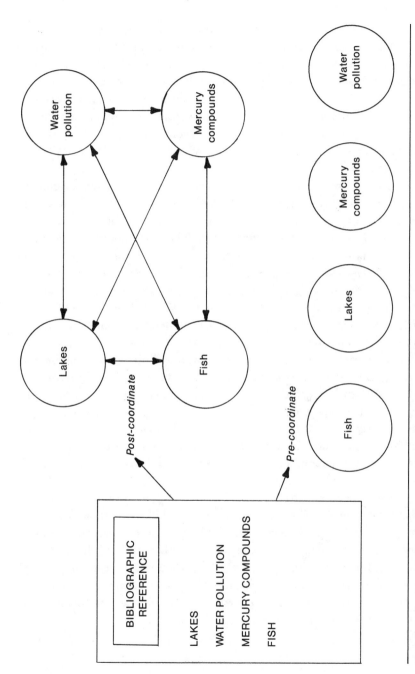

Exhibit 3 Comparison of pre-coordinate and post-coordinate systems.

string. For instance, in Exhibit 3, the index entry FISH, LAKES, MERCU-RY COMPOUNDS, WATER POLLUTION allows retrieval only if the user enters the index under FISH, the other terms being subdivisions or modifiers of this term. This type of index is referred to as pre-coordinate: Classes are coordinated (combined) in a particular sequence at the time the index is constructed; the user of the index cannot freely combine classes and cannot conveniently retrieve a document from any aspect not explicitly provided for in the construction of the index.

Entries can be duplicated in a pre-coordinate index, and a number of procedures exist for arriving at the set of required entries (or, in some cases, a single entry with cross-references) in a systematic manner, possibly through computer programs. These methods include systematic rotation, as used in the indexes of *Excerpta Medica* and *Applied Mechanics Reviews* (Juhasz et al., 1980); the SLIC index (Sharp, 1966); chain indexing (Wilson, 1971); preferred ordering, as used, for example, in the *British Technology Index* (Coates, 1960); and PRECIS (Foskett, 1982). By duplicating entries in a pre-coordinate index, one can provide multiple access points, but, for reasons of space and cost, there tends to be an upper limit on the number of access points possible, which is much less true for the post-coordinate index. Moreover, regardless of how many access points are provided, the pre-coordinate index still fails to give the user the ability to freely manipulate classes that the post-coordinate system does. It is for this reason that the two types are sometimes referred to as *manipulative* (post-coordinate) and *nonmanipulative* (pre-coordinate) (Bernier, 1956).

In the pre-coordinate example in Exhibit 3, an alphabetic subject index is assumed. Similar limitations would apply to a pre-coordinate index in which the terms used are notations derived from a classification schedule. For example, the index entry could look like AbEfGccKp, where Ab represents "fish," Ef "lakes," and so on.

Vocabulary control is as applicable to pre-coordinate systems as it is to post-coordinate systems. Nevertheless, the emphasis of this book is vocabulary control in post-coordinate systems.

3 *Vocabulary Structure and Display*

In general, a controlled vocabulary should have two complementary components: some systematic organization of terms and an alphabetic listing of these terms. The components can be separate or completely integrated.

OVERT CLASSIFICATIONS

One possible way to systematically display a vocabulary is as a "tree structure," which closely resembles the genealogical family tree. An example appears in Exhibit 4. Note that the display reflects true genus/species relationships: "Moving picture cameras" is one of four species of "cameras"; "cine cameras" is one of two species of "moving picture cameras"; and so on. One of the terms, "underwater cine cameras," actually has two genera—underwater cameras and cine cameras.

If a vocabulary were displayed in this way, each tree (hierarchy) would occupy a separate page. The resulting printed tool would resemble an atlas, each page being a "map" of the terminology of a

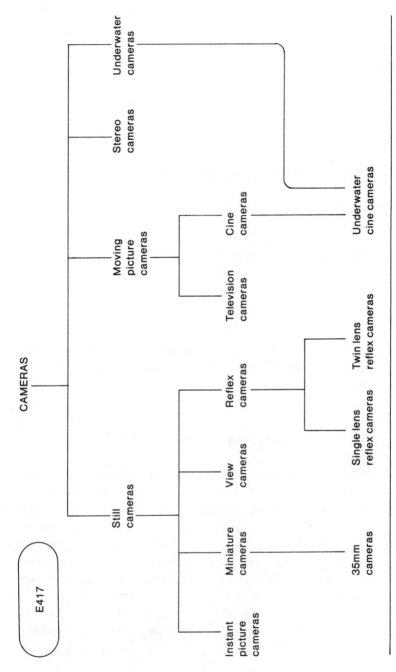

Exhibit 4   Tree structure display. Reprinted from *Guidelines for the Establishment and Development of Monolingual Thesauri* (1981) by permission of Unesco.

particular subject; the map in Exhibit 4 is identified by the number E417. Some form of cross-referencing could be built into the maps to link related maps (in much the same way that one road map will lead to another), although no such references are given in this exhibit. For example, the entire "cameras" map could be linked to another map, "photography"; "underwater cameras" could be linked to "underwater exploration"; and so on. Even if such references were built into the maps, an alphabetic index to the maps would still be necessary. Exhibit 5 shows sample entries from such an index. Note that this index does more than refer to the map on which a particular term appears; it provides cross-references to related maps, so that photography is linked to cameras, underwater cameras to diving, and so on. The convention used is RT, which means "related term."

The sample index entries also show synonym control. "Land cameras" and "view cameras" are treated as synonymous; the user enter-

```
35mm CAMERAS    E417

CAMERAS    E417
   RT: Photography    R562

CINE CAMERAS    E417
   RT: Cinema    R668

CINEMA    R668
   RT: Cine cameras    E417

DIVING    T473
   RT: Underwater cameras    E417

INSTANT PICTURE CAMERAS    E417
   SN: Cameras which produce a
       finished print directly

Land cameras    USE    VIEW CAMERAS

MINIATURE CAMERAS    E417

MOVING PICTURE CAMERAS    E417

PHOTOGRAPHY    R562
   RT: CAMERAS    E417

REFLEX CAMERAS    E417

SINGLE LENS REFLEX CAMERAS    E417
```

```
STEREO CAMERAS    E417

STILL CAMERAS    E417

TELEVISION    R685
   RT: Television cameras    E417

TELEVISION CAMERAS    E417
   RT: Television    R685

TWIN LENS REFLEX CAMERAS    E417

UNDERWATER CAMERAS    E417
   RT: Diving    T473

UNDERWATER CINE CAMERAS    E417

VIEW CAMERAS    E417
   SN: Cameras with through-the-lens
       focusing and a range of
       movements of the lens plane
       relative to the film plane
   UF: Land cameras
```

Exhibit 5 Example of entries from alphabetic index to a tree structure display. Reprinted from *Guidelines for the Establishment and Development of Monolingual Thesauri* [1981] by permission of Unesco.

ing the list under the former term is referred to ("use") the latter. This relationship is reciprocated: Under "view cameras," one is told that this term is used for ("UF") land cameras. Finally, terms whose meanings may not be immediately obvious are given a scope note ("SN"), a brief definition of how the term is used within the system to which this vocabulary relates.

The vocabulary depicted in Exhibits 4 and 5 satisfies all the objectives of a controlled vocabulary: Synonyms are controlled, and related terms are brought together to help the indexer and searcher select the most appropriate term to represent a particular topic and to help the searcher identify *all* terms needed to complete a comprehensive search on some subject. The paradigmatic relationship is taken care of by the tree structure of the index language, and the syntagmatic relationship is covered by the related terms. Moreover, the vocabulary has both systematic display and alphabetic display components.

The vocabulary illustrated can be considered a type of classification scheme with complementary alphabetic index. It is a perfectly acceptable way to implement a controlled vocabulary, with two exceptions. First, for very large hierarchies, display problems might be encountered (e.g., cameras could be one element of a much larger "equipment" hierarchy). Second, if the vocabulary is extensive, this method of display might be uneconomical because of the amount of space it occupies.

A more common type of classification scheme (resembling bibliographic classification schemes used in libraries) is shown in Exhibit 6. In Exhibit 6A, the tree structure of Exhibit 4 is presented as a "systematic" display. This is more compact than the tree structure, but it does have disadvantages. Even though indentation is used to show hierarchical levels, these levels are not as easily grasped as they are in the tree structure. Moreover, it is not immediately obvious that "underwater cine cameras" is subordinate to both "cine cameras" and "underwater cameras"; in fact, the term appears in two places, which is both confusing and ambiguous, since in one place it is given the notation 305 and in another, 317.

Exhibit 6A also illustrates an important point that seems to confuse some students of library science. The numbering system ("notation") that appears alongside the terms serves only to maintain the sequence of the printed systematic display and to act as a convenient "shorthand" to represent the terms (especially on the spines of books arranged on library shelves). The exhibit would be just as much a classification of camera terminology if the notation were removed, just as Exhibit 4—without notation—is a true classification of this terminology presented in a different way.

The systematic display of Exhibit 6A also requires an alphabetic index, illustrated in Exhibit 6B. Unlike Exhibits 4 and 5, however, Exhibits 6A and 6B are not perfectly complementary. There is considerable redundancy because the RT references and even the scope notes are duplicated in the two components. Nevertheless, the vocabulary depicted does satisfy the requirements for a controlled vocabulary, as stated in Chapter 1.

COVERT CLASSIFICATIONS

A third display possibility is shown in Exhibit 7. In this case, the terms from Exhibit 4 have been rearranged in alphabetic order and interspersed with terms from other hierarchies. The most important thing to note about this display is that it, too, perfectly reproduces the hierarchy of Exhibit 4. In this case, the genus of a term is referred to as a "broader term" (BT) and each species of a term is referred to as a "narrower term" (NT). One can see, for example, that "Reflex cameras" is a species of "still cameras" (i.e., it acknowledges "Still cameras" as its genus or BT) and that "reflex cameras" has two species (NTs). These relationships perfectly reciprocate: "Underwater cameras" shows "cameras" as its BT, and "cameras" shows "underwater cameras" as one of its NTs.

Although the display is overtly alphabetic, it is obvious that this BT/NT relationship constitutes a covert classification. In fact, it would not have been possible to arrive at this display without first developing the hierarchy shown in Exhibit 4. Exhibit 4 can be derived from Exhibit 7, and Exhibit 7 from Exhibit 4. Furthermore, it is possible to write a computer program to derive the BT/NT structure of Exhibit 7 from the tree structure of Exhibit 4 and vice versa.

A

301 OPTICAL EQUIPMENT
302 CAMERAS
     RT: Photography 824
     By medium
303 MOVING PICTURE CAMERAS
304 CINE CAMERAS
     RT: CINEMA 895
305 UNDERWATER CINE CAMERAS
306 TELEVISION CAMERAS
     RT: Television 897
307 STEREO CAMERAS
308 STILL CAMERAS
309 INSTANT PICTURE CAMERAS
     SN: Cameras which produce
     a finished print
     directly
310 MINIATURE CAMERAS
311 35mm CAMERAS
312 REFLEX CAMERAS
313 SINGLE LENS REFLEX CAMERAS
314 TWIN LENS REFLEX CAMERAS
315 VIEW CAMERAS
     SN: Cameras with through-

B

35mm CAMERAS 311
CAMERAS 302
     RT: Photography 824
CINE CAMERAS 304
     RT: Cinema 895
CINEMA 895
     RT: Cine cameras 304
DIVING 931
     RT: Underwater cameras 316
INSTANT PICTURE CAMERAS 309
     SN: Cameras which produce a
     finished print directly
Land cameras *USE* VIEW CAMERAS 315
MICROSCOPES 318
MINIATURE CAMERAS 310
MOVING PICTURE CAMERAS 303
OPTICAL EQUIPMENT 301
PHOTOGRAPHY 824
     RT: Cameras 302

the-lens focusing and
a range of movements
of the lens plane
relative to the film
plane

    UF: Land cameras

316 UNDERWATER CAMERAS
    RT: Diving 931
317 UNDERWATER CINE CAMERAS
318 MICROSCOPES

REFLEX CAMERAS 312

SINGLE LENS REFLEX CAMERAS 313

STEREO CAMERAS 307

STILL CAMERAS 308

TELEVISION 897
    RT: Television cameras 306

TELEVISION CAMERAS 306
    RT: Television 897

TWIN LENS REFLEX CAMERAS 314

UNDERWATER CAMERAS 316
    RT: Diving 931

UNDERWATER CINE CAMERAS 305; 317

VIEW CAMERAS 315
    SN: Cameras with through-the-lens
    focusing and a range of
    movements of the lens plane
    relative to the film plane
    UF: Land cameras

Exhibit 6 A: Systematic display. **B:** Alphabetic index to systematic display. Reprinted from *Guidelines for the Establishment and Development of Monolingual Thesauri* (1981) by permission of Unesco.

35mm CAMERAS
   BT: MINIATURE CAMERAS

CAMERAS
   BT: OPTICAL EQUIPMENT
   NT: MOVING PICTURE CAMERAS
      STEREO CAMERAS
      STILL CAMERAS
      UNDERWATER CAMERAS
   RT: PHOTOGRAPHY

CINE CAMERAS
   BT: MOVING PICTURE CAMERAS
   NT: UNDERWATER CINE CAMERAS
   RT: CINEMA

CINEMA
   RT: CINE CAMERAS

DIVING
   RT: UNDERWATER CAMERAS

INSTANT PICTURE CAMERAS
   SN: Cameras which produce a
   .   finished print·directly
   BT: STILL CAMERAS

Land cameras *USE* VIEW CAMERAS

MICROSCOPES
   BT: OPTICAL EQUIPMENT

MINIATURE CAMERAS
   BT: STILL CAMERAS
   NT: 35mm CAMERAS

MOVING PICTURE CAMERAS
   BT: CAMERAS
   NT: CINE CAMERAS
      TELEVISION CAMERAS

OPTICAL EQUIPMENT
   NT: CAMERAS
      MICROSCOPES

PHOTOGRAPHY
   RT: CAMERAS

REFLEX CAMERAS
   BT: STILL CAMERAS
   NT: SINGLE LENS REFLEX CAMERAS
      TWIN LENS REFLEX CAMERAS

SINGLE LENS REFLEX CAMERAS
   BT: REFLEX CAMERAS

STEREO CAMERAS
   BT: CAMERAS

STILL CAMERAS
   BT: CAMERAS
   NT: INSTANT PICTURE CAMERAS
      MINIATURE CAMERAS
      REFLEX CAMERAS
      VIEW CAMERAS

TELEVISION
   RT: TELEVISION CAMERAS

TELEVISION CAMERAS
   SN: Cameras for both broadcasting
      and videotape recording
   BT: MOVING PICTURE CAMERAS
   RT: TELEVISION

TWIN LENS REFLEX CAMERAS
   BT: REFLEX CAMERAS

UNDERWATER CAMERAS
   BT: CAMERAS
   NT: UNDERWATER CINE CAMERAS
   RT: DIVING

UNDERWATER CINE CAMERAS
   BT: CINE CAMERAS
      UNDERWATER CAMERAS

VIEW CAMERAS
   SN: Cameras with through-the-lens
      focusing and a range of movements
      of the lens plane relative to the
      film plane
   UF: Land cameras
   BT: STILL CAMERAS

Exhibit 7   Alphabetic display with covert classification. Reprinted from *Guidelines for the Establishment and Development of Monolingual Thesauri* (1981) by permission of Unesco.

Note that Exhibit 7 also incorporates the synonym control (*use* reference), the RT structure, and the scope notes seen in the earlier displays. It also satisfies the requirements for a controlled vocabulary. Moreover, since the display is alphabetic, with the hierarchy covertly embedded through a cross-reference structure, it satisfies these requirements in a single display; that is, alphabetic and systematic displays are combined. Of course, one still cannot take in the complete hierarchy in a single glance as one can with a tree structure; the hierarchy can only be reconstructed by following the BT/NT paths. For this reason, it might be useful to retain some overtly hierarchical display (Exhibit 4 or Exhibit 6A without the notation and the redundant elements) as a complement to Exhibit 7.

Exhibit 7 is a typical *thesaurus* display. As demonstrated, a properly constructed thesaurus is usually overtly alphabetic and covertly systematic. Exhibit 7 contains a hierarchical classification that is as perfect as those of Exhibits 4 and 6A.

The next several chapters cover the construction of thesauri—the collection of the raw material (i.e., terms) and the organization of this raw material to form a consistent and effective tool for information retrieval. An underlying assumption is that the construction of a *new* thesaurus is necessary. Actually, an information center would be well advised to consider the possibility that some existing thesaurus could be adopted or adapted to meet local needs. Another possibility would be to construct a microthesaurus to fit within the hierarchical structure of some more general thesaurus. Such approaches would probably be less expensive than building a completely new tool; moreover, they promote compatibility and avoid the proliferation of similar, overlapping vocabularies.

4 Gathering the Raw Material

Chapter 3 presented several ways in which the vocabulary of a subject field can be displayed. Now let us turn to how this vocabulary can be derived.

Exhibit 4 suggests one possible way of establishing terminology: a "top down" approach. Once the "top" term (*summum genus*) of a particular hierarchy has been identified, the various levels of subdivisions are established through intellectual effort. A number of thesauri have been built this way. In some cases, committees of subject experts identify the major classes in their areas of specialization and then arrive at a consensus on how these classes should be subdivided.

Although this approach seems attractive at first glance, there are problems associated with it. For instance, when working more-or-less in a vacuum, it is difficult to identify all the subdivisions or even all the major classes that would be needed to cover a field comprehensively. Moreover, it is sometimes difficult to determine how specific terms should be to best serve the intended audience.

The "bottom up" approach to thesaurus construction tends to be more reliable than the "top down" approach. In this case, the thesaurus maker first gathers raw material—the terms that actually occur in a subject field—and then groups like terms together, thus identifying the major aspects or facets of the field. These facets can then be subdivided, not according to theoretical principles, but in a way that comfortably and logically accommodates all the terms that have been collected. Clearly, this approach is quite empirical.

LITERARY WARRANT

Where are the terms to be derived from? Here the principle of *literary warrant*—also known as *bibliographic warrant*—must be observed. This principle was first enunciated by Hulme (1911) more than 70 years ago. Hulme was concerned with bibliographic classification schemes as used to arrange books on library shelves when he put forward this principle. In essence, he said that a subdivision (i.e., class number) in such a scheme could only be justified (warranted) if at least one book on that subject was known to exist. In other words, the classification scheme should not be philosophically or theoretically based; it should be empirically derived from the published literature. The prime example of this is the classification scheme of the Library of Congress: The first scheme was compiled to fit the books actually on the shelves of the library at that time and to reflect how these books seemed to group themselves into useful clusters. The scheme continues to be updated on the principle of literary warrant and is expanded to meet the needs of the library as new materials are published and acquired.

The principle of literary warrant is equally applicable to thesaurus construction: An index term is justified only if it is known to occur in the literature of the subject field. In practice, however, the principle is best extended as follows: A term is justified only if it occurs often enough in the literature to be considered significant and useful for retrieval purposes.

How, then, can one derive terms from the literature of some subject field? The best way is to consult sources in which the terminology of the field appears in a highly compact form. Obvious tools are dictionaries, glossaries, encyclopedias, handbooks, and comprehensive textbooks, providing that these are up-to-date. Better still might be an abstracting publication if one exists in the subject area to be covered.

Suppose, for example, that one must compile a thesaurus to index literature on the manufacture, marketing, and sale of toys (i.e., literature of interest to the toy industry) and that a *Toy Abstracts* has been published since 1978. Working in a purely manual mode, one might begin with the last issue of *Toy Abstracts* available and, working backwards, examine the text of titles and abstracts, looking for significant words and phrases. Each word or phrase is transferred to a card. At the same time, the compiler notes other useful information on this card—possible BTs, NTs, RTs, synonyms, or SNs suggested by the abstracts. Of course, many hours will be spent before the amount of work begins to level off. Thus, this is a viable procedure for compiling a thesaurus on a small scale, and it certainly provides literary warrant, but it is most impractical for putting together a thesaurus in a very broad subject field. A better procedure would be to have the thesaurus compiler (who should have some knowledge of the subject matter being dealt with) underline the words and phrases selected. Significant words and phrases should be underlined regardless of how frequently they have previously occurred. They can then be transcribed by a typist.

The typist should create a file in machine-readable form. A simple program can then be used to produce two ranked lists of terms in descending order of frequency of occurrence: one list for single-word terms and one for multiword terms. It is desirable to keep these separate because the frequency score that might make a multiword term significant will be much lower than the frequency scores of the significant single-word terms. The ranked lists would have literary warrant, and, in general, the more frequently occurring terms would be the strongest candidates for inclusion in the thesaurus. Moreover, in choosing among terms that are synonymous or nearly synonymous, the ranked lists can be of great help: The term that occurs most frequently will usually be the one selected.

If the full text of the abstracts can be obtained in machine-readable form, a lot of work can be saved, since it will no longer be necessary to peruse the abstracts to select terms. A ranked list of all words occurring, with frequency counts, will be easy to generate. Since single-word occurrences are not the only interest, however, it will be necessary to develop a more complex program for identifying significantly occurring phrases and ranking them by frequency.

With further machine processing, another valuable tabulation can be generated. For at least the high-frequency words and phrases, other words or phrases that occur most frequently with them (in titles or abstracts) can be determined. Thus, a type of "profile" emerges, as in the following example:

$$
\begin{array}{ll}
\text{A} & 674 \\
\text{B} & 82 \\
\text{F} & 69 \\
\text{K} & 44 \\
\text{O} & 31 \\
\text{Q} & 19 \\
\end{array}
$$

This shows that term A has occurred 674 times in abstracts, that term B has co-occurred with term A 82 times, and so on. Clearly, a table of this kind has potential value in identifying useful relationships (BT/NT or RT) among the terms.

USER WARRANT

Deriving terms from the type of literature that is to be indexed clearly satisfies the requirement for literary warrant (i.e., an index term is justified only if it is known to occur in the literature). There is another requirement that is frequently overlooked, however. This can be referred to as *user warrant:* A term is justified for inclusion in an index only if it is of interest to the users of the information service. User warrant is especially important in establishing the appropriate level of specificity in the vocabulary. In a particular facet of the subject being dealt with, the terms occurring in the literature may be more specific than the users really need. For example, in a retrieval system for applied mechanics, it might be sufficient to provide for such general materials terms as STEEL, ALUMINUM, PLASTICS,

CERAMICS, and so on, even though highly specific terms (e.g., CHROMIUM-NICKEL-VANADIUM STEELS) may occur in the literature.

To satisfy the requirement for user warrant implies that one must collect terms from the potential users of an information service— terms that represent their particular subject interests. How can this be accomplished?

If the information service for which the thesaurus is being developed has existed for some time, then it probably has maintained records of past information requests. If so, these records will be a rich source of terminology reflecting the information needs of system users. On the other hand, if the information service is new, or if no such records have been kept, similar information might be available from other information centers covering the same general subject areas. Even if no records are available, interviews or questionnaires can be administered to potential users to derive terminology reflecting their precise subject interests. A mailed questionnaire could be applied to a random sample of potential users or to a complete population if this group was small.

The questionnaire (or interview) should seek at least the following types of information:

1. A full job description for the respondent (particularly appropriate, perhaps, for an industrial respondent) that relates his or her duties and responsibilities in the organization. The job description should be in the respondent's own words.

2. A statement, again in the respondent's own words, of his or her professional or research interests. This should be as detailed as possible.

3. If the respondent is an author, titles of publications he or she has written. In fact, one should collect copies of these reports or articles, because they will be an extremely valuable source of relevant terminology.

Terms collected in this way should be processed as discussed in the preceding section. Preferably, they would be put into machine-readable form so that frequency counts could be produced.

Ideally, one should gather terms from both the literature and the users so that the thesaurus has user warrant as well as literary warrant. The two inputs are merged, although the source of the input for each term (users and frequency of mention versus literature and frequency of occurrence) should be distinguished. This makes it possible to identify terms occurring often in both sources, as well as terms occurring frequently in one source but not the other.

If one can get the users of a system to cooperate fully (as one might, for example, if developing a thesaurus for use by a single organization), another approach is possible: Have the users select terms from the literature. If practical, this is probably the best approach of all. Potential users are supplied (or supply themselves) with, say, five or six journal articles, conference papers, or other items that closely reflect their current professional interests. They submit these articles to the thesaurus compiler after they have underlined or highlighted in the text the terms that *make these items important to them.* In this way, the requirements for literary and user warrant are satisfied in a single step. The input is put into machine-readable form for processing. Of course, a rather large number of individuals must be involved before the vocabulary collected can be considered fully representative of both literature and user interests.

This approach has been used in thesaurus construction by Dym (1967) and Pickford (1968), among others. Louzada (1979) used a variation in which she required her users to underline terms in the text and then transcribe these terms onto a form, putting them in rank order according to their own perceptions of their significance. In addition, and perhaps more important, she asked each respondent to define the term appearing at the top of the ranking. This was helpful for understanding how the terms were used by the community surveyed, as well as for identifying possibly ambiguous terms and for developing appropriate scope notes where needed.

A thesaurus is a dynamic tool; it is never likely to be complete. One cannot wait for completeness before organizing the terms he has collected into at least a first draft. The organization of terms into a coherent thesaurus structure is the subject of Chapters 6 and 7.

5 Standards and Guidelines

Although the possibility of some form of thesaurus for controlling vocabulary in information retrieval systems had been discussed earlier, the first true thesaurus of this type appears to have been developed by the Engineering Information Center of E. I. Dupont de Nemours around 1959 (Holm and Rasmussen, 1961). As experience was gained in thesaurus construction, it was recorded and codified, eventually leading to the appearance of guidelines and standards for the process. A possible evolution of these standards is suggested in Exhibit 8. The paths traced cannot all be considered truly definitive, since it is not completely clear who influenced whom in all cases. Nevertheless, the diagram depicts the evolutionary process as I have interpreted it. Two main lines of influence are evident: The alphabetic subject indexing influence is attributable mostly to the United States, and the bibliographic classification influence comes mostly from the United Kingdom.

Charles Ammi Cutter was the first to present rules for the construction of alphabetic subject headings; the original edition of his

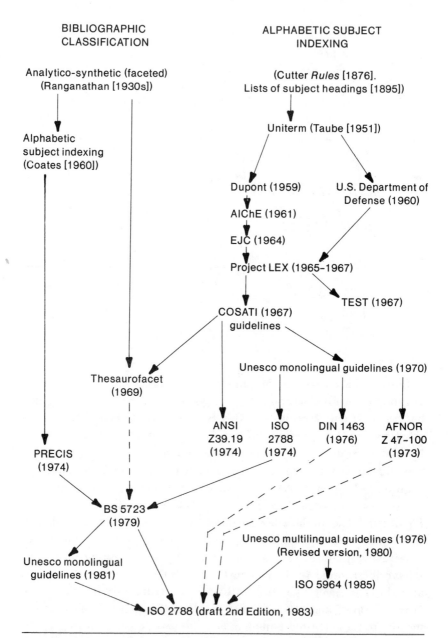

Exhibit 8   Evolution of thesaurus standards (dotted lines depict weaker influences).

Rules for a Dictionary Catalogue appeared in 1876. These eminently sensible rules are still worth our study today. The first controlled vocabulary for alphabetic subject catalogs was the *American Library Association's List of Subject Headings for Use in Dictionary Catalogs,* published in 1895. In Exhibit 8, these early developments are placed within brackets. This is because, although one might suppose that they would have influenced thesaurus development, they appear not to have done so. At least, Holm and Rasmussen made no acknowledgement to subject heading practice, and no direct influence is discernible in the first thesaurus.

On the other hand, the Uniterm system, introduced by Mortimer Taube in 1951, may be considered largely responsible for the appearance of the thesaurus. The major characteristic of this system was the representation of subject matter by single words ("uniterms") extracted from the text of the documents without any form of control. The sheer simplicity of this approach was beguiling, and Taube's ideas were adopted by some influential governmental and industrial organizations in the United States in the 1950s. The Uniterm system was first implemented through use of typed or handwritten cards; later, some punched card systems were used. Unfortunately, systems without any vocabulary control, especially those based on single words, tend to break down because of the large number of term manipulations that may be needed (a problem that disappears when computers are applied to information retrieval); this, in fact, was exactly what happened. The first thesaurus was introduced to impose control on what was essentially a Uniterm system. The influence of Taube is apparent in the large number of single-word terms that can be found in many early thesauri—at least those produced in the United States; he may also have influenced the early standards for thesaurus construction.

The major information center within the U.S. Department of Defense (at that time the Armed Services Technical Information Agency—ASTIA) produced its first thesaurus in 1960, and, in 1961, the American Institute of Chemical Engineers (AIChE) published the *Chemical Engineering Thesaurus.* This was a direct derivative of the work of Dupont and was the first thesaurus to be widely offered for public sale. The *Thesaurus of Engineering Terms,* published by the

Engineers Joint Council (EJC) in 1964, was based on the AIChE the-saurus but was expanded to cover engineering as a whole. The first guidelines for thesaurus construction appear to have emanated from the work of Dupont, AIChE, and EJC (Wall, 1962); Engineers Joint Council, 1965).

The two sources—that is, industry (engineering) and defense—came together in Project LEX (1965–1967), which was funded by the Department of Defense, but with considerable participation from in-dustry. The result was the publication of the *Thesaurus of Engineering and Scientific Terms (TEST)* in 1967. The guidelines for thesaurus construction that emerged from Project LEX were endorsed and pub-lished by the Committee on Scientific and Technical Information (COSATI), an official committee of the U.S. Federal Council for Sci-ence and Technology. Accompanying this publication was a strong recommendation that the COSATI guidelines be followed in the-saurus construction throughout agencies of the U.S. government.

The American national standard for thesaurus construction (ANSI—American National Standards Institute—Z39.19, 1974) can be considered a direct derivative of experience gained in these vari-ous projects. The first version of the Unesco *Guidelines for the Estab-lishment and Development of Monolingual Scientific and Technical The-sauri,* issued in 1970, also developed from this experience. In nearly all respects, the Unesco guidelines are compatible with the ANSI standard. The Unesco guidelines subsequently formed the basis for the first international standard on thesaurus construction (ISO—International Organization for Standardization—2788), issued in 1974, and also influenced the French (AFNOR—Association française de normalization) and German (DIN—Deutsches Institut für Nor-mung) standards.

On the left-hand side of Exhibit 8, one sees that the major in-fluence stems from the theories of bibliographic classification, most particularly from the approach to analytico-synthetic (faceted) classi-fication put forward by the Indian librarian Ranganathan in the 1930s. Not only did Ranganathan's principles lead to a series of spe-cialized classification schemes (mostly produced in the United Kingdom) in a variety of subject areas, they also had a profound effect on alphabetic subject indexing. These influences can be traced from the work of Coates (1960) to the appearance of PRECIS in 1974. At the same time, the influences of faceted classification and the conventional thesaurus were brought together in the thesaurofacet (1969), an attempt to create a tool that achieves the best of both worlds.

In the British Standards (BS 5723) on thesaurus construction, published in 1979, some influence from all these sources is evident; the strongest influences, however, stem from PRECIS and ISO. The second edition of the Unesco (i.e., UNISIST) guidelines (1981) also exhibits the influence of U.S. standards and experience, along with some of the philosophy of and experience from work in the United Kingdom on alphabetic subject indexing; the major influence, however, is that of BS 5723.

On a somewhat different track, the Unesco guidelines for multilingual thesauri, issued in 1976 and revised in 1979, led to the ISO standard ISO 5964, issued in 1985. Both sets of guidelines—monolingual and multilingual—seem to have influenced the new ISO standard for monolingual thesauri (1983).

In this book, no attempt has been made to analyze or compare these various standards (a partial analysis and comparison has already been made by Somers, 1981). In the next several chapters, however, the principles of thesaurus construction discussed are all compatible with international guidelines, unless otherwise noted.

6 *Organization of Terms: The Hierarchical Relationship*

Once terms have been collected through the procedures discussed in Chapter 4, they must be organized into a coherent and cohesive structure. Suppose that one is constructing a thesaurus in the field of library science, that terms have been collected from *Library and Information Science Abstracts,* and that they have been recorded on cards. After collection has ceased (because a point of diminishing returns appears to have been reached), the cards must be put into groups of "like" terms. For example, one pile of cards represents kinds of libraries; another represents the kinds of materials with which libraries deal, a third indicates the types of services that libraries provide; and so on.

This process is illustrated in Exhibit 9. What has occurred is the division of the terminology of library science into a series of aspects or facets. Some of the piles will be relatively large because that particular facet is a large one; other piles might be quite small. In fact, one might need to create a (hopefully) small miscellaneous pile to accommodate terms that do not seem to fall particularly well into any of the major facets.

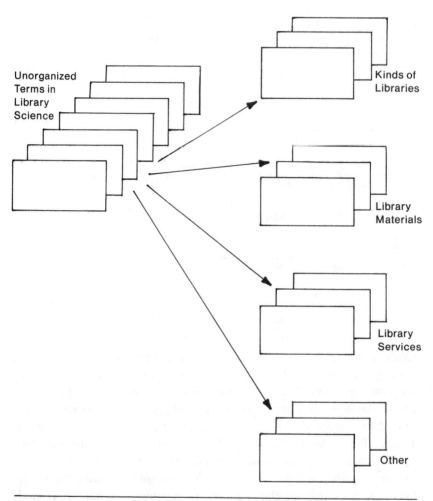

Exhibit 9   Applying facet analysis to terms.

After the facets have been identified in this way, each must be organized into hierarchies. It is impossible to arrive at an effective thesaurus structure without first constructing a classification scheme. Exhibit 10 shows partial hierarchies within two facets of library science. This is a true classification of a portion of the terminology of library science; having a notation associated with the terms is not an essential element of a classification scheme. The classificatory

LIBRARIES	LIBRARY MATERIALS

LIBRARIES

  PUBLIC LIBRARIES
    CITY LIBRARIES
    RURAL LIBRARIES

  ACADEMIC LIBRARIES
    COLLEGE LIBRARIES
      JUNIOR COLLEGE LIBRARIES
    UNIVERSITY LIBRARIES

  SCHOOL LIBRARIES
    PRIMARY SCHOOL LIBRARIES
    SECONDARY SCHOOL LIBRARIES

  SPECIAL LIBRARIES
    ACADEMIC SPECIAL LIBRARIES
    INDUSTRIAL LIBRARIES

  NATIONAL LIBRARIES

LIBRARY MATERIALS

  PRINT ON PAPER

  MICROFORMS
    MICROCARD
    MICROFICHE
      ULTRAMICROFICHE
    MICROFILM

  AUDIOVISUAL MATERIALS
    FILMS
    FILMSTRIPS
    VIDEODISKS
    VIDEOTAPES

Exhibit 10   Partial hierarchies for two facets of library science.

structure is overt, and the levels are clear from the degrees of indentation. To derive a thesaurus structure from the terms in Exhibit 10 will involve sorting the terms into alphabetic order and using the BT/NT conventions under each term to maintain the hierarchical relationships already established.

An example of this is given in Exhibit 11. Whereas Exhibit 10 is an overt classification, the entries of Exhibit 11 reflect a covert classification. Nevertheless, if the entire set of thesaurus entries were derived, the result would be no less a classification scheme than Exhibit 10. The entries of Exhibit 11 could be derived from Exhibit 10 by computer program, just as Exhibit 10 could be generated from a complete set of thesaurus entries.

In comparing the two exhibits, however, it is obvious that the thesaurus entries reflect only one hierarchical step up and one down. For example, ACADEMIC LIBRARIES (Exhibit 11) shows COLLEGE LIBRARIES as one of its narrower terms but does not show JUNIOR COLLEGE LIBRARIES, which is an NT only under COLLEGE LIBRARIES.

This "one step up, one step down" approach is recommended for a printed thesaurus, mainly to conserve space. Some thesauri, however, do not adopt such a convention. Instead, they list all levels of narrower terms under each entry, as in the following example:

LIBRARIES
  NT   ACADEMIC LIBRARIES
        ACADEMIC SPECIAL LIBRARIES
        CITY LIBRARIES
        COLLEGE LIBRARIES
        INDUSTRIAL LIBRARIES
        JUNIOR COLLEGE LIBRARIES
        NATIONAL LIBRARIES
        PRIMARY SCHOOL LIBRARIES
        PUBLIC LIBRARIES
        RURAL LIBRARIES
        SCHOOL LIBRARIES
        SECONDARY SCHOOL LIBRARIES
        SPECIAL LIBRARIES
        UNIVERSITY LIBRARIES

This type of display wastes space, and the mixing of hierarchical levels is confusing rather than helpful. A better display is one that

---

ACADEMIC LIBRARIES
    BT   LIBRARIES
    NT   COLLEGE LIBRARIES
            UNIVERSITY LIBRARIES

COLLEGE LIBRARIES
    BT   ACADEMIC LIBRARIES
    NT   JUNIOR COLLEGE LIBRARIES

MICROFICHE
    BT   MICROFORMS
    NT   ULTRAMICROFICHE

MICROFORMS
    BT   LIBRARY MATERIALS
    NT   MICROCARD
            MICROFICHE
            MICROFILM

Exhibit 11   Sample thesaurus entries derived from Exhibit 10 (hierarchical relationship only).

presents the narrower terms in a type of alphabetico-classed approach, as follows:

```
LIBRARIES
    NT   ACADEMIC LIBRARIES
             COLLEGE LIBRARIES
                 JUNIOR COLLEGE LIBRARIES
             UNIVERSITY LIBRARIES
         NATIONAL LIBRARIES
         PUBLIC LIBRARIES
             CITY LIBRARIES
             RURAL LIBRARIES
         SCHOOL LIBRARIES
             PRIMARY SCHOOL LIBRARIES
             SECONDARY SCHOOL LIBRARIES
         SPECIAL LIBRARIES
             ACADEMIC SPECIAL LIBRARIES
             INDUSTRIAL LIBRARIES
```

This, too, wastes space, but it at least reveals the levels of hierarchy at a glance.

Of course, a thesaurus intended solely for on-line display does not face the same space constraints. In such a case, it would make more sense to display all levels of the hierarchy below any term for which the user requests a thesaurus expansion.

The hierarchies of Exhibit 10 and the thesaurus entries derived from them are based strictly on a genus/species relationship. In general, the BT/NT relationship should always be one of genus/species; that is, the species term must represent a "kind of" the genus term. If it does not, it is probably not a legitimate NT. Consider the following entry, taken from an actual thesaurus:

```
LAUNCHING
    NT   CATAPULTS
         GUIDED MISSILE LAUNCHERS
         ROCKET LAUNCHERS
         TORPEDO LAUNCHERS
         UNDERWATER LAUNCHING
```

Only the last term represents a true species (i.e., a kind of launching); the others should really be grouped under the broader term LAUNCHING DEVICES.

A mistake sometimes made by students is to confuse the thing/kind relationship (the true BT/NT relationship) with the thing/application or thing/derivative relationship: APPLE PIES is not a legitimate NT under APPLES, although it is under PIES.

In most circumstances, the whole/part (partitive) relationship is also not a legitimate BT/NT relationship; that is, BICYCLE WHEELS is a legitimate NT under WHEELS but not under BICYCLES. There are some subject areas, however, where the partitive relationship, by convention, is treated as though it were a generic relationship. The most notable examples are anatomy and geography. The following types of entries can be considered acceptable:

RESPIRATORY SYSTEM	CHILE
NT BRONCHI	NT SANTIAGO
LUNGS	VALPARAISO

although, clearly, lungs are not kinds of respiratory systems and Valparaiso is not a kind of Chile.

The Unesco guidelines recognize two further classes in which the whole/part relationship can be treated as a legitimate BT/NT relationship: "fields of discourse" (BIOLOGY could be an NT under SCIENCE) and "social structures" (e.g., CORPS could be an NT under ARMIES).

In other subject areas, if a compelling reason exists for grouping parts under the whole, it is desirable that the genus/species relationship and the whole/part relationship be kept separate. The Unesco guidelines allow a distinction to be made between the NTG (narrower term generic) and NTP (narrower term partitive) relationships. An example of an entry following this convention is

HOUSES
NTG   BILEVEL HOUSES
SINGLE-LEVEL HOUSES
TRILEVEL HOUSES

NTP   CEILINGS
FLOORS
ROOFS
WALLS

This is acceptable, but there are other solutions. For example, these part terms could be grouped under a different BT (e.g., STRUCTURAL ELEMENTS). The preceding entry would then be transformed into

> HOUSES
> > NT   BILEVEL HOUSES
> > SINGLE-LEVEL HOUSES
> > TRILEVEL HOUSES
>
> > RT   STRUCTURAL ELEMENTS

If the NTP/NTG distinction is made, the distinction must also be made at the BT level (e.g., Bi-level houses—BTG Houses, Ceilings—BTP Houses).

The Unesco guidelines also recognize another legitimate BT/NT relationship—"instance." The following type of entry is acceptable:

> PRE-RAPHAELITES
> > NT   DANTE GABRIEL ROSSETTI
> > WILLIAM HOLMAN HUNT
> > JOHN EVERETT MILLAIS

Rossetti is not really a kind of pre-Raphaelite, but rather an example of one. Clearly, this sort of relationship will be an important one for thesauri in many areas of the humanities.

In general, most thesaurus terms will have only one BT. If a thesaurus is encountered in which a large proportion of the terms appear in several hierarchies (i.e., have more than one BT), it is likely that the tool has been poorly constructed.

Of course, there will be cases in which a term can appear in more than one hierarchy, especially in a multidisciplinary thesaurus. For example, DIAMONDS could be an NT under CUTTING TOOLS as well as under GEMS.

The scope of the thesaurus, and the intended audience, should govern all decisions. In a thesaurus on dentistry, for example, the term GOLD will be an NT under FILLING MATERIALS; it would make little sense to create a "metals" or "precious metals" hierarchy. On the other hand, in a general thesaurus, GOLD should appear in a metals hierarchy rather than in a hierarchy representing an application of gold, although, under certain circumstances (as in the diamonds example), it could be justified in both. If in doubt, one should generally put a term in the hierarchy to which it always relates; for example, diamonds are always gems but not always cutting tools.

In a thesaurus, unlike a faceted classification scheme, it is legitimate to group together as NTs a number of terms derived from the genus (BT) by the application of different principles of division, as in the following example:

           PIPES
               NT   CIRCULAR PIPES
                     METAL PIPES
                     NONCIRCULAR PIPES
                     PLASTICS PIPES
                     STEAM PIPES
                     WATER PIPES

Three different principles of division — shape, material, and application — are evident here. In a faceted classification, the terms would be grouped by principle, and the principle would be explicitly stated:

           PIPES
               (by shape)
               CIRCULAR PIPES
               NONCIRCULAR PIPES
               (by material)
               METAL PIPES
               PLASTICS PIPES
               (by application)
               STEAM PIPES
               WATER PIPES

Although this is necessary in a faceted classification since notations are to be combined in a particular sequence to express a more complex entity (e.g., noncircular plastics pipes for carrying water), this refinement is not really needed in a thesaurus from which terms may be freely assigned to a document with no sequence implied; an article on the above topic would be indexed under WATER PIPES, PLASTICS PIPES, and NONCIRCULAR PIPES.

Nevertheless, for very large hierarchies, it may indeed be convenient to arrange NTs by principle of division:

TOYS
    NT (by materials)
        CLOTH TOYS
        METAL TOYS
        PLASTICS TOYS
        RUBBER TOYS
        WOODEN TOYS
    NT (by age groups)
        ADULT TOYS
        BABY TOYS
        CHILDREN'S TOYS
    NT (by locomotion)
        CLOCKWORK TOYS
        ELECTRIC TOYS
        PULL TOYS
        PUSH TOYS

This type of organization is permitted by the Unesco guidelines, where the principle of division as stated in the thesaurus is referred to as a "node label" or a "facet indicator."

The hierarchies of a typical thesaurus are unlikely to be symmetrical; some will be large, whereas others will be quite small. In fact, some "hierarchies" could conceivably consist of a single term. For example, a thesaurus on library science might include such terms as DETERIORATION or EFFECTIVENESS, which do not fit into any of the major hierarchies. In general, however, such "floating" terms should be minimized. In fact, it may be desirable to create an artificial genus term to allow the grouping of a category of terms that might otherwise be difficult to organize effectively:

GENERAL PROPERTIES
NT   COLOR
      DURABILITY
      SHAPE
      SIZE

The hierarchical relationship is relatively clear-cut, and rather precise guidelines can be formulated to ensure that the BT/NT relationship is consistently applied. The associative relationship, much less clear-cut, is discussed in Chapter 7.

7 *Organization of Terms: The Associative Relationship*

The associative relationship (represented in the thesaurus by RT, meaning "related term") is not a hierarchical relationship. In fact, the one thing definite about this relationship is that it should *not* be used to link terms that appear in the same hierarchy. Some published thesauri do link sibling members of a hierarchy (e.g., COLLEGE LIBRARIES RT UNIVERSITY LIBRARIES), but this is unnecessary; the relationship is provided for by moving up to the common BT:

        ACADEMIC LIBRARIES
            BT   LIBRARIES
            NT   COLLEGE LIBRARIES
                  UNIVERSITY LIBRARIES

The Unesco guidelines do allow for the linking of siblings where the meanings of these terms partially overlap or are otherwise unclear (e.g., DONKEYS shows MULES as an RT, and vice versa), but even this seems somewhat redundant.

The associative relationship is syntagmatic or a posteriori. Unfortunately, it is not possible to establish precise rules for this relationship in quite the same way that one can for the hierarchical relationship. The best one can say is that any two terms whose meanings are related, but that appear in different thesaurus hierarchies, are possible candidates for linking by the RT reference.

Some authors have suggested the possibility of arriving at useful RTs through a type of associative game resembling the "free association" used in certain types of psychological testing (e.g., Papier and Cortelyou, 1962), but such a procedure seems unnecessary and artificial.

Generation of tables of term co-occurrences from an appropriate data base, as suggested in Chapter 4, can indicate which terms are "related" in an associative sense. If this is not possible, the thesaurus builder can rely on common sense and on his knowledge of the subject matter.

Nevertheless, it is possible to identify certain types of interterm relationships that seem particularly strong candidates for the application of the RT link. These are

1. Between a "thing" and its application

      ADHESIVES
        RT   BONDING

and the converse,

      BONDING
        RT   ADHESIVES

2. Between an effect and a cause (and vice versa)

      BRITTLE FRACTURE
        RT   HYDROGEN EMBRITTLEMENT

3. Between a "thing" and a property strongly associated with it

      RUBBER
        RT   ELASTICITY

4. Between a raw material and a product

>   KAOLIN
>   RT   CHINA

5. Between two complementary activities

>   TEACHING
>   RT   LEARNING

6. Between certain opposites

>   LIFE
>   RT   DEATH

7. Between an activity and a property associated with it

>   BENDING
>   RT   PLASTICITY

8. Between an activity and an agent of that activity

>   SMOKING
>   RT   CIGARETTES
>   TOBACCO

9. Between an activity and a product of that activity

>   WEAVING
>   RT   CLOTH

10. Between a thing and its parts (where not provided for in some other way)

>   AIRPLANES
>   RT   FUSELAGE

Unesco's guidelines give further examples, as do Barhydt and Schmidt (1968), Gerd (1980), and Willetts (1975).

The acid test in all cases is simply, "Is it likely that someone seeking information indexed under term A might also be interested in information indexed under term B?" If the answer is yes, then A and B should be linked by the RT reference, providing that the relationship is not already made explicit by the BT/NT structure.

Although it is not an absolute requirement that the RT relationship be reciprocal, it is usually desirable to make it so, if for no other reason than to facilitate thesaurus maintenance: When A shows B as its RT, but B does not acknowledge A as an RT, there is danger that if B is subsequently deleted, a blind reference will remain under A.

In the clear distinction it makes between the BT/NT and the RT relationships, the thesaurus demonstrates definite superiority over lists of subject headings as traditionally used in libraries. In the list of subject headings, both relationships are taken care of by a single reference — *see also* — as in the following example:

> FRACTURE
>   *see also* BRITTLE FRACTURE
>   BRITTLENESS
>   CRACKING
>   HYDROGEN EMBRITTLEMENT

Moreover, in conventional subject heading practice, the reference is made from the general to the specific but rarely in the opposite direction. Thus, one would probably find the reference JOINING *see also* WELDING, but not WELDING *see also* JOINING. In other words, the relationship is not explicitly reciprocal. Unlike a properly constructed thesaurus, the list of subject headings is not a perfect hierarchical classification, and one cannot automatically derive such a classification from a list of subject headings.

The thesaurus of the American Petroleum Institute (1982) is unusual in that it recognizes *see also* references as well as RTs, the former being used much more extensively than the latter. The *see also* relationship here appears more casual than the RT relationship. In fact, when term A is assigned to a document by an indexer, term B is automatically assigned to that document ("autoposted") if B is listed as an RT under A. Since some *see also* references also result in autoposting, the situation is a little confusing. Actually, it is the *see also* reference in this thesaurus that serves the associative relationship. The RT reference is really used to link a term to a hierarchy other than the one in which it has been placed; RT here really means "additional broader term."

8 *Terms: Form and Compounding*

Chapters 1–7 have discussed the organization of terms without explicitly specifying the form in which terms should appear. Various aspects of "form" need to be considered.

Most thesaurus terms will consist of nouns or of nouns and modifiers (i.e., noun phrases). Most noun phrases will be adjectival phrases, but some prepositional phrases may also be justified. The following are all acceptable:

> BIRDS (noun)
> EXTINCT BIRDS (adjectival phrase)
> BIRDS OF PREY (prepositional phrase)

Active verbs should not be used, but gerunds are perfectly acceptable. Thus, RUN is not permitted but RUNNING is.

In general, adjectives should not appear in a thesaurus unless attached to nouns. In certain thesauri, however, a need may exist for some general adjectives that could potentially modify many of the

51

other terms in the vocabulary. Examples might include "manual" and "automatic." It is best to keep such unattached adjectives to a minimum.

For the sake of consistency, terms should always appear in direct rather than inverted form (PRIMARY SCHOOLS, not SCHOOLS, PRIMARY). This rule should be followed rigidly, even if it occasionally leads to some unusual access points, such as VERY HIGH FREQUENCY or SIXTEEN MILLIMETER FILMS. Students of thesaurus construction are sometimes tempted to invert terms to bring together a group of related terms that would otherwise be separated alphabetically, as in the following example:

> AIRCRAFT
> AIRCRAFT, CIVIL
> AIRCRAFT, MILITARY
> AIRCRAFT, PASSENGER
> AIRCRAFT, RECONNAISSANCE

This is unnecessary in a true thesaurus structure—it is the purpose of the BT/NT relationship to achieve this collocation. Inverted forms do occur in lists of subject headings, including the National Library of Medicine's *Medical Subject Headings,* which is sometimes erroneously referred to as a thesaurus. Since these are not thesauri, they lack a true BT/NT structure for grouping terms. In a thesaurus, entries such as

> AIRCRAFT
> NT   CIVIL AIRCRAFT
>   MILITARY AIRCRAFT

and

> MILITARY AIRCRAFT
> NT   FIGHTER AIRCRAFT
>   RECONNAISSANCE AIRCRAFT

completely obviate the need for inversion.

The thesaurus maker must also be consistent in the use of singular/plural forms. Most nouns appear in the plural form (MICE rather than MOUSE, DOGS rather than DOG). A distinction is to be made, however, between nouns of quantity ("count nouns") and nouns of volume. Nouns of quantity are those representing entities for which one would normally ask "How many are there?"; these should always appear in the plural form. Nouns of volume, on the other hand, are those representing entities for which one would normally ask "How much is there?"; these should be in the singular form. Thus, one should use PAPERS (how many are there?) if the term refers to contributions made to conferences or to the manuscripts of an author but PAPER (how much paper?) when the term refers to a material.

Occasionally, exceptions to the rule may make sense for a particular thesaurus. This is especially true for nouns usually thought of in the singular form. Consider, for example, a thesaurus on violins and violin playing. It is appropriate to use the term STRINGS, since a violin has several of them, but to use the singular BRIDGE because each violin has only one. The same argument applies to anatomical terms. It is obviously logical to use EARS and EYES but to retain HEAD and NOSE. Unesco's guidelines give more examples of when to use the singular versus the plural form, but most decisions involve nothing more than common sense. For adjectival nouns such as BRITTLENESS, of course, no plural forms exist.

A more difficult problem (perhaps the most difficult one facing the thesaurus compiler) is to decide how much pre-coordination (some refer to it as "compounding") to use. Take the expression "jet engine noise." Should this compound be retained or should it be split into "jet engines" and "noise" or even into "jets" and "engines" and "noise"? Intuitively, one may feel that splitting into single words (uniterms) is not very useful and that the pair JET ENGINES and NOISE is "about right." One should not rely solely on intuition, however. The problem is not trivial because decisions on compounding have a profound effect on the character of the hierarchies formed in the thesaurus.

Again, the scope of the thesaurus must guide such decisions. For example, in a thesaurus devoted exclusively to jet engines, the term NOISE can reasonably be interpreted to mean "jet engine noise." Needless redundancy in specialized thesauri should be avoided. In a thesaurus on library science, there would be little point in beginning many of the terms with the word "library." In this context, the term COOPERATION implies library cooperation, BUILDINGS implies library buildings; and so on. The construction of a specialized thesaurus is in many ways easier than the construction of a more general one, not only because less term ambiguity is likely to occur but also because certain concepts are easier to handle within a limited context. For example, in a thesaurus on toys, an entry such as

> AUDIENCE
> NT   ADULTS
>   CHILDREN
>   HANDICAPPED
>   INFANTS

appears meaningful, whereas this grouping may make little sense in a thesaurus devoted to a wider subject area.

The guidelines on thesaurus construction published by the British Standards Institution were the first to address in detail the treatment of compounds. The major influence on the British standard appears to be syntactical factoring as developed by Derek Austin for PRECIS. Since Austin was one of the coauthors of the second edition of the Unesco *Guidelines,* it is hardly surprising that these principles are also evident there. Because Unesco's guidelines are detailed and somewhat complicated, they deserve considerable attention.

A distinction is made in the guidelines between *semantic factoring* and *syntactical factoring.*

Semantic factoring involves the analysis of a word into the largest number of ideas implied. Thus, a word such as "urinalysis" factors into "urine" and "analysis," whereas "magnetohydrodynamics" factors into "fluid flow," "magnetism" and "electrical conductivity." Controlled vocabularies have been constructed on this principle (see especially Perry and Kent, 1958), but it can no longer be recommended.

Syntactical factoring involves the splitting of compound terms into component terms that could appear in the thesaurus in their own right (e.g., "jet engine noise" into "jet engines" and "noise"). According to the guidelines, most index terms can be divided into a "focus" and a "difference." This is merely the distinction between a genus term (the noun component of a compound) and a term that identifies one of its species (i.e., one derived from the genus by applying a particular principle of division). The following are examples:

Compound	Focus (genus term)	Difference (species term)
FRENCH LITERATURE	LITERATURE	FRENCH
CLOCKWORK TOYS	TOYS	CLOCKWORK
BIRDS OF PREY	BIRDS	OF PREY

According to the Unesco guidelines, a term should be retained as a compound when

1. *The difference does not have (or no longer has) the same meaning as when standing alone.* Thus, TRADE WINDS cannot be factored into "trade" and "winds" since, in this compound, "trade" takes on a meaning different from the noun "trade." This principle should be extended to include the case in which the difference has no real meaning on its own. Although "clockwork toys" might conceivably be factored, "pull toys" cannot be.

2. *The difference suggests a resemblance to some entity or phenomenon unrelated to the focus.* "Butterfly valves" cannot be factored into "butterflies" and "valves," nor can "tiger lilies" be reduced to "tigers" and "lilies."

3. *The compound has a missing but implicit noun.* For example, "fire escapes" suggests escapes for fires but really means escapes for people from fires.

4. *The difference does not represent a "true" species of the focus.* A "clothes horse" is not a kind of horse and a "shoe tree" is not a kind of tree. This type of difference can be referred to as *syncategorematic.*

5. *The component terms, taken alone, are ambiguous.* "Plate glass" cannot be factored because the components, when combined in a search, could refer to glass plates.

6. *The compound consists of, or includes, a proper name.* For example, "Markovian processes" or "Monroe doctrine" should not be factored.

7. *The compound occurs so frequently in the literature that it would make little sense to split it.* An example might be "pressure vessels."

On the other hand, according to the Unesco guidelines, the following types of compounds should be split:

1. *When the focus represents a property or part, and the difference represents the possessor of the property or the sum of the parts.* "Soil acidity" should not be a term, although "acid soils" could be. Likewise, "compressor blades" is probably best split into "blades" and "compressors." In this connection, it should be noted that some compounds masquerade as true species when, in fact, they are not. For example, "gas turbine corrosion" is not a kind of corrosion but, rather, corrosion occurring in a particular place. Such terms as "stress corrosion" and "fretting corrosion," on the other hand, are true forms of corrosion. These can be retained as compounds, but "gas turbine corrosion" must be split into "corrosion" and "gas turbines."

2. *Compounds representing a transitive action modified by the name of the entity on which the action is performed.* "Steel casting" is not acceptable, although "cast steel" is. Care must be taken in applying this rule. For example, it hardly makes sense to split a term such as "bird watching." The guidelines explicitly suggest that "office managment" should be split. Again, however, this seems unjustifiable because of the frequency with which this term occurs as a compound.

3. *Compounds representing an intransitive action modified by the performer of the action.* "Bird migration" would not be retained as a compound, although "migrating birds" could be.

A critique of these principles, as they appear in the British Standard, can be found in Jones (1981).

Although not specifically mentioned in the Unesco guidelines, there is another type of compound that should always be factored: the compound representing two different principles of division. "Children's picture books" should be factored into "children's books" and "picture books." If this rule is observed, much polyhierarchicalism can be avoided and most thesaurus terms will have only a single BT. Returning to Exhibits 4–7, for example, the term "underwater cine cameras" should really be factored. It must always be kept in mind that the thesaurus is intended for use in post-coordinate systems; consequently, many compound ideas are best expressed through the joint use of two or more components. An article on "underwater cine cameras," therefore, should be indexed under "underwater cameras" and "cine cameras."

9 *The Entry Vocabulary*

As discussed in Chapter 7, the *see also* reference of the list of subject headings has no exact equivalent in the thesaurus, since what it attempts to achieve is partly covered by the RT and partly by the BT/NT relationships. On the other hand, the *see* reference of the list of subject headings is directly equivalent to the *use* reference of the thesaurus. Whereas the RT and BT/NT references (*see also* in subject heading practice) direct from a term that is used to a related term that also is used, the *use* (or *see*) reference directs from an unused term (sometimes called a *nondescriptor*) to a used term. *Use* references provide additional entry points into the vocabulary and, hence, are sometimes referred to as *entry terms* or as forming an *entry vocabulary.*

The *use* reference serves two purposes: to direct from a term not used in indexing to another term that is more-or-less "synonymous" and to direct from a specific term, not used in indexing, to the appropriate more general term.

SYNONYMY

Words or phrases that are *exactly* equivalent are not that common. In information retrieval, one deals more with near synonyms than with exact synonyms. A pragmatic definition is that two terms can be considered synonymous if, in representing subject matter, the distinction between them is either not worth making or is too difficult to make. An example from the field of applied mechanics might be "plates" and "panels."

There are, of course, some categories of terms that can be considered truly synonymous. The most obvious are abbreviations and acronyms. In general, the complete term is preferred and the abbreviation used as an entry term when it, too, is likely to be a point of access for some users:

VERY HIGH FREQUENCY
UF   VHF

VHF *use* VERY HIGH FREQUENCY

Note that the relationship reciprocates: VERY HIGH FREQUENCY shows that it is *used for* (UF) the abbreviation VHF.

In some cases, an abbreviation or acronym is so commonly used that most people have forgotten what it stands for. It seems unnecessarily pedantic to use "LIGHT AMPLIFICATION BY STIMULATED EMISSION OF RADIATION" in place of LASER, and who can remember what RADAR actually stands for? In such cases, the abbreviation or acronym is preferred, with the full term used as an entry term if this is deemed necessary.

There are other cases when choice will be dictated by who is to use the tool. The reference LSD *use* LYSERGIC ACID DIETHYLAMIDE seems sensible in a medical thesaurus, but the reverse reference is preferred in a thesaurus used to index popular literature such as magazine articles.

As long ago as 1876, Cutter, in his *Rules for a Dictionary Catalog,* emphasized that the preferred term should be the one most likely to be used by members of the community to be served. This is still sound advice in deciding among synonyms. In a "popular" thesaurus, popular terms should be used ("stamp collecting" rather than "philately"), whereas more scientific terms are preferable when the thesaurus is to be used by a scholarly community. Actually, it makes little difference which form is selected so long as the alternative also appears as an entry term. Nevertheless, consistency is important: System users will be confused if abbreviations are sometimes preferred and sometimes not and the decisions seem arbitrary or capricious.

It has been pointed out that direct entry of phrases, rather than inversion, is preferable. There will rarely be need for even a *use* reference from the inverted form. For example, there is no need for AIRCRAFT, MILITARY *use* MILITARY AIRCRAFT, since AIRCRAFT will show MILITARY AIRCRAFT as one of its NTs. An exception can be made in the case of prepositional phrases. For instance, EQUATIONS OF MOTION should have a reference in the form of MOTION, EQUATIONS OF *use* EQUATIONS OF MOTION.

So far, only one-to-one mapping of terms has been considered (A *use* B); one-to-many mapping (A *use* Q and R) may also be needed on occasion. For example, it might be desirable to make entries of the following types:

ULTRASONIC DEGREASING *use* DEGREASING and ULTRASONICS
JET LAG *use* AIR TRAVEL and CIRCADIAN RHYTHMS

In such cases, it will be necessary to use some punctuation convention to indicate that a particular term is only one of two or more terms referred to. For example,

CIRCADIAN RHYTHMS
UF + JET LAG

where the + reveals that JET LAG is mapped to at least one other term in addition to CIRCADIAN RHYTHMS.

How many of these one-to-many mappings are necessary will depend largely on how much factoring of compound terms occurs, as discussed in Chapter 8.

The term *quasi-synonym* deserves some explanation at this point. It is loosely used, but Mandersloot et al. (1970) give it a precise connotation. Two terms are quasi-synonyms if they represent opposite extremes on a continuum of values. A good example is the pair "roughness" and "smoothness." Clearly, roughness is the absence of smoothness and vice versa, and a report discussing the effect of surface roughness on fluid flow over plates could be considered to deal equally with smoothness effects. Quasi-synonyms are treated as synonyms:

ROUGHNESS *use* SMOOTHNESS

THE SPECIFIC TO GENERAL REFERENCE

The second purpose of *use* is to refer from a specific term, not used for indexing, to the appropriate more generic term or terms:

CONCORDE *use* SUPERSONIC AIRCRAFT and PASSENGER AIRCRAFT
ARGON ARC WELDING *use* SHIELDED ARC WELDING
TERRIERS *use* DOGS

The assumption here is that, although literature exists on these subjects in the data base, it is not necessary to index those particular topics at this level of specificity. Nevertheless, the entry term serves two useful purposes: It tends to ensure the consistent representation of subject matter (e.g., that all indexers choose both SUPERSONIC AIRCRAFT and PASSENGER AIRCRAFT when articles on the Concorde are encountered), and it tells the searcher precisely where to look and informs him that literature on the specific subject does exist in the data base.

"USE" AND "SEE"

A few thesauri have distinguished between *use* and *see* references.*
In the *EURATOM Thesaurus* (1966–1967), for example, both refer-
ences occur. Moreover, there are actually two kinds of *use* references.
In the example

JASON *use* RESEARCH REACTORS

one may index under the specific reactor name if one wishes. If so,
the generic descriptor referred to must also be used. On the other
hand, in the example

—ION CHAMBERS *use* IONIZATION CHAMBERS

the dash indicates a forbidden term. The indexer may not use this
term; he must use the descriptor referred to.

The *see* reference indicates optional assignment (whereas the *use*
reference indicates compulsory assignment). It is used particularly
with words that have many possible contexts:

LAMPS *see* INFRARED RADIATION
or LIGHT
or ULTRAVIOLET RADIATION

This means that one should probably index a document on ultraviolet lamps under both LAMPS and ULTRAVIOLET RADIATION.

The *SPINES Thesaurus* (1976) is another thesaurus in which both
see and *use* references occur. The *use* reference directs from a term to
one or more other terms that must be used in its place:

RESEARCH AND DEVELOPMENT *use* R&D

---

*The distinction is not one approved in the majority of standards or guidelines for
thesaurus construction.

BERTIELLA

BERTIELLA (B1) 1967
genus under Cestoda; tapeworms found
in primates and occasionally in
domestic animals and man (MeSH
definition)

bertiellasis
Index CESTODE INFECTIONS (IM) (68)
BERTIELLA (IM) (68)

Bertolotti's syndrome
(Ruhl & Sokoloff: A Thesaurus of
Rheumatology)
Index SCIATICA (IM) (68)
SPINAL DISEASES (IM) (68)

BESNOITIASIS (C1,C15) 1968
syn. globidiosis
infection with protozoa of the genus
Besnoitia (Globidium) (MeSH definition)

Bessau's nutrient
an infant nutrient facilitating the
growth of intestinal Lactobacillus
bifidus flora (Gyermekgyogyaszat
9:299 Oct-Nov 58)
Index LACTOBACILLUS *growth &
developement (IM) (68)
INTESTINES *microbiology (IM) (68)

bigarrure

beutacultura (It)
xsubmerged cultures ə
Index CULTURE MEDIA (68)

Bewegungsbestrahlung
xmoving-beam irradiation ə

Bezold-Jarisch reflex
respiratory arrest, bradycardia and
lowering of blood pressure
Index RESPIRATORY INSUFFICIENCY (IM)(68)
BRADYCARDIA (IM) (68)
BLOOD PRESSURE (IM) (68)

BF1 virus
virus isolated from bovine feces which
is cytopathogenic for tissue culture
cells (C R Soc Biol (Par) 153:1653
1959)
Index VERTEBRATE VIRUSES (68)

BGA virus
blue-green algae virus (J Bact 88:771,
Sep 64)
Index PLANT VIRUSES (IM) (68)
ALGAE (NIM) (68)

bharal
Index ARTIODACTYLA (68)

beta-inhibitor
  a virus inhibitor which migrates
  electrophoretically with the fast
  gamma globulin or the slow-moving
  beta-globulins (Proc Soc Exp Biol Med
  126:176, Oct 67)
  Index VIRUSES (IM) (68)   (NIM)
        VIRUS INHIBITORS (Prov)   (68)

beta-radiography
  utilizes the effect of the emission of
  electrons in the absorption of x-rays
  to produce a charge pattern on an
  insulating plate placed in contact with
  a lead surface (Radiography,Lond 23:
  281, Oct 57)
  Index RADIOGRAPHY (68)

Betz cells
  cerebral cortical neurons with efferent
  axons in the medullary pyramids
  (J Physiol 166:313, Apr 63)
  Index CEREBRAL CORTEX *cytology (IM) (68)
      NEURONS   (IM)   (68)

BHK cells
  cell cultures of hamster cells
  Index TISSUE CULTURE (68)

BICUSPID (A3) 1965
  (premolar) one of the eight teeth in
  man, four in each jaw, between the
  cuspids and the first molars; usually
  has two cusps; replaces the molars of
  the deciduous dentition (MeSH definition)

Biesalski-Mayer technic
  tendon transplant in peroneus
  muscle (Afrigue Fr Chir, Jun-Aug
  54)
  Index TENDONS *transplantation (68)

bigarrure (Fr)
  = mottled enamel >
  Index MOTTLED ENAMEL (68)

Exhibit 12   Excerpt from MEDLARS Integrated Authority File.

The *see* reference, on the other hand, recognizes that a term can have more than one context. It directs from one term to a choice of terms that are to be used in its place:

INNOVATION PROCESSES *see* R&D
or TECHNOLOGY TRANSFER

The makers of the *Urban Thesaurus* (1968) do not believe in the use of preferred synonyms. Any synonym may be used; all are linked together by an OR indicator:

RECTANGULAR PLAN
    OR   GRIDIRON PLAN
    OR   GRID PATTERN
    OR   GRID PLAN
    RT   PLANNING
           STREET SYSTEMS

They justify this decision (see p. 10 of the thesaurus) on the grounds that "it would be presumptuous to suggest preferred terms where a number of disciplines and professions are using the same thesaurus, each having its own set of preferred terms for nearly identical concepts." Unfortunately, the thesaurus is confusing, in that each synonymous term is not given the same set of relationships with other terms in the vocabulary. RECTANGULAR PLAN shows STREET SYSTEMS as an RT, whereas one synonym, GRIDIRON PLAN, shows STREET SYSTEMS as a BT and a second synonym, GRID PLAN, has URBAN FORM as its BT. No relationship is shown between URBAN FORM and either RECTANGULAR PLAN or GRIDIRON PLAN. Such inconsistencies are confusing and difficult to justify.

A distinction has been made between "suggestive" vocabularies and "prescriptive" vocabularies. The former give the indexer more latitude in choice of terms (A *use* Q or R), whereas the latter tend to remove all choice. The less prescriptive a vocabulary, the less consistency will occur in indexing.

A published thesaurus usually incorporates a limited entry vocabulary in the form of *see* or *use* references. A large information center may also issue a separate entry vocabulary for in-house use by indexers, searchers, and lexicographers. Such a vocabulary may be available in several forms, such as card file, loose-leaf, machine-readable for printout or on-line display, and microfilm. A specimen page from an entry vocabulary once issued by the National Library of Medicine (it is no longer updated) and known as the Integrated Authority File is illustrated in Exhibit 12. The file includes definitions or scope notes for descriptors in uppercase letters. For nondescriptors, it presents indexing directions and sometimes gives definitions. Foreign terminology is included along with English terms. Note that much of the mapping is one-to-many. *Bertielliasis,* for instance, must be indexed by the terms CESTODE INFECTIONS and BERTIELLA. The joint use of these terms defines this infection uniquely. BF1 virus, on the other hand, is only mapped to the more general VERTEBRATE VIRUSES and is thus not uniquely defined in the vocabulary.

10 *Homography and Scope Notes*

A *homograph* is a string of characters that has more than one meaning (e.g., "guy"); it also may have more than one pronunciation (e.g., "lead" and "lead"). A *homonym* is a character string that has more than one meaning but only one pronunciation (e.g., "plant"). *Homophone* refers to character strings that are different but that are pronounced identically (e.g., "cell" and "sell"). Homophones are not yet a problem in information retrieval (although they could be if spoken interrogation of data bases becomes possible), but homographs (including homonyms) can create difficulties.

Fortunately, homography is much less of a problem than it might appear to be at first sight. Early writings on information retrieval made it more of an issue than it should have been. The classic example was "venetian blinds," which might retrieve documents on blind Venetians. Although clever, this is somewhat absurd. Homography is a problem mainly at the single-term level. For example, "strikes" could retrieve items on labor disputes, on military actions, or on certain sporting activities. But information retrieval rarely involves the

69

use of words in isolation. The combination "strikes" and "unions," in a search strategy, is unlikely to retrieve items on baseball, and the combination "strikes" and "terrorists" is unlikely to retrieve items on baseball or on labor disputes.

The scope of a thesaurus devoted exclusively to a limited subject area reduces possible ambiguity. "Strikes" hardly needs explication in a thesaurus devoted to labor and industrial relations. Where possible ambiguity does exist, it is easily resolved with a parenthetical qualifier:

TANKS (CONTAINERS)
TANKS (VEHICLES)

Such qualifiers can be considered miniature scope notes; however, the qualifier is an integral part of the descriptor, whereas a true scope note is a completely separate statement preceded by the abbreviation SN:

> GOTHIC ROMANCE
> SN   A type of novel, popular in the late eighteenth and early nineteenth centuries, in which the principal elements are violence, horror, and the supernatural. The setting is frequently a ruined Gothic castle or abbey.

Not every descriptor needs a scope note but, rather, only those whose scope might be unclear to the thesaurus user. These would include unusual terms, including foreign-language terms, very recent terms, and terms that are used in a way that is different from common usage.

Furthermore, a scope note need not be a true definition. It is merely a guide to how a particular term should or should not be used. Barhydt and Schmidt (1968) recognize four different uses of scope notes:

1. *Positive limitation in the scope of a term:*

> RETRAINING
> Training for a change in occupation.

Such a note limits scope of the term and distinguishes it from other related terms such as REHABILITATION.

2. *Negative limitation:*

LICENSING

Excluding school accreditation and teacher certification.

Such a scope note not only excludes, but also may direct a user to concepts he might have had in mind when approaching the thesaurus under LICENSING. This could be made more explicit:

Excludes aspects covered by the descriptors SCHOOL ACCREDITATION and TEACHER CERTIFICATION.

3. *True definition:*

SPACE ERROR

Tendency to be biased by the spatial position of stimuli in relation to the observer.

4. *Combination of definition and positive limitation:*

PLAYBACK

Of a visual or sound recording enabling a person to evaluate or react to his own recorded performance.

Some thesauri carry a few general terms that are only to be used as a last resort. Such terms may be given a scope note of the following type:

SHELLS
  SN   Use only for general discussions on shell theory where no particular configuration is involved. In all other cases, prefer the specific terms, for example, CYLINDRICAL SHELLS, HEMISPHERICAL SHELLS, REINFORCED SHELLS.

The context in which a term appears in a thesaurus also reduces both ambiguity and the need for qualifiers or scope notes. For example, if the term TANKS is shown to have WEAPONS as its broader term, the meaning is clear from the context.

11 *Thesaurus Display*

If a descriptor has all the elements previously identified, the thesaurus entry will look like this:

POSITION FINDING INSTRUMENTS
    SN   Instruments used to locate aircraft, ships, or other objects in relation to a specific reference point or points
    UF   Position indicators
    BT   INSTRUMENTS
    NT   COMPASSES
           GROUND POSITION INDICATORS
           PLAN POSITION INDICATORS
           SEXTANTS
           TARGET POSITION INDICATORS
    RT   DETECTION
           TRACKING

Not all entries will have all elements. Most terms will have one BT, and many will have one or more NTs. The occurrence of other elements will be less regular. The elements in the example are presented in the sequence generally recommended by thesaurus standards; note that within each list (BT, NT, RT), the terms are arranged alphabetically.

The alphabetic display of terms in a properly constructed thesaurus will reflect a perfect hierarchical classification. Nevertheless, the alphabetic display does have limitations: It is difficult to get a complete picture of all the terms in a large hierarchy or all the terms in a broad subject category. To give the entire picture, one or more additional displays are usually provided to complement the alphabetic display. These complementary displays can be illustrated by considering the *UNBIS Thesaurus* (1981), developed by the Dag Hammarskjöld Library of the United Nations. Here are two typical entries from this thesaurus:

MANPOWER	INTERNATIONAL COMMERCIAL
12.01.00	ARBITRATION
UF: LABOUR FORCE	01.07.02
BT: HUMAN RESOURCES	BT: COMMERCIAL ARBITRATION
RT: LABOUR	RT: ARBITRAL AWARDS
MANPOWER NEEDS	INTERNATIONAL TRADE
POPULATION	TT: DISPUTE SETTLEMENT
PRODUCTIVE LIFE SPAN	
TT: HUMAN RESOURCES	

This is a fairly conventional set-up except that

–The subject category in which the descriptor appears—e.g., 12.01.00—is given.

–The abbreviation TT gives the "top term" in the hierarchy from which the descriptor is drawn. Thus, for each descriptor, one will usually find the term immediately above it (BT) and the TT. For the term MANPOWER, the BT and TT are the same (i.e., the term immediately above MANPOWER is the top term of the hierarchy).

Exhibit 13 shows a specimen page from the *UNBIS Thesaurus* categorized list of terms. Under each broad subject category—in this case the first in the list, 01.01.00 — all the terms appear in alphabetic order, together with scope notes and *use* references.

Exhibit 14 presents a sample from the hierarchical list. Each top term is arranged alphabetically, and, below it, the entire hierarchy appears, with the various levels shown through indentation. The alphabetic display serves as the entry point to the complementary displays, since, for each descriptor, both top term and subject category code are given.

Exhibit 15 illustrates a permuted word display in a KWOC (keyword out of context) format. This is a useful supplement because it shows every occurrence of a particular word in the vocabulary, whatever position the word occupies in a descriptor.

GRAPHIC DISPLAYS

In the conventional thesaurus, the alphabetic display is the major display and the others are supplements to it. A different way of presenting a thesaurus — the graphic display — is popular in Europe but has never been adopted with enthusiasm in the United States. Exhibit 16 shows a page from a hypothetical thesaurus. Here the hierarchy of camera terms, first encountered in Chapter 3, is presented in a graphic format known as an *arrowgraph*. The top term of the hierarchy (CAMERA) appears at the center. By following the arrows, it is possible to pick out the various levels of the hierarchy. Thus, one can readily see that CAMERAS has four immediately narrower terms; that one of these — STILL CAMERAS — has four narrower terms of its own; and so on. Looked at another way, one sees that 35MM CAMERAS is a subdivision of MINIATURE CAMERAS, which is a subdivision of STILL CAMERAS, which is a subdivision of CAMERAS, the top term.

Various terms in the display are linked to other displays (e.g., CINE CAMERAS points to CINEMA) in much the same way that one map in an atlas leads to another. In fact, this type of display is frequently referred to as a map of terminology.

01.
POLITICAL AFFAIRS

01.01.00
POLITICAL CONDITIONS,
INSTITUTIONS, MOVEMENTS

AERIAL HIJACKING
USE: HIJACKING OF AIRCRAFT
ALLEGIANCE
ANTICOMMUNIST MOVEMENTS
ASSASSINATION
AUTARCHY
AUTHORITARIANISM
SN: A political style characterized by obedience of subordinate to superior, reliance on threats of punishment and aversion to consultation and persuasion
AUTHORITY
BILL DRAFTING
BLACK POWER
BUREAUCRACY
CABINET OFFICERS
CABINET SYSTEM
USE: PARLIAMENTARY GOVERNMENT
CAPITALISM
CIVIL DISOBEDIENCE
SN: Refusal to obey laws regarded as morally unjust, ordinarily by nonviolent resistance
CIVIL SUPREMACY OVER THE MILITARY
USE: CIVIL-MILITARY RELATIONS
CIVIL WAR
CIVIL-MILITARY RELATIONS
CLASS STRUGGLE
COALITION GOVERNMENTS
COMMISSIONS OF INQUIRY
SN: Includes international commissions
COMMUNES (CHINA)
SN: Large-scale enterprise which includes collectivized agriculture, industry, social services and local government functions
COMMUNISM
COMMUNIST PARTIES
COMMUNIST REVISIONISM
COMMUNIST STATE
SN: Use for theoretical works on the future communist state. Do not confuse with

GOVERNMENT INVESTIGATIONS
GOVERNORS
HEADS OF STATE
HIJACKING OF AIRCRAFT
HOSTAGE HOLDING
USE: HOSTAGES
HOSTAGE TAKING
USE: HOSTAGES
HOSTAGES
IDEOLOGY
INTELLIGENCE SERVICES
INTEREST GROUPS
USE: PRESSURE GROUPS
INTERNAL SECURITY
INTERNATIONAL TERRORISM
USE: TERRORISM
INTERSTATE AGREEMENTS
SN: Use for agreements between states, provinces etc., within a single country
INTERSTATE COMPACTS
USE: INTERSTATE AGREEMENTS
INTERSTATE RELATIONS
ISRAEL AND THE DIASPORA
USE: ZIONISM
LEADERSHIP
LEGISLATIVE BODIES
LEGISLATIVE HEARINGS
LEGISLATIVE POWER
LEGITIMACY OF GOVERNMENTS
LENINISM
LIBERALISM
LOBBYING
LOCAL GOVERNMENT
SN: Any subnational unit of government
MARTIAL LAW
MARXISM
METROPOLITAN GOVERNMENT
MILITARY GOVERNMENT
MISCONDUCT IN OFFICE
SN: Criminal offences committed by government officials in or on the occasion of the performance of their duties
MONARCHY
MUNICIPAL GOVERNMENT
NATIONAL SOCIALISM
USE: NAZISM
NATIONALISM

POLITICAL TRIALS
SN: Used for trials conducted for political reasons or in a politicized manner
POLITICAL VIOLENCE
POLITICS
USE: POLITICS AND GOVERNMENT
POLITICS AND GOVERNMENT
SN: Use only for general discussions of the governmental structure and political processes of a particular country
POLITICS AND WAR
POWER (SOCIAL SCIENCES)
USE: POLITICAL POWER
PRESIDENTS
PRESSURE GROUPS
PRIME MINISTERS
PROPAGANDA
PROPORTIONAL REPRESENTATION
PROTEST MOVEMENTS
PUBLIC MEETINGS
REGIONALISM
SN: Use only in the subnational sense
REPRESENTATIVE GOVERNMENT
RESISTANCE TO GOVERNMENT
USE: CIVIL DISOBEDIENCE
POLITICAL VIOLENCE
REVOLUTIONARIES
REVOLUTIONS
RIGHT AND LEFT (POLITICAL SCIENCE)
RIOTS
SN: Group acts of violence, prejudicial to public law and order
SECRET SERVICE
USE: INTELLIGENCE SERVICES
SEDITION
USE: SUBVERSIVE ACTIVITIES
SEPARATION OF POWERS
SMALL STATES
SOCIALISM
SOCIALIST PARTIES
SOVIETS
STATE CONSTITUTIONS
USE: Use for constitutions of U.S. states, German laender, etc.
STATE GOVERNMENTS
SN: Subnational governments, in federal systems
STATE OF SIEGE

COMMUNIST STRATEGY
  SN: Political strategy
COMMUNITY LEADERSHIP
COMMUNITY ORGANIZATION
COMMUNITY POWER
COMPARATIVE GOVERNMENT
CONSERVATISM
CONSTITUTIONS
CORPORATE STATE
  SN: Systems of government based on functional representation
CORRUPTION IN POLITICS
  USE: POLITICAL CORRUPTION
COUNTERREVOLUTION
CURRENT EVENTS
DECENTRALIZATION IN GOVERNMENT
DEMOCRACY
DICTATORS
  USE: DICTATORSHIP
DICTATORSHIP
DIVISION OF POWERS
  USE: FEDERAL GOVERNMENT
ELECTION DISTRICTS
ELECTIONS
EMERGENCY LEGISLATION
EMERGENCY POWERS
ESPIONAGE
EUROCOMMUNISM
EXECUTIVE POWER
EXECUTIVE PRIVILEGE
  SN: With respect to government information
EXTRALEGAL EXECUTIONS
  SN: Killing of political opponents or suspected offenders by armed forces, law enforcement officials, etc. or paramilitary or political groups enjoying the support of governmental agencies
FASCISM
FEDERAL GOVERNMENT
FEDERAL-CITY RELATIONS
FEUDALISM
FORUMS (DISCUSSION AND DEBATE)
  USE: GROUP COMMUNICATION
      PUBLIC MEETINGS
GOVERNMENT AND THE PRESS

NEWLY-INDEPENDENT STATES
NONVIOLENCE
OFFICIAL SECRETS
PACIFISM
  SN: Opposition to war as a means of settling disputes among nations
PANCHAYAT
PARLIAMENT
  USE: LEGISLATIVE BODIES
PARLIAMENTARY GOVERNMENT
PARLIAMENTARY PRACTICE
PARLIAMENTARY PROCEDURE
  USE: PARLIAMENTARY PRACTICE
PARLIAMENTARY SYSTEMS
  USE: PARLIAMENTARY GOVERNMENT
PASSIVE RESISTANCE TO GOVERNMENT
  USE: CIVIL DISOBEDIENCE
      NONVIOLENCE
PATRIOTISM
PEASANT MOVEMENTS
PEASANT UPRISINGS
  USE: PEASANT MOVEMENTS
POLITICAL CONVENTIONS
POLITICAL CORRUPTION
POLITICAL CRIMES
  SN: Use for crimes committed for political reasons. Treatment of persons as criminals for political acts should be indexed with terms such as "political prisoners," "political trials," etc.
POLITICAL ETHICS
POLITICAL MOVEMENTS
POLITICAL OPPOSITION
POLITICAL PARTICIPATION
POLITICAL PARTIES
POLITICAL POWER
POLITICAL PRISONERS
POLITICAL PSYCHOLOGY
POLITICAL REPRESENTATION
POLITICAL SCIENCE
POLITICAL SOCIALIZATION
  SN: The process of bringing a formerly inactive group into active political participation
POLITICAL SOCIOLOGY
POLITICAL SYSTEMS

USE: STATES' RIGHTS
STATES
  SN: Includes theoretical works on the nature of the State
STATES' RIGHTS
  SN: The rights of subnational states in federal systems
STATESMEN
STUDENT MOVEMENTS
SUBVERSIVE ACTIVITIES
SYNDICALISM
  SN: Refers to political movements for government based on trade unions
TERRORISM
TOTALITARIANISM
  SN: Highly centralized government exercising control over all organized social activities and permitting no rival centres of power
TREASON
TRIALS (POLITICAL CRIMES AND OFFENCES)
  USE: POLITICAL TRIALS
UNDERGROUND MOVEMENTS
  SN: Political opposition groups unwilling or unable to come out into the open, often resistance groups in occupied territory
UNLAWFUL INTERFERENCE WITH INTERNAT CIVIL AVIATION
  USE: HIJACKING OF AIRCRAFT
VETO
VOTER REGISTRATION
VOTING
WAR AND EMERGENCY LEGISLATION
  USE: EMERGENCY LEGISLATION
WAR AND EMERGENCY POWERS
  USE: EMERGENCY POWERS
ZIONISM

01.02.00
INTERNATIONAL RELATIONS

AFRO-ASIAN POLITICS
ALLIANCES
AMBASSADORS

Exhibit 13 Example from the categorized lists of the *UNBIS Thesaurus*. New York, United Nations, 1981. (Publication Sales No. E.81.I.17). Reproduced by permission.

COMMUNICATION (cont.)

.... OCEANIAN NEWSPAPERS
.... POLISH NEWSPAPERS
.... PORTUGUESE NEWSPAPERS
.... SLAVIC NEWSPAPERS
.... SOUTH AFRICAN NEWSPAPERS
.... SPANISH NEWSPAPERS
.... SWEDISH NEWSPAPERS
.... SWISS NEWSPAPERS
.. PERIODICALS
... AMERICAN PERIODICALS
... ARABIC PERIODICALS
... BELGIAN PERIODICALS
... BERMUDIAN PERIODICALS
... CANADIAN PERIODICALS
... CHINESE PERIODICALS
... ENGLISH PERIODICALS
... EPHEMERAL PERIODICALS
... FRENCH PERIODICALS
... GERMAN PERIODICALS
... HUNGARIAN PERIODICALS
... JAPANESE PERIODICALS
... LATIN AMERICAN PERIODICALS
... PANAMANIAN PERIODICALS
... NIGERIAN PERIODICALS
... PHILIPPINE PERIODICALS
... POLISH PERIODICALS
... PORTUGUESE PERIODICALS
... RUSSIAN PERIODICALS
... SCHOLARLY PERIODICALS
... SLAVIC PERIODICALS
... SPANISH PERIODICALS
... SWEDISH PERIODICALS
... SWISS PERIODICALS
... YUGOSLAV PERIODICALS
.. PUBLISHING
... BOOK INDUSTRY
... MICROPUBLISHING
... MUSIC PUBLISHING
... NEWSPAPER PUBLISHING
... PERIODICALS PUBLISHING
.. RADIO
... EDUCATIONAL RADIO
.. TELEVISION
... CABLE TELEVISION
... EDUCATIONAL TELEVISION
.. MICROFORMS

.. PROPAGANDA
.. PUBLIC RELATIONS
... PUBLIC RELATIONS AND POLITICS
.. PUBLICITY
.. REPORT WRITING
.. TECHNICAL WRITING

COMMUNICATIONS

.. POSTAL SERVICES
... AIR MAIL SERVICES
... PARCELS POST
.. TELECOMMUNICATION
... AERONAUTICAL TELECOMMUNICATION
.... AERONAUTICAL RADIO SERVICES
... RADIO BROADCASTING
... RADIO COMMUNICATIONS
... REMOTE SENSING
... SATELLITE COMMUNICATION
... TELEGRAPH
... TELEPHONE
... TELETYPE
... TELEVISION BROADCASTING

COMMUNISM

.. EUROCOMMUNISM

COMPENSATION

.. DAMAGES

COMPETITION

.. GOVERNMENT COMPETITION
.. INTERNATIONAL COMPETITION
.. UNFAIR COMPETITION

COMPUTER PROGRAMMING

.. MICROPROGRAMMING

CONFLICT

.. SOCIAL CONFLICT

CONSTITUTIONS

.. STATE CONSTITUTIONS

CONSTRUCTION

.. BRIDGE CONSTRUCTION
.. CONCRETE CONSTRUCTION

CRIMINAL JUSTICE

.. CORRECTIONAL SYSTEMS
... COMMUNITY BASED CORRECTIONS
... JUVENILE CORRECTIONS
.... JUVENILE DETENTION HOMES
... PARDON
... PAROLE
... PRISON LABOUR
... PRISONS
.... REFORMATORIES
.. CRIMINAL PROCEDURE
... INDICTMENTS
... PRELIMINARY EXAMINATIONS
... PROSECUTION
... SEARCHES AND SEIZURES
.. LAW ENFORCEMENT
... NARCOTICS LAW ENFORCEMENT

CROPS

.. FIELD CROPS
.. FORAGE CROPS
.. TROPICAL CROPS

CULTIVATION SYSTEMS

.. CROP DIVERSIFICATION
.. CROP ROTATION
.. DRY FARMING
.. IRRIGATION FARMING
.. NUCLEAR AGRICULTURE
.. ORGANIC FARMING
.. SHIFTING CULTIVATION

CULTURAL PROPERTY

.. ART WORKS
.. HISTORIC SITES AND MONUMENTS
... NUBIAN HISTORIC SITES AND MONUMENTS

CULTURE

.. ART AND LITERATURE
.. ART AND SCIENCE
.. ART AND SOCIETY
.. ART AND STATE
.. ARTS
... MUSIC
.... FOLK MUSIC
.... FOLK SONGS
... PERFORMING ARTS

. . . COMPUTER OUTPUT MICROFORMS
. . . MICROCARDS
. . . MICROFICHE
. . . MICROFILMS
. . NONBOOK MATERIALS
. . AUDIOVISUAL MATERIALS
. . FILMS
. . . CHILDREN'S FILMS
. . . CINEMATOGRAPHIC WORKS
. . . DOCUMENTARY FILMS
. . . EDUCATIONAL FILMS
. . FILMSTRIPS
. . MAPS
. . . AERONAUTICAL CHARTS
. . . BATHYMETRIC CHARTS
. . . CADASTRAL MAPS
. . . GEOLOGICAL MAPS
. . . INTERNATIONAL MAP OF THE WORLD
          ON THE MILLIONTH SCALE (IMW)
. . . MILITARY MAPS
. . . NAUTICAL CHARTS
. . . ROAD MAPS
. . . TOPOGRAPHIC MAPS
. . . TROPICAL MAPS
. . . WEATHER MAPS
. . PHOTOGRAPHS
. . PHONORECORDS
. . PHONOTAPES
. . VIDEO RECORDINGS
. INFORMATION NETWORKS
. . LIBRARY INFORMATION NETWORKS
. ORAL COMMUNICATION

COMMUNICATION PROCESS
. GROUP COMMUNICATION
. INFORMATION TRANSFER
. DATA TRANSMISSION
. . FACSIMILE TELEGRAPH TRANSMISSION
. INFORMATION EXCHANGE
. INTERCULTURAL COMMUNICATION
. INTERPERSONAL COMMUNICATION
. MASS COMMUNICATION
. ADVERTISING
. . INDUSTRIAL ADVERTISING

. EARTHQUAKE RESISTANT CONSTRUCTION
. INDUSTRIALIZED BUILDING

CONSULTANTS
. INDUSTRIAL CONSULTING
. MANAGEMENT CONSULTANTS

CONSUMER GOODS
. CLOTHING
. FURNITURE
. HOUSEHOLD APPLIANCES

CONSUMPTION
. ENERGY CONSUMPTION
. FOOD CONSUMPTION
. WATER CONSUMPTION

CONTRACEPTIVES
. CHEMICAL CONTRACEPTIVES
. INTRAUTERINE CONTRACEPTIVES
. ORAL CONTRACEPTIVES

COPYING PROCESSES
. PHOTOCOPYING

COPYRIGHT
. INTERNATIONAL COPYRIGHT

CORPORATIONS
. CONGLOMERATE CORPORATIONS
. HOLDING COMPANIES
. NONPROFIT CORPORATIONS

CORRUPT PRACTICES
. ILLICIT PAYMENTS

CREDIT
. AGRICULTURAL CREDIT
. COMMERCIAL CREDIT
. BANKERS' COMMERCIAL CREDITS
. EXPORT CREDITS
. IMPORT CREDITS
. CONSUMER CREDIT
. DEVELOPMENT CREDITS

. . CINEMA
. . DANCE
. . OPERA
. . THEATRE
. . DRAMA
. . RADIO PLAYS
. VISUAL ARTS
. FINE ARTS
. . ARCHITECTURE
. . . ARCHITECTURAL ACOUSTICS
. . . DOMESTIC ARCHITECTURE
. . . INDUSTRIAL ARCHITECTURE
. . . MECHANICAL DRAWING
. . . MODERN ARCHITECTURE
. . . MURAL PAINTING AND DECORATION
. . PAINTING
. . . PORTRAITS
. . . PICTURES
. . PLASTIC ARTS
. . GRAPHIC ARTS
. . . COMMERCIAL ART
. . REPRODUCTIVE ARTS
. . PHOTOGRAPHY
. . . AERIAL PHOTOGRAPHY
. . . COLOUR PHOTOGRAPHY
. . . LUNAR PHOTOGRAPHY
. . . MICROPHOTOGRAPHY
. . PRINTING
. . . LITHOGRAPHY
. LITERATURE
. . AFRICAN LITERATURE
. . AMERICAN LITERATURE
. . AMERICAN POETRY
. . ARABIC LITERATURE
. . ASIAN LITERATURE
. . . CHINESE LITERATURE
. . . INDIAN LITERATURE
. . . JAPANESE LITERATURE
. . . PAKISTANI LITERATURE
. . AUSTRALIAN LITERATURE
. . BLACK LITERATURE
. . CATHOLIC LITERATURE
. . CHILDREN'S LITERATURE
. . ENGLISH LITERATURE
. . ENGLISH POETRY

Exhibit 14 Sample page from the hierarchical list of the *UNBIS Thesaurus*. New York, United Nations, 1981. (Publication Sales No. E.81.I.17). Reproduced by permission.

ABACA
04.02.02 ABACA

ABANDONED
14.03.00 ABANDONED CHILDREN

ABBREVIATIONS
15.01.01 ABBREVIATIONS

ABILITY
05.02.00 EXECUTIVE ABILITY

ABOARD
06.02.00 CRIMES ABOARD AIRCRAFT

ABORIGINES
08.03.01 AUSTRALIAN ABORIGINES

ABORTION
08.02.00 ABORTION
08.02.00 ABORTION POLICY
08.02.00 ABORTION TECHNIQUES
08.02.00 ILLEGAL ABORTION
08.02.00 LEGAL ABORTION

ABROAD
11.03.00 STUDY ABROAD
07.04.00 TRADE REPRESENTATION ABROAD

ABSENCE
12.03.00 LEAVE OF ABSENCE

ABSENTEEISM
12.04.00 ABSENTEEISM

ABSORPTIVE
02.04.00 ABSORPTIVE CAPACITY

ABSTINENCE
08.02.00 SEXUAL ABSTINENCE

ABSTRACTING
15.05.00 ABSTRACTING
15.05.00 ABSTRACTING AND INDEXING SERVICES

ABSTRACTS
18.00.00 ABSTRACTS

13.02.00 NUCLEAR ACCIDENTS
10.04.00 RADIATION ACCIDENTS
06.03.00 RAILWAY ACCIDENTS
06.03.00 TRAFFIC ACCIDENTS

ACCOMMODATIONS
18.00.00 ACCOMMODATIONS

ACCOUNT
18.00.00 SPECIAL ACCOUNT

ACCOUNTING
05.02.00 ACCOUNTING
02.09.00 ACCOUNTING AND REPORTING
02.02.00 FLOW OF FUNDS ACCOUNTING
02.06.01 GOVERNMENT ACCOUNTING
05.02.00 INCOME ACCOUNTING
05.02.00 PRODUCTIVITY ACCOUNTING
02.06.02 TAX ACCOUNTING

ACCOUNTS
18.00.00 ACCOUNTS ...
18.00.00 ACCOUNTS OF EXECUTING AGENCIES ...
05.02.00 ACCOUNTS RECEIVABLE
02.02.00 NATIONAL ACCOUNTS
14.05.01 SOCIAL ACCOUNTS

ACCULTURATION
14.05.03 ACCULTURATION

ACETYLENE
05.04.00 ACETYLENE

ACHIEVEMENT
18.00.00 ACHIEVEMENT INDICATORS
11.01.00 ACHIEVEMENT MOTIVATION

ACID
03.04.00 ACID RAIN

ACOUSTIC
05.05.00 ACOUSTIC ENGINEERING

ACOUSTICS
09.02.00 ARCHITECTURAL ACOUSTICS
16.04.00 UNDERWATER ACOUSTICS

18.00.00 NGO ACTIVITIES ...
18.00.00 OPERATIONAL ACTIVITIES ...
18.00.00 OUTER SPACE ACTIVITIES ...
18.00.00 PROJECT ACTIVITIES
18.00.00 SPECIALIZED AGENCIES ACTIVITIES ...
01.01.00 SUBVERSIVE ACTIVITIES
18.00.00 UN SYSTEM ACTIVITIES ...

ACTIVITY
01.04.00 MILITARY ACTIVITY
16.03.00 SEISMIC ACTIVITY

ACTS
02.05.00 ADMINISTRATIVE ACTS
01.07.00 JUDICIAL REVIEW OF ADMINISTRATIVE ACTS
01.07.00 JURISTIC ACTS

AD
18.00.00 AD HOC WORKING GROUPS

ADDED
02.06.02 VALUE ADDED TAX

ADDICTS
14.04.01 DRUG ADDICTS

ADDRESS
18.00.00 ADDRESS TO ... SESSION OF ...
14.06.00 FORMS OF ADDRESS
06.06.00 TELEGRAPH CODE ADDRESS

ADDRESSES
18.00.00 ADDRESSES, ESSAYS, ETC.

ADEN
17.08.01 GULF OF ADEN

ADJOURNMENT
18.00.00 ADJOURNMENT

ADJUSTMENT
18.00.00 ADJUSTMENT
18.00.00 ADJUSTMENT FOR CURRENCY CHANGES
07.05.00 ADJUSTMENT PROCESS
18.00.00 COST OF LIVING ADJUSTMENT

ABUSE
02.05.00 ABUSE OF ADMINISTRATIVE POWER
14.04.02 CHILD ABUSE
14.04.01 DRUG ABUSE
14.04.01 DRUGS OF ABUSE

ACADEMIC
11.03.00 ACADEMIC DEGREES
14.02.02 ACADEMIC FREEDOM

ACADEMIES
06.04.00 MARITIME TRAINING ACADEMIES

ACCELERATORS
16.08.00 PARTICLE ACCELERATORS

ACCESS
18.00.00 ACCESS FOR DEVELOPING COUNTRIES
01.07.03 ACCESS TO THE SEA
07.01.00 MARKET ACCESS

ACCESSIONS
18.00.00 ACCESSIONS
18.00.00 ACCESSIONS AND RATIFICATIONS

ACCIDENT
05.08.00 ACCIDENT INSURANCE
01.07.00 ACCIDENT LAW
10.05.00 ACCIDENT PREVENTION
06.02.00 AIRCRAFT ACCIDENT INVESTIGATION
06.02.00 AIRCRAFT ACCIDENT PREVENTION

ACCIDENTS
10.05.00 ACCIDENTS
06.02.00 AIRCRAFT ACCIDENTS
12.03.00 INDUSTRIAL ACCIDENTS
06.02.00 LIABILITY FOR AIRCRAFT ACCIDENTS
06.04.00 LIABILITY FOR MARINE ACCIDENTS
15.06.00 LIABILITY FOR SPORTS ACCIDENTS
06.04.00 MARINE ACCIDENTS

ACQUISITIONS
15.05.00 CO-OPERATIVE ACQUISITIONS
15.05.00 LIBRARY ACQUISITIONS

ACRONYMS
15.01.01 ACRONYMS

ACT
01.07.00 ACT OF STATE
18.00.00 CONSTITUENT ACT
18.00.00 FINAL ACT

ACTION
18.00.00 ACTION BY ...
12.03.00 AFFIRMATIVE ACTION PROGRAMMES
07.03.00 ESCAPE CLAUSE ACTION
18.00.00 INTERNATIONAL ACTION
18.00.00 NATIONAL ACTION
18.00.00 PLAN OF ACTION
18.00.00 PROGRAMME OF ACTION
18.00.00 PROGRAMME OF ACTION (DRAFT)
18.00.00 REGIONAL ACTION
18.00.00 REGIONAL PLAN OF ACTION
14.05.03 SOCIAL ACTION
18.00.00 WORLD PLAN OF ACTION

ACTIONS
01.07.00 ACTIONS AND DEFENCES
01.07.00 LIMITATION OF ACTIONS (CIVIL LAW)
01.07.00 LIMITATION OF ACTIONS (CRIMINAL LAW)
01.07.00 PREJUDICIAL ACTIONS

ACTIVITIES
18.00.00 ACTIVITIES ...
18.00.00 FUND-RAISING ACTIVITIES
18.00.00 INCOME PRODUCING ACTIVITIES
12.04.00 INTERNATIONAL LABOUR ACTIVITIES
18.00.00. NATIONAL AND INTERNATIONAL ACTIVITIES ...

18.00.00 POST ADJUSTMENT
14.05.02 SOCIAL ADJUSTMENT
07.03.00 TRADE ADJUSTMENT ASSISTANCE

ADMINISTRATION
18.00.00 ADMINISTRATION
18.00.00 ADMINISTRATION AND MANAGEMENT
01.07.00 ADMINISTRATION OF ESTATES
01.07.00 ADMINISTRATION OF JUSTICE
04.01.01 AGRICULTURAL ADMINISTRATION
07.04.00 CUSTOMS ADMINISTRATION
02.04.00 DEVELOPMENT ADMINISTRATION
11.01.00 EDUCATIONAL ADMINISTRATION
05.01.01 INDUSTRIAL ADMINISTRATION
12.04.00 LABOUR ADMINISTRATION
15.05.00 LIBRARY ADMINISTRATION
02.05.00 PUBLIC ADMINISTRATION
10.02.00 PUBLIC HEALTH ADMINISTRATION
14.05.04 SOCIAL WORK ADMINISTRATION
11.05.00 STUDENT PARTICIPATION IN ADMINISTRATION
02.06.02 TAX ADMINISTRATION

ADMINISTRATIVE
02.05.00 ABUSE OF ADMINISTRATIVE POWER
02.05.00 ADMINISTRATIVE ACTS
02.05.00 ADMINISTRATIVE AGENCIES
18.00.00 ADMINISTRATIVE AND BUDGETARY QUESTIONS
02.05.00 ADMINISTRATIVE AND POLITICAL DIVISIONS
18.00.00 ADMINISTRATIVE ASPECTS
18.00.00 ADMINISTRATIVE BACKSTOPPING
18.00.00 ADMINISTRATIVE BUDGET ...
18.00.00 ADMINISTRATIVE BUDGETS
01.07.00 ADMINISTRATIVE COURTS AND TRIBUNALS
02.05.00 ADMINISTRATIVE DISCRETION
02.05.00 ADMINISTRATIVE ECONOMIC COUNCILS
18.00.00 ADMINISTRATIVE EXPENSES ...
02.05.00 ADMINISTRATIVE FEES
02.05.00 ADMINISTRATIVE LAW

Exhibit 15 KWOC display from the *UNBIS Thesaurus*. New York, United Nations, 1981. (Publication Sales No. E.81.I.17). Reproduced by permission.

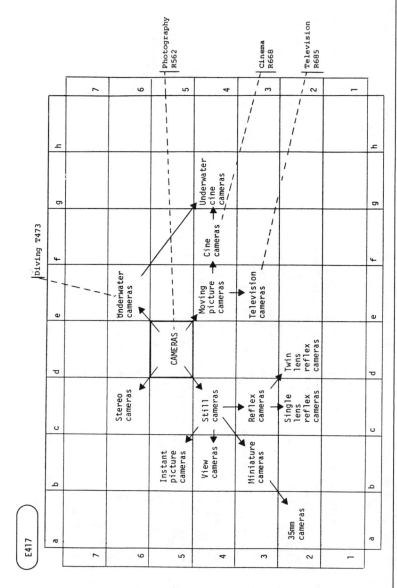

Exhibit 16 Example of graphic display. From *Guidelines for the Establishment and Development of Monolingual Thesauri*, ©1981. Reproduced by permission of Unesco.

An alphabetic index to these maps is obviously needed; such an index is shown in Exhibit 17. This is more than an index, of course, since it includes all the elements of a full thesaurus.

Over the years, various forms of graphic display have been tried. Four different formats are illustrated in Exhibits 18–21.

The *TDCK Circular Thesaurus System* (1963), shown in Exhibit 18, appears to be the first of its type and was one of the first thesauri of any kind. Term displays take the form of concentric circles, each circle representing a level of the hierarchy, with the top term (in this

---

35mm CAMERAS E417.a2
    BT: Miniature cameras

CAMERAS E417.d5
    RT: Photography R562

CINE CAMERAS E417.f4
    BT: Moving picture cameras
    NT: Underwater cine cameras
    RT: Cinema R668

CINEMA R668.d5
    RT: Cine cameras E417

DIVING T473.g5
    RT: Underwater cameras E417

INSTANT PICTURE CAMERAS E417.b5
    SN: Cameras which produce a
        finished print directly
    BT: Still cameras

Land cameras *USE* VIEW CAMERAS

MINIATURE CAMERAS E417.b3
    BT: Still cameras
    NT: 35mm cameras

MOVING PICTURE CAMERAS E417.e4
    BT: Cameras
    NT: Cine cameras
        Television cameras

PHOTOGRAPHY R562.d5
    RT: Cameras E417

REFLEX CAMERAS E417.c3
    BT: Still cameras
    NT: Single lens reflex cameras
        Twin lens reflex cameras

SINGLE LENS REFLEX CAMERAS E417.c2
    BT: Reflex cameras

STEREO CAMERAS E417.c6
    BT: Cameras

STILL CAMERAS E417.c4
    BT: Cameras
    NT: Instant picture cameras
        Miniature cameras
        Reflex cameras
        View cameras

TELEVISION R685.d5
    RT: Television cameras E417

TELEVISION CAMERAS E417.e3
    BT: Moving picture cameras
    RT: Television R685

TWIN LENS REFLEX CAMERAS E417.d2
    BT: Reflex cameras

UNDERWATER CAMERAS E417.e6
    BT: Cameras
    NT: Underwater cine cameras
    RT: Diving T473

UNDERWATER CINE CAMERAS E417.g4
    BT: Cine cameras
        Underwater cameras

VIEW CAMERAS E417.b4
    SN: Cameras with through-the-lens
        focusing and a range of
        movements of the lens plane
        relative to the film plane
    UF: Land cameras
    BT: Still cameras

Exhibit 17 Alphabetic complement to graphic display in Exhibit 16. From *Guidelines for the Establishment and Development of Monolingual Thesauri*, ©1981. Reproduced by permission of Unesco.

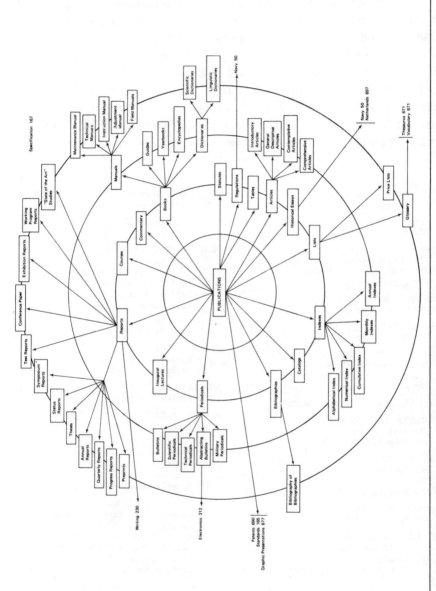

Exhibit 18 Specimen page from *TDCK Circular Thesaurus System*. Reprinted by permission of the Wetenschappelijk en Technisch Documentatie- en Informatiecentrum voor de Krijgsmacht.

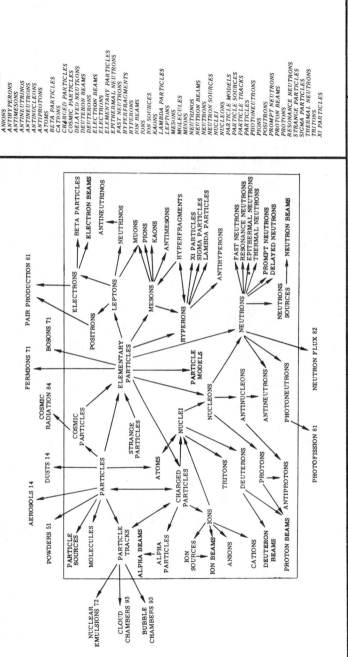

Exhibit 19 Specimen page from *EURATOM Thesaurus*, 1st Edition. Reprinted by permission of the Commission of the European Communities.

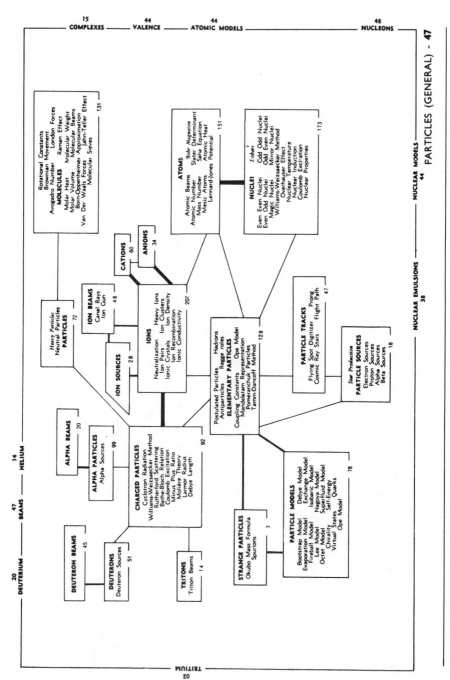

Exhibit 20 Specimen page from *EURATOM Thesaurus*, 2nd Edition. Note modification of graphic display used in 1st Edition. Reproduced by permission of the Commission of the European Communities.

A2   FURNACES

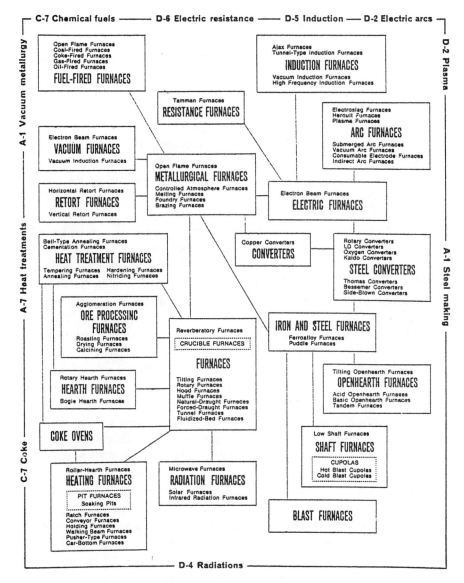

Exhibit 21   Graphic display used in the *Metallurgy Thesaurus* (1974). Reprinted by permission of the Commission of the European Communities.

exhibit, PUBLICATIONS) at the center. The first edition of the *TDCK Circular Thesaurus* displayed more than 10,000 terms in this way. According to Rolling (1979), the thesaurus is still updated regularly.

Perhaps better known are the graphic displays of the *EURATOM Thesaurus* (1966–1967), the justification for which is well presented by Rolling (1971). This thesaurus includes both alphabetic and graphic displays. Because the graphic display is used, the alphabetic display needs neither cross-references nor hierarchy. The graphic display used in the first edition (Exhibit 19) consists of arrowgraphs. Within each keyword group, the hierarchical and associative relationships are represented by arrows. These replace the cross-referencing encountered in a conventional thesaurus. Some arrows point to related keywords in other graphs. For example, NEUTRONS is related to NEUTRON FLUX, which appears in chart 82. The direction of the arrows is usually from the higher to the lower generic level; related keywords of the same generic level are linked with two-way arrows. In the second edition of the thesaurus, a modified display was adopted (Exhibit 20). Here, semantically related terms are grouped to form clusters (domains) around the keywords, which appear in uppercase letters. Nonkeyword *accepted* terms (synonyms and terms at lower generic levels—the *use* references in a conventional thesaurus) are in lowercase letters, and *forbidden* words are italicized. The difference between these two is that the *accepted* terms may be used in indexing and searching, whereas the *forbidden* terms may not. The *see also* or RT references of the classic thesaurus are replaced by links between terms in the arrowgraphs, with the thickness of the line indicating the strength of the link—that is, the strength of the "semantic relationship." Related graphs are referred to along the periphery of each diagram. Thus, DEUTERON BEAMS is connected to DEUTERIUM, which appears in graph 20, relating to radioisotopes. According to Colbach (1970), these displays "do away with the need for extensive cross-referencing and scope notes defining the conceptual coverage of the keywords, since the scope of every keyword is defined by the surrounding nonkeyword terminology and limited by the existence of its keyword neighbors" (pp. 587–588).

Finally, Exhibit 21 gives another format, from the *Metallurgy Thesaurus* (1974), a trilingual tool in the field of metallurgy. This thesaurus is similar to one used by the French Road Research Laboratory (Van Dijk, 1966). In these tools, a superimposable transparency can be used to show term equivalencies in various languages.

Graphic display is effective in all forms of communication. It has appeal in the thesaurus context because, like the faceted classification scheme, it brings related terms into physical proximity and allows an indexer or searcher to view a complete conspectus of these associations at a glance. The alphabetic display does not allow this; to get the full picture, we must dodge backward and forward as the related term references direct us. Extremely large hierarchies involving multiple relationships and levels, however, are difficult to display intelligibly in graphic form. Moreover, they tend to waste space.

Another thesaurus produced within the United Nations, the *SPINES Thesaurus* (1976), has several unique features. Exhibits 22 and 23 illustrate the alphabetic structured list and the graphic display, respectively. The alphabetic component of the thesaurus explicitly identifies all levels of BTs and NTs for each descriptor and gives scope notes, RTs, and *use* references. As mentioned in Chapter 9, a distinction is made between the *use* and *see* references (whose reciprocal is *sf*, seen from), the latter giving a choice of descriptors to replace the nondescriptor (entry term).

The graphic display uses polygons, subpolygons and sub-subpolygons in an attempt to clarify various hierarchical levels. Related polygons are linked by an "associative relation," a type of RT reference. A complete page of the graphic display ("chart") may include several interrelated polygons, although the example in Exhibit 23 shows only one complete polygon. (I find this particular graphic display to be more confusing than helpful.)

THE THESAUROFACET

The complementary alphabetic and graphic displays depicted in Exhibits 16 and 17 represent an attempt to combine the advantages of the conventional thesaurus with those of the hierarchical classification scheme. Another such attempt can be seen in the thesauro-

Top descriptor entry

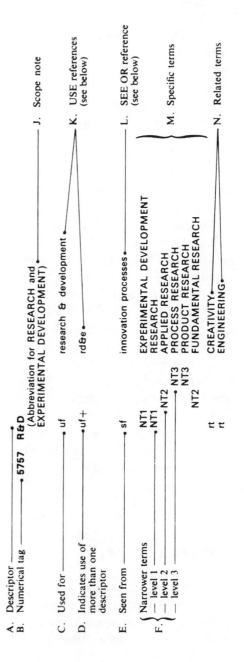

A. Descriptor
B. Numerical tag ——— 5757 R&D
(Abbreviation for RESEARCH and
EXPERIMENTAL DEVELOPMENT)

J. Scope note

C. Used for ——— uf ——— research & development

K. USE references
(see below) ——— uf+ rd&e

D. Indicates use of more than one descriptor

E. Seen from ——— sf ——— innovation processes

L. SEE OR reference
(see below)

F. Narrower terms
— level 1 ——— NT1   EXPERIMENTAL DEVELOPMENT
              NT1   RESEARCH
— level 2 ——— NT2   APPLIED RESEARCH
              NT3   PROCESS RESEARCH
              NT3   PRODUCT RESEARCH
— level 3 ——— NT2   FUNDAMENTAL RESEARCH

M. Specific terms

N. Related terms ——— rt   CREATIVITY
                     rt   ENGINEERING

Intermediate descriptor entry

435   APPLIED RESEARCH

G. Broader terms
— level 1 ——— bt1   RESEARCH

O. Generic terms

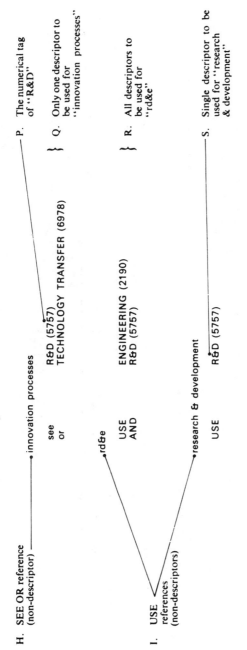

NT1   PRODUCT RESEARCH
rt   EXPERIMENTAL DEVELOPMENT
rt   FUNDAMENTAL RESEARCH

Non-descriptor entries

H. SEE OR reference ——————— innovation processes
   (non-descriptor)

       see   R&D (5757)
       or   TECHNOLOGY TRANSFER (6978)

         • rd&e

I. USE   USE   ENGINEERING (2190)
   references   AND   R&D (5757)
   (non-descriptors)

       • research & development

         USE   R&D (5757)

P. The numerical tag of "R&D"

Q. Only one descriptor to be used for "innovation processes"

R. All descriptors to be used for "rd&e"

S. Single descriptor to be used for "research & development"

Exhibit 22 Alphabetic display illustrative of the *SPINES Thesaurus*. From *SPINES Thesaurus*, ©1976. Reproduced by permission of Unesco.

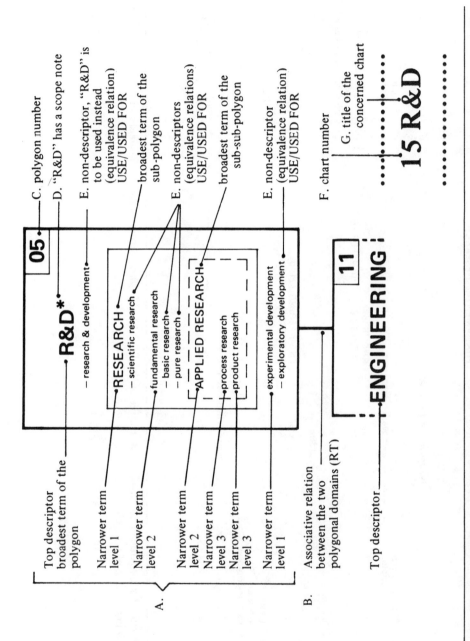

Exhibit 23 Polygonal display illustrative of the *SPINES Thesaurus*. From *SPINES Thesaurus*, ©1976. Reprinted by permission of Unesco.

facet, which combines the alphabetic thesaurus with a faceted hierarchical scheme.

Some entries from a hypothetical thesaurofacet are shown in Exhibit 24. Note that these two parts fully complement one another. The faceted component takes care of the hierarchical relationship (i.e., the BT/NT structure), and all other relationships appear in the thesaurus component. The thesaurus component gives the notation for each term so that the user can go to the faceted component to see the hierarchical relationship. In the faceted classification, a term appears only once; however, if a term can legitimately appear in more than one hierarchy, the secondary relationships are given in the thesaurus, using the convention BT (A), which stands for "additional broader term." The thesaurofacet has an obvious advantage over other thesaurus forms: It can be used for arranging books on the shelves of a special library as well as for indexing the items in a data base. Moreover, shelf arrangement and data base will be fully compatible.

The first thesaurofacet was produced by Aitchison et al. (1969). Containing 16,000 approved terms and 7,000 "entry terms," it completely integrated the faceted classification (Exhibit 25) and the thesaurus (Exhibit 26). Both look fairly conventional. *Use* references control synonyms and provide entries for specific terms that are not used for indexing or searching. The UF reciprocals also appear. Against each descriptor in the thesaurus is its class number. Thus,

Faceted display		*Thesaurus display*
L	Libraries	City libraries Ldc
La	Academic libraries	UF Municipal libraries
Lac	College libraries	RT City government Qp
Lah	University libraries	
Ld	Public libraries	Industrial libraries Li
Ldc	City libraries	BT (A) Industrial information
Ldf	Rural libraries	services Rj
Li	Industrial libraries	
Lk	Government libraries	Municipal libraries
		use City libraries Ldc

Exhibit 24 Examples from a hypothetical thesaurofacet in library science.

96

Electron tubes   MA

	Electron wave tubes
MBE	
MBF	Travelling wave tubes
MBH	Backward wave tubes
MBJ	Carcinotrons
MBM	Magnetrons
MBP	Velocity modulated tubes
MBQ	Klystrons
MBT	**Electron beam deflection tubes**
MBV	Indicator tubes (tuning)
MBW	Trochotrons
MC	Cathode ray tubes
MC2	Image converter tubes
MC4	Image intensifiers
MC6	Storage tubes
MCE	Television camera tubes
MCI	Television colour camera tubes
MCL	Television picture tubes
MCO	Television colour picture tubes
MCQ	**X ray tubes**
MCS	**Phototubes**
	Photomultipliers
MCT	**Electron multipliers**
MCW	· Photomultipliers MCT

By number of electrodes:

MD	Diodes (tubes)
	· Plasma diodes (tubes) MAR

· Electron tube oscillators   LL, MA
· Electron tube rectifiers   JPL

By components:

MF	Electron tube components
	· Electrodes KP
	· Electron guns EHT
	· Electron lenses EHL
	· Fluorescent screens DWQ
MF3	Grids (tube components)
MF5	Filaments (tube components)
MF6	Heaters (tube components)

By techniques:

MFM	Electron tube production techniques
	Combine with appropriate notation from Production engineering and other schedules
	· Brazing TQ
	· Glass metal seals QNS
	· Soldering TQO
	· Vacuum engineering PV
	· Welding TN

Semiconductors

MG	· Crystals FB

MD5	(Thyratrons ...) Multielectrode tubes
	· Trochotrons MBW
MD6	Phasitrons
MD7	Reactance tubes
MDA	Tetrodes
MDB	Dynatrons
MDC	Resnatrons
MDG	Pentodes
MDH	Pentagrid converters
MDL	Multiple unit tubes

By application:

	· Storage tubes MC6	MCE
	· Television camera tubes	MCL
	· Television picture tubes	
MER	Counting tubes	
	· Indicator tubes (numerical)	MB7
MET	· Trochotrons MBW	
	Dekatrons	

For other applications combine notation for Electron tubes with application For manual systems the preferred order is application followed by tube. but permuted entries may be made. for example

· Electron tube amplifiers	LE/MA
· Electron tube demodulators	LW/MA
· Electron tube mixers	LX/MA
· Electron tube modulators	LV/MA

SEMICONDUCTOR MATERIALS

MG2	SEMICONDUCTOR MATERIALS
MGB	Binary semiconductor materials
MGC	Ternary semiconductor materials
MGF	Intrinsic semiconductor materials
MGG	Extrinsic semiconductor materials
MGJ	Impurity elements
MGK	Acceptors
MGL	Donors
MGN	N type semiconductor materials
MGP	P type semiconductor materials
MGR	Bulk semiconductor materials
MGS	Multivalley semiconductor materials
MGV	Mixed valence semiconductor materials
MGW	Seminsulators

For individual semiconductor materials combine with the notation from the materials schedules. for example :—

MG2/GLR	Silicon semiconductor materials
MG2/GLS	Germanium semiconductor materials
MG2/HFG/HLP	Gallium arsenide semiconductor materials

SEMICONDUCTOR DEVICES

MH	SEMICONDUCTOR DEVICES
	· Semiconductor amplifiers LE/MH
	· Semiconductor demodulators LW/MH
	· Semiconductor lasers MOF
	· Semiconductor masers MNL
	· Semiconductor modulators LV·MH

Exhibit 2.5 Specimen page from faceted classification portion of Aitchison et al.'s *Thesaurofacet* (1969). Reprinted by permission of GEC Power Engineering Ltd.

Teletypewriters
    Telegraph receivers
    Telegraph transmitters
  BT(A) Automatic typewriters
    Typewriters

Television   NH
  RT Television and radio manufacturing
      industries
    Television broadcasting
    Television films
    Television recording
    Television telephone calling
      apparatus
    Vehicular communications

Television Aerials   NSN
  RT Television masts
    Television receivers
    Television stations
    Television transmission systems
    Television transmitters
    Towers
  BT(A) Television apparatus

Television and Radio Manufacturing
  Industries   ZKFW
  UF Radio industry
  RT Radio
    Television

Television Apparatus   NJ
  RT Television switching
  NT(A) Colour television apparatus
    Fluorescent screens
    Radiofrequency transformers
    Telecine equipment
    Television aerials
    Television receivers
    Television recording cameras
    Television telephone calling
      apparatus
    Television transmitters
    Vison mixers

Television Broadcasting   ZLSJD
  RT Colour television
    Subscription television
    Television

    Equalising pulses
    Horizontal deflection oscillators
    Limiters
    Phase detectors
    Scanning circuits
    Synchronising pulse generators
    Synchronising separators
    Television time bases
    Vertical deflection oscillators
    Videofrequency amplifiers
    Vision mixers

Television Colour Camera Tubes   MCI
  UF Colour camera tubes (colour television)
    Colour cell
    Pick up tubes (colour television)
    Plumbicons
  RT Colour television cameras
  BT(A) Colour television apparatus

Television Colour Picture Tubes   MCO
  UF Apple tubes
    Banana tubes
    Colour picture tubes (television)
    Display tubes (television colour)
    Chromatrons
    Flat picture tubes
    Gabar tubes
    Kaiser Aiten thin tubes
    Kinescope (colour)
    Reflected beam kinescope
    Shadowmask tubes
    Television display tubes (colour)
  RT Colour television receivers

Television Communication Systems use
Television Transmission Systems

Television Display Tubes (colour) use
Television Colour Picture Tubes

Television Distribution Systems use
Television Transmission Systems

Television Fields   ENS
  RT Interlaced scanning
    Television scanning

  RT Towers (television)
    Radio towers
    Television aerials
    Television transmission systems
    Television transmitters
    Television transmitting aerials
    Towers
  BT(A) Masts

Television Modulation   NH2
  RT Chrominance modulators
    Colour television transmisson
      systems
    Colour television transmitters
    Television transmitters
  BT(A) Modulation

Television Networks   NHA
  RT Television links
  BT(A) Communication networks

Television Picture Tubes   MCL
  UF Display tubes (television)
    Kinescope
    Picture tubes (television)
  RT Fluorescent screens
    Phosphors
    Raster
    Television receivers
  BT(A) Television apparatus

Television Receiver Control   NIQ
  RT Television receivers
    Television synchronisation
    Tuning
  NT(A) Colour television receiver control

Television Receivers   NVU
  RT Fluorescent screens
    Television aerials
    Television circuits
    Television picture tubes
    Television receiver control
    Television receiving aerials
    Television reception
    Television synchronisation
  BT(A) Television apparatus

Television Screens use
Fluorescent Screens

Television Signal Frequency use
Videofrequency

Television Signals   NHE
  UF Signals (television)
  NT(A) Colour signals

Television Standards Convertors   NJ7
  UF Convertors (television standard)
    Image transfer standards convertors
    Standard convertors television
  RT Bandwidth compression
    Low pass filters
    Magnetic recording

Television Standard Signals   NHJ
  JF Colour television standard signals
  RT Colour signals
    Standardisation
  BT(A) Standards

Television Stations   NJD
  UF Stations (television)
  RT Television aerials
    Television broadcasting
    Television transmission systems
    Television transmitters
    Television transmitting aerials

Television Studio Apparatus   NJH
  UF Control rooms (television)
    Sound control (television)
    Vison control (television)
  RT Optical television recording
    Television films
  NT(A) Luminaires
    Microphones
    Sound mixers
    Telecine equipment
    Television cameras
    Television recording cameras
    Vison mixers

Television Studios   NJF
  UF Studios (television)

Television Time Bases

systems

Television Cameras NJ3
RT Television camera tubes
   Television transmitters
NT(A) Colour television cameras
   Television recording cameras
BT(A) Television studio apparatus

Television Camera Tubes MCE
UF Camera tubes (television)
   Emitrons
   Iconoscopes
   Image iconoscopes
   Image orthicons
   Orthicons
   Pick up tubes (television)
   Vidicons
RT Phototubes
   Photomultipliers
   Television cameras
BT(A) Television apparatus

Television Centres use
Television Studios

Television Channels NHC
UF Channels (television)
RT Television links

Television Circuits NJA
RT Clamping circuits
   Television interference
   Television receivers
   Television scanning
   Television synchronisation
   Television transmitters
   Video circuits
NT(A) Colour television circuits
   Combining amplifiers

Films (television) WIG
RT Optical television recording
   Photographic film
   Telecine equipment
   Television
   Television studio apparatus
BT(A) Films

Television Guidance WIG

Television Interference NI4
RT Snow (spurious signals)
   Television circuits
   Television transmission systems
NT(A) Colour television interference
   Crossview
BT(A) Interference (radio wave)

Television Interference Suppression NI4/MXS
Synth
S RT Television interference
S NT(A) Colour television interference
   suppression
S BT(A) Interference suppression

Television Links NJN
UF Links (television)
   Point to point television links
RT Vision links
   Communication satellites
   Microwave communication systems
   Radio links
   Radio towers
   Television channels
   Television networks

Television Masts NJK
UF Television towers

NT(A) Communal television aerials

Television Reception NI
RT Signal detection
   Signal processing
   Television receivers
NT(A) Colour television reception
BT(A) Reception

Television Reception Quality NI2
NT(A) Colour television reception
   quality
BT(A) Reception quality

Television Recording WRH
UF Video recording (television)
RT Recording receivers
   Television
   Video tape recorders

Television Recording Cameras WRW
UF Recording cameras (television)
   Telecine cameras
RT Optical television recording
BT(A) Television apparatus
   Television cameras
   Television studio apparatus

Television Rediffusion use
Television Wire Transmission Systems

Television Relay Systems use
Television Links

Television Scanning NIB
RT Raster
   Television circuits
   Television fields
NT(A) Colour television scanning
   Interlaced scanning
BT(A) Scanning

Television Switching MM6
UF Switching (television)
   Video switching
RT Switches
   Television apparatus

Television Synchronisation NIE
UF Synchronising signals
RT Hold control
   Horizontal deflection oscillators
   Oscillators
   Sweep generators
   Synchronising separators
   Television circuits
   Television receiver control
   Television receivers
   Television time bases
   Television transmitters
   Vertical deflection oscillators
NT(A) Colour television synchronisation
BT(A) Synchronisation (electric)

Television Systems NJM
NT(A) Television telephone calling
   apparatus
   Television wire transmission
   systems
   Walkie-lookies

Television Telephone Calling Apparatus N70
RT Television wire transmission
   systems
BT(A) Television apparatus
   Television systems

Television Time Bases LKJ
UF Frame generators
   Line generators

Exhibit 26 Specimen page from the thesaurus portion of Aitchison et al.'s *Thesaurofacet* (1969). Reprinted by permission of GEC Power Engineering Ltd.

TELEVISION CAMERA TUBES is given the class number MCE. In the classification schedules, the faceted display reveals the complete hierarchy of broader terms (CATHODE RAY TUBES, ELECTRON BEAM DEFLECTION TUBES, ELECTRON TUBES) and narrower terms (TELEVISION COLOR CAMERA TUBES). It also shows the terms that are most closely related, that is, the coequal terms in the same array (e.g., STORAGE TUBES, IMAGE CONVERTER TUBES) and the terms subsidiary to these. The advantage over the conventional thesaurus is that the display shows all these relations for any term at a glance and shows the correct relations among these terms.

The thesaurus section of Aitchison et al.'s *Thesaurofacet* also contains some RTs and BTs but does not duplicate any feature of the classified section. The related terms are terms from other facets. TELEVISION CAMERA TUBES is shown to be related to PHOTOTUBES, PHOTOMULTIPLIERS, and TELEVISION CAMERAS. None of these belongs in the same array as TELEVISION CAMERA TUBES and thus might well be overlooked if the faceted display alone were used.

The related terms shown in the thesaurus are not terms related hierarchically. The thesaurus displays other relationships (e.g., between a whole and a part or between an object and its properties). Likewise, the thesaurus does not display the same BT relationship shown in the faceted structure. The faceted display shows only the principal hierarchy. Others are revealed in the thesaurus. In the case of TELEVISION CAMERA TUBES, the additional hierarchy, indicated by the abbreviation BT (A), is the hierarchy of TELEVISION APPARATUS.

The thesaurus similarly lists additional narrower terms, indicated by NT (A). As an illustration, consider the term JETS. This appears in the faceted schedules as follows:

CWJ   Jets
CWK   Jet Streams
CWL   Plumes
CWM   Wall jets
CWO   Couette flow
CWP   Jet mixing
CWQ   Propulsive jets

This is the primary JETS hierarchy; the JETS listed here are all fluid dynamic jets. But there are other types of jets, and these additional hierarchical linkages are shown as NT (A)s under JETS in the thesaurus:

> JETS
> NT(A) JETS (HOVERCRAFT)
> PLASMA JETS

Used jointly, the classification scheme and the thesaurus reveal the "multiple hierarchical linkage" of terms.

In the *Thesaurofacet*, the thesaurus replaces the alphabetic subject index that would normally accompany the schedules in a conventional faceted classification. Likewise, the faceted classification replaces the usual hierarchical structure built into a thesaurus by means of BT/NT references. In a sense, the *Thesaurofacet* achieves the best of all worlds. It benefits from careful facet analysis and thus consistently displays the most important relationships between terms and provides consistent control of synonyms. The faceted schedules facilitate generic search, and the thesaurus portion facilitates immediate access to a specific term and also provides interterm relationships that cut across the faceted structure. The tool can be used equally well as a terminological authority in a pre-coordinate system (using notational synthesis) or a post-coordinate system.

Since the *Thesaurofacet* was published, a number of vocabularies built on the same principles have appeared. These vary somewhat from the original in the degree of interdependency between the faceted and alphabetic components. The *Unesco Thesaurus* (1977), compiled by Jean Aitchison, the architect of the original thesaurofacet, is one example.

The *ROOT Thesaurus* (1981) is perhaps the most elaborate of the tools to combine a faceted classification with an alphabetic display of terms. Exhibits 27 and 28 show examples from the two major displays. In Exhibit 27, the facets into which a subject is divided are clearly and explicitly indicated ("By property," "By additive," and so on). The thesaurus uses some special conventions, as follows (p. 102):

JOK	Gasoline
	= High-grade gasoline
	= Petrol
	* < Automotive fuels JFR
	* – Petrol engines NGK.R
	(By property)
JOK.K	Antiknock ratings
JOK.KK	Octane number
	* – Isooctane DQC.CIJ
	(By additive)
JOK.S	Gasoline additives
	= Petrol additives
	* < Additives TJP
	* – Lead alkyls DWB.B
JOK.SO	Antiknock additives
JON	Bitumens
	* – Construction materials RXH
JON.C	Natural bitumens
JON.E	Asphalts
	* – Asphaltic cement VUC.QH
	* -- Tarmacadam RXH.T
JON.EF	Mastic asphalts
JON.ER	Rolled asphalts
JON.G	Asphaltene
JON.J	Cut-back bitumens
JON.N	Fluxed bitumens
JON.Q	Reinforced bitumens
JON.S	Bituminous products
	= Bituminous materials
	* > Bituminous cement VUC.Q
JON.SO	Bituminous felts
JOQ	Tars
	* > Coal tar JKT
	* – Tarmacadam RXH.T
JOT	Pitch (petroleum product)
JOW	Mineral waxes
	= Waxes (mineral)
JOW.G	Petroleum jelly
	≔ Petrolatum
	(By application)
JOY	Flux oil
	* < Fluxes (materials) TOY

Exhibit 27   Specimen hierarchies from the faceted component of the *ROOT Thesaurus* (1981). Reprinted by permission of the British Standards Institution.

Geothermal power   JEJ
    <   Fuelless energy sources
   * −   Geothermal-electric power
           stations   KDN.CP

Heavy fuel oil   JOB.BH
    <   Fuel oil

High-grade gasoline
    →   Gasoline   JOK

Hydrogen
    +   Gas generators
   = **   Hydrogen generators   JQK.GH

**Hydrogen generators   JQK.GH
    →   Gas generators
       +   Hydrogen

Kerosine   JOB.BB
    =   Paraffin
    <   Fuel oil

Light fuel oil   JOB.BG
    <   Fuel oil

Lignite   JFD.D
    =   Brown coal
    <   Coal

Ligroin   JOB.BD
    <   Fuel oil

Liquefied natural gas   JFE.L
    <   Natural gas

Liquefied petroleum gas   JQG
    =   LPG
    −   Gas technology
   * <   Gaseous fuels   JFJ
   * <   Liquefied gases   CIL.LL
   * <   Petroleum products   JN/JO
   * −   Butane   DQC.CE
   * −   Pentane   DQC.CF
   * −   Propane   DQC.CD

Liquid fuel appliances   JFI.G
    −   Liquid fuels
   * −   Oil-fuelled devices   JOB.BV

Liquid fuels   JFI
    <   Fuels
    −   Liquid fuel appliances
   * >   Fuel oil   JOB.B

LPG
    →   Liquefied petroleum gas   JQG

Manually-operated devices   JET
    −   Fuelless energy sources
   * −   Manual control systems   MCE

Manufactured gas   JQE
    >   Town gas
    −   Gas technology
   * <   Gases   DGD.E
   * >   Acetylene   DQD.QB
   * >   Coal gas   JKI
   * >   Water gas   JKM
   * −   Coal gasification   JJG

Mastic asphalts   JON.EF
    <   Asphalts

Mineral oils   JOB
[Excluding crude petroleum]
    =   Oils (mineral)
    >   Fuel oil
    >   Residual oil
    −   Petroleum products
   * −   Coolants   TMF
   * −   Hydraulic fluids   NIE.H
   * −   Insulating oils   KNY.JC
   * −   Lubricating oils   VMM
   * −   Vegetable and animal oils
           technology   VM

Mineral waxes   JOW
    =   Waxes (mineral)
    <   Petroleum products
    >   Petroleum jelly

Motor Fuels
    →   Automotive fuels   JFR

Natural bitumens   JON.C
    <   Bitumens

Natural gas   JFE
    <   Fossil fuels
    >   Liquefied natural gas
   * <   Gases   DGD.E
   * −   Gas technology   JQ
   * −   Natural gas extraction   SFN

Nuclear containment structures   JSK
    =   Containment structures
           (nuclear)
    −   Nuclear technology

Nuclear energy
    →   Nuclear power   JG

Nuclear Engineering
    →   Nuclear technology   JS

Nuclear fuel processing   JSP
    −   Nuclear technology
   * −   Nuclear fuels   JGG

Nuclear fuels   JGG
    =   Fissile materials
    −   Nuclear power
   * <   Fuels   JF

Exhibit 28   Specimen entries from the alphabetic display of the *ROOT Thesaurus* (1981). Reprinted by permission of the British Standards Institution.

=	a nonpreferred synonym
* <	an additional broader term from elsewhere in the display (e.g., GASOLINE ADDITIVES can be considered a narrower term under TJP, ADDITIVES, as well as a subdivision of GASOLINE).
* >	an additional narrower term from another part of the display
* −	an additional related term from another part of the display

The alphabetic section of the *ROOT Thesaurus* (Exhibit 28) gives only one level of hierarchy. The following conventions are used:

=	a nonpreferred synonym
<	a broader term in the same part of the display (e.g., LIGNITE is shown to be a narrower term under COAL)
>	a narrower term in the same part of the display (e.g., FUEL OIL is a narrower term under MINERAL OILS)
−	a related term in the same part of the display (e.g., LIQUID FUEL APPLIANCES is related to LIQUID FUELS)
* <	a broader term in another display
* >	a narrower term in another display
* −	a related term in another display

Nondescriptors are handled in one of two ways. The first example,

HIGH-GRADE GASOLINE

→ GASOLINE   JOK

indicates that the former topic is to be indexed under the latter term. The second example,

        **HYDROGEN GENERATORS JQK.GH
       →GAS GENERATORS
       +HYDROGEN

indicates a "synthesized term": The term HYDROGEN GENERATORS is not to be used; instead, this concept is to be indexed under GAS GENERATORS and HYDROGEN (note that the entry under HYDROGEN shows that this term + GAS GENERATORS is to be used to represent HYDROGEN GENERATORS). The special symbols used in place of BT, NT, RT, and *use* make the structure independent of language.

The entire scheme is ingenious, and great care has gone into its construction. One wonders, however, if such sophistication of structure is really needed in most information retrieval applications. It is certainly a far cry from natural language, which is discussed in Chapter 17.

12 *Vocabulary Growth and Updating*

A controlled vocabulary cannot be static; it must grow. A vocabulary developed by drawing terms from the literature will grow very quickly at first but will gradually level off. How large the vocabulary will be depends not only on the subject field but also on the specificity of the terms and their type. A vocabulary with a large amount of compounding will tend to be larger and to grow more quickly than one that involves little compounding.

The rate of vocabulary growth will also depend on what the terms are describing. The growth curve shown in Exhibit 29, taken from Wadington (1958), is unusual in that no plateau had been reached after 10,000 documents had been indexed. The true subject descriptors, however, began to level off early. Most of the continued growth was in "materials" terms. These are mainly terms for chemicals and specific chemical compounds. Clearly, this type of vocabulary could be very large and could continue to grow steadily, so long as documents on new chemical compounds are encountered in indexing.

At some point in the development of a thesaurus, it may be desirable to estimate its completeness to determine whether it can be put

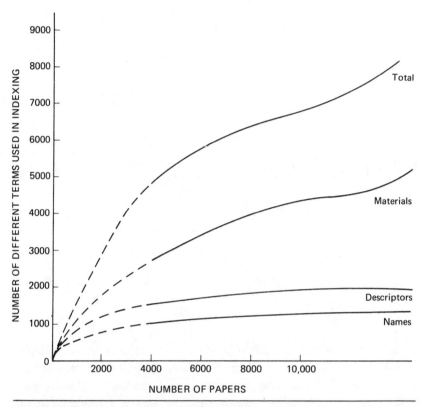

Exhibit 29   Growth curve showing rate of addition of terms of various types. From Wadington (1958), copyright John Wiley & Sons, Inc., by permission of the publisher.

into service. This can be done by taking a random sample of recently published items and checking to see to what extent they can be indexed completely and precisely. A formalized procedure is recommended, as follows:

1. Draw a random sample of, say, 100 papers from the latest issues of relevant periodicals.

2. Develop an indexing form in two columns. On the left, the indexers write down phrases representing their conceptual analyses of the papers. On the right, they translate these into the most appropri-

ate terms available in the thesaurus. For reasons of objectivity, the indexers should not have been directly involved in the process of thesaurus construction.

3. A team comprising the indexers and the thesaurus compilers scores the test on the basis of the proportion of the total number of concepts that can be translated completely and precisely (i.e., at the required level of specificity) into thesaurus terms.

This type of test, inexpensive to implement, can be used not only to estimate completeness but to check on the specificity of terms throughout the thesaurus and to reveal other defects or problems associated with the use of the draft. A more mathematically precise procedure is described by Snow (1965), but it is unnecessarily elaborate for the purposes of this book.

UPDATING THE VOCABULARY

Once a vocabulary has grown to a leveling-off point, continued gradual growth to increase specificity and to accommodate new topics is to be expected, but there should not be any sudden bursts of growth unless the information center happens to move into completely new subject areas. The continued growth of the vocabulary should come from within the system and should be based on literary and user warrant: New terms will be derived from the indexing and searching operations. They will be terms needed to express items of subject matter occurring in documents and in requests that cannot be expressed in the terms of the present vocabulary. This is the principal criterion governing the addition of new terms to a vocabulary.

In a large information center or network of information centers, a vocabulary control group (sometimes called a "lexicographic staff") may be created to review the vocabulary on a continuous basis and, in particular, to consider recommendations for new terms made by indexers and searchers.

If an indexer encounters a topic that cannot adequately be represented in the vocabulary, he may generate a new "candidate" descriptor. Justification for the new descriptor is based on the subject analyst's own expertise, thesaurus rules and conventions, handbooks, and other reference materials. The candidate descriptor may be entered on the indexing form, on a special input form, or directly at an on-line terminal. It is reviewed by the vocabulary control group for compliance with thesaurus rules and overlap with existing terms, among other factors. In some systems, a new descriptor is introduced for a trial period; its use patterns (manner and frequency of use) are observed and it is then retained or discarded.

Besides adding new terms to the vocabulary, thesaurus updating will also include some term deletion, although the amount of deletion is unlikely to equal the amount of addition. A term may be deleted and replaced by a synonymous or nearly synonymous expression. This is likely to reflect a change in the accepted terminology of the field. Alternatively, a term may be deleted and referred by a *use* reference to another term of broader scope.

The decision to delete a specific term and map to a broader one is usually based on the fact that the specific term has not been used much in indexing and therefore would not be missed. Statistics of indexing use are valuable indicators in vocabulary updating operations and are maintained in most systems. Strangely enough, statistics on term usage in searching are less frequently kept; yet, in a sense, these are more important. However often a term is used in indexing, it is unjustified if, over a two-year period (for instance), it has never been used in searching. This might indicate that the term is unnecessarily specific, but indexers use it because it is available and documents exist on the specific topic. Even so, requests are never made this specifically in the particular subject area, so a term at this level of specificity is redundant. On the other hand, a term that has not been used in searching might indicate a discrepancy between the scope of the collection and the interests of the clientele.

A controlled vocabulary must be tailored to the types of requests made to the retrieval system. Furthermore, system users must make initial requests in their own natural-language terms and not in the terms of the system vocabulary, and their requests should be recorded and analyzed for input to vocabulary-updating procedures. It is highly undesirable to require a user to make an initial request in the terms of a controlled vocabulary because the request will be unnaturally constrained by the terminology of the system; that is, the user will ask not for what he wants but for what he thinks the system can give him, which may be quite removed from his actual information needs. Also, if users always phrase requests in the terminology of the system, one will tend not to become aware of inadequacies in the system caused by lack of specificity in the vocabulary. For example, many users might like to be able to search on terms indicating specific oxides or groups of oxides (e.g., alkaline earth oxides), but they do not make their requests this specific. Instead, they say OXIDES, because this is the only descriptor existing in this area. Consequently, the information service is not made aware that, to meet user needs adequately, the descriptor requires further subdivision.

For vocabulary-updating purposes (as well as for other reasons), it is desirable that all requests made to a retrieval system be initially recorded in the user's own words (on a search request form or at an on-line terminal) and that the translation into system terminology take place *after* the natural-language statement is recorded.

Addition of new terms to a vocabulary, at least on a provisional basis, will occur continuously. But term deletion involves the analysis of statistics on term usage, which can be done only through complete, periodic vocabulary-review procedures. Sometimes, such review is done annually, leading to the production of a revised edition of the thesaurus.

Although continuous vocabulary review is essential if a retrieval system is to remain responsive to user needs, changes in terminology over time do complicate the searching process when many years of a data base are involved. By using a computer to maintain term histories, however, such searching problems are minimized. The role of the computer in vocabulary control is dealt with in Chapter 13.

13 *The Role of the Computer*

Computers play a valuable role in vocabulary control. They can be used to

1. Gather terms in the initial stages of thesaurus building
2. Expand the structure of a thesaurus, check for consistency, and generate alternative displays
3. Generate a printed tool
4. Facilitate updating and maintenance
5. Allow the vocabulary to interface with indexing and searching operations
6. Allow the vocabulary to interface with the production of a printed index
7. Allow for on-line vocabulary display

The gathering of terms is discussed in Chapter 2. Terms can be derived from machine-readable data bases and ranked lists produced on the basis of frequency of occurrence. Even if terms are not derived from machine-readable sources, it is often advantageous to put them in machine-readable form for sorting and counting and for possible production of co-occurrence tables.

Because the construction of a conventional thesaurus is mainly an intellectual activity, computer processing of terms contributes to this task only in minor ways. For example, by sorting and printing all terms according to final words (WELDING, GAS WELDING, SHIELDED ARC WELDING) or even by the roots of these words, the computer can perhaps aid in the identification of facets or hierarchies.

Once the thesaurus compiler has organized the vocabulary into facets and hierarchies, however, computer processing is extremely valuable, if not essential. As an example, consider the partial hierarchy displayed in Exhibit 30, where a simple notation is used to represent hierarchical levels. With these data, the computer can print a hierarchical display such as that shown in Exhibit 14; a permuted word display such as that shown in Exhibit 15; and, providing each hierarchy has been placed in a particular subject category, a categorized display such as that in Exhibit 13. More important, however, a computer program can be used to generate a perfectly consistent alphabetic display (as in Exhibit 31) with all BTs, NTs, RTs and *use* references reciprocated. Furthermore, the thesaurus data in machine-readable form can be input to a photocomposition device so that the final printout of all displays is of high typographic quality.

1	LIBRARIES
11	ACADEMIC LIBRARIES RT HIGHER EDUCATION
112	COLLEGE LIBRARIES
1121	JUNIOR COLLEGE LIBRARIES
113	UNIVERSITY LIBRARIES
12	PUBLIC LIBRARIES
13	SPECIAL LIBRARIES

Exhibit 30   Thesaurus input from which various displays can be generated by computer.

ACADEMIC LIBRARIES
    BT   LIBRARIES
    NT   COLLEGE LIBRARIES
          UNIVERSITY LIBRARIES
    RT   HIGHER EDUCATION

COLLEGE LIBRARIES
    BT   ACADEMIC LIBRARIES
    NT   JUNIOR COLLEGE LIBRARIES

HIGHER EDUCATION
    RT   ACADEMIC LIBRARIES

JUNIOR COLLEGE LIBRARIES
    BT   COLLEGE LIBRARIES

LIBRARIES
    NT   ACADEMIC LIBRARIES
          PUBLIC LIBRARIES
          SPECIAL LIBRARIES

Exhibit 31   Sample thesaurus entries generated by computer from the data of Exhibit 30.

THESAURUS MAINTENANCE

In addition to producing a thesaurus and presenting it in a number of output formats, computer programs can be used to maintain the thesaurus. Terms can be added at any time. The addition of a new term, in the appropriate way, will cause the term to be incorporated into the thesaurus structure in its correct position and the necessary reciprocals generated. When a term is deleted from the thesaurus, the programs will check all the term reciprocals and delete all references to this term automatically. If the spelling of a term is changed, the programs will alter the spelling in all the appropriate places. If additional cross-references are added to a term, the programs will automatically generate the necessary reciprocals for these. Similarly, the computer will make all needed thesaurus alterations when a scope note is changed or when a term is moved from one subject category to another. Chepkasov (1977) has prepared a detailed description of a thesaurus maintenance program used by the International Atomic Energy Agency. The program takes care of all changes caused by the addition or deletion of a term, including references to the term in the scope notes of other terms. The program is now operating on-line.

THE MASTER VOCABULARY FILE

Just as the computer plays a valuable role in generating a printed thesaurus, the machine-readable thesaurus has important functions in the operation of a retrieval system. The machine-readable thesaurus is a fully authoritative record of the system vocabulary, and it is completely up-to-date. Let us call it the "master vocabulary file" (MVF). In addition to providing thesaurus printouts of various types, the MVF has the following functions in a computer-based retrieval system:

1. It checks for consistency and acceptability of terms used by indexers and searchers. Should an indexer or searcher use a term that is not recognized by the MVF, the input record or search input will be rejected with an appropriate notification. In addition to checking for appearance and spelling of descriptors, the MVF can be used to check on acceptability of combinations. For example, it can check on the validity of descriptor/subheading combinations.

2. In some systems, the MVF may undertake certain automatic mapping activities. For example, the indexer or searcher may be allowed to use any of several synonyms recognized in the thesaurus, the MVF automatically substituting the preferred term. Only when a term used by the indexer or searcher is completely unrecognized will the input be rejected. Mapping can be from synonymous expressions (e.g., ASPIRIN *use* ACETYLSALICYLIC ACID) or from combinations (e.g., LUNG PHYSIOLOGY *use* LUNG/PHYSIOLOGY, where PHYSIOLOGY has become a subheading under LUNG).

3. A special form of mapping is associated with term history. Vocabularies used in indexing and searching do not remain static.

Changes are made over time, usually to make the vocabulary increasingly specific or to reflect current preferences in terminology. It is difficult and tedious to maintain the history of a large vocabulary by manual processes. The computer can do this very easily. Suppose, for example, that the term CIRCADIAN RHYTHM was first introduced into the vocabulary on 5/9/75. Prior to that date, the more generic term PERIODICITY was used for this specific concept. The printed thesaurus now shows CIRCADIAN RHYTHM as an accepted term so the indexer has no problem in handling documents on this topic. But what about the searcher? He must use the term PERIODICITY for material prior to 5/9/75 if he wishes a comprehensive search. The MVF can be used to generate printouts showing terminological changes; this would mean that the searcher must always consult such printouts and use all variants (with date restrictions) in conducting a search. An alternative would be to have the searcher use only the latest descriptor, allowing the search programs to substitute earlier versions automatically. Thus, in this example, if the searcher used CIRCADIAN RHYTHM, the search program would automatically substitute PERIODICITY in searching records input before 5/9/75.

4. The MVF maintains certain useful statistics that would be difficult, if not impossible, to keep up manually. First and foremost, it maintains a record of the number of "postings" under each term— that is, the number of times the term has been used in indexing. Such data can be presented in printouts or displayed on-line. Information on the frequency with which a term has been used in indexing is valuable in the searching operation because it allows the searcher to estimate how many citations will be retrieved in response to a particular search strategy or, at the very least, shows the maximum number of citations that could possibly be retrieved.

Statistics on frequency of assignment in indexing are important also in vocabulary-control activities. A descriptor that has been used infrequently in the past year may be a good candidate for deletion from the vocabulary.

Statistics on frequency of use of terms in searching also are extremely valuable in vocabulary control (perhaps even more valuable than the statistics on indexing use); these are used less frequently in automated systems than are statistics on frequency of assignment, although they are no more difficult to collect.

5. A record of the complete hierarchical structure of the vocabulary should appear on the MVF. This facilitates the conduct of generic searches. Only the parent term need be specified in searching, its descendants being substituted automatically from the MVF. This procedure is used in MEDLINE (the National Library of Medicine's Medical Literature Analysis and Retrieval System Online), where the hierarchical structure of the vocabulary is fully recorded on the MVF and in print in *Medical Subject Headings Tree Structures* (Exhibit 32).

Suppose one wanted to conduct a search on some aspect of tuberculosis and was interested in all types of tuberculosis. Without the MVF, he would need to incorporate all tuberculosis terms in an *or* relationship: TUBERCULOSIS *or* TUBERCULOSIS, AVIAN *or* TUBERCULOSIS, BOVINE *or* TUBERCULOSIS, . . . , and so on. Considering that there are some 30 terms to choose from, this would be a tedious and unnecessary procedure. To accomplish such a generic search in MEDLINE, where it is referred to as an *explosion,* one need enter only the appropriate generic term or its category number. In this instance, if the command EXPLODE C1.252.40.552.846 is entered on-line, the MVF will automatically expand to include all subdivisions and incorporate these automatically, in an *or* relationship, into the search strategy.

6. Using statistics on frequency of term assignment in indexing, the MVF may be used in the automatic optimization of a search strategy. Consider the Boolean strategy (A *or* B) *and* (L *or* M *or* N) *and* Y. To satisfy this search formula, a citation must have been indexed under either term A *or* B *and* (L *or* M *or* N), *and also* under term Y. Suppose that Y is a very broad term and has been used 10,000 times; A and B have collectively been used 750 times; and L, M, and N have collectively been used only 84 times. In searching the system, it would be most efficient to read the shortest list of document numbers first, then to compare it with the next shortest list, and so on, leaving comparison with the largest list for the last step in the process. From postings statistics on the MVF, an efficient search program can automatically optimize the strategy; that is, it can identify the least heavily posted component, the next least heavily posted, and so forth, ordering the strategy in ascending order of posting and manipulating files in this sequence to economize on computer time.

	C1 (Tree)		
TUBERCULOSIS			
TUBERCULOMA	C1.252.40.552.846		
TUBERCULOSIS, AVIAN	C1.252.40.552.846.493		
TUBERCULOSIS, BOVINE	C1.252.40.552.846.516	C22.131.921	
TUBERCULOSIS, CARDIOVASCULAR	C1.252.40.552.846.538	C22.196.927	
PERICARDITIS, TUBERCULOUS	C1.252.40.552.846.561	C14.826	
TUBERCULOSIS, CUTANEOUS	C1.252.40.552.846.561.595	C14.826.595	
ERYTHEMA INDURATUM	C1.252.40.552.846.583	C17.838.887	
LUPUS	C1.252.40.552.846.583.329	C17.838.887.	
TUBERCULOSIS, ENDOCRINE	C1.252.40.552.846.583.603	C17.838.887.	
TUBERCULOSIS, GASTROINTESTINAL	C1.252.40.552.846.606	C19.927	
TUBERCULOSIS, HEPATIC	C1.252.40.552.846.628	C6.405.831	
TUBERCULOSIS IN CHILDHOOD	C1.252.40.552.846.651	C6.552.933	
TUBERCULOSIS, LARYNGEAL	C1.252.40.552.846.674		
TUBERCULOSIS, LYMPH NODE	C1.252.40.552.846.696	C8.730.884	C9.400.860
TUBERCULOSIS, MENINGEAL	C1.252.40.552.846.719	C15.604.921	
TUBERCULOSIS, MILIARY	C1.252.40.552.846.741	C10.228.228.	
TUBERCULOSIS, OCULAR	C1.252.40.552.846.764		
TUBERCULOSIS, ORAL	C1.252.40.552.846.786	C11.915	
TUBERCULOSIS, OSTEOARTICULAR	C1.252.40.552.846.809	C7.465.943	
TUBERCULOSIS, SPINAL	C1.252.40.552.846.831	C5.116.165.	
TUBERCULOSIS, PERITONEAL	C1.252.40.552.846.831.722	C5.116.165.	C5.878.909
TUBERCULOSIS, PLEURAL	C1.252.40.552.846.854	C6.772.922	
EMPYEMA, TUBERCULOUS	C1.252.40.552.846.877	C8.528.928	
TUBERCULOSIS, PULMONARY	C1.252.40.552.846.877.405	C8.528.238.	C8.730.912.
SILICOTUBERCULOSIS	C1.252.40.552.846.899	C8.381.922	C8.730.939.
	C1.252.40.552.846.899.669	C8.381.655,	
		C21.447.800.	
TUBERCULOSIS, SPLENIC	C1.252.40.552.846.922	C15.604.744.	
TUBERCULOSIS, UROGENITAL	C1.252.40.552.846.944	C12.672	C13.371.803
TUBERCULOSIS, FEMALE GENITAL	C1.252.40.552.846.944.596	C13.371.803.	
TUBERCULOSIS, MALE GENITAL	C1.252.40.552.846.944.721	C12.294.889	C12.672.721
TUBERCULOSIS, RENAL	C1.252.40.552.846.944.847	C12.672.847	C12.777.419.

Exhibit 32 Example from the *Medical Subject Headings Tree Structures*, as used by the National Library of Medicine.

7. The MVF can be used to generate automatically *see* and *see also* references in printed indexes. For example, if an entry is to appear in the printed index under DECORATION, the reference INTERIOR DECORATION *see* DECORATION (where these two terms have been treated as synonymous and linked by *use*) is generated automatically and will appear in the printed index. Likewise, if DEMODULATORS and MODULATORS are both used as headings in an issue of a printed index, because they are linked by RT indicators in the machine thesaurus, the printed *see also* references are generated automatically.

ON-LINE DISPLAY

In an on-line information system, both the indexer and the searcher will need to consult an alphabetic display of the vocabulary; in other words, on at least some occasions, they will need to verify that a particular term does exist in a data base. The capability of displaying a vocabulary alphabetically is fairly common in existing on-line systems. In response to a command such as NEIGHBOR or EXPAND, the system will display, for any term entered, the term itself together with the terms that immediately precede and follow it in alphabetic sequence. A sample is shown in Exhibit 33. To the right of each term appears a figure indicating the number of postings for that term. Note that the term entered by the searcher (FLEXIBLE) has no postings data associated with it. This means that this particular term does not appear in the data base. Nevertheless, the system displays

1	FLASHBACK	8
2	FLAW DETECTION	207
3	FLAWS	82
4	FLEXIBILITY	24
5	FLEXIBLE	
6	FLEXIBLE FILAMENTS	43
7	FLEXIBLE WALLS	58
8	FLEXURAL LOADING	109
9	FLEXURAL WAVES	124

Exhibit 33   Alphabetic display of terms on-line.

those terms that are closest to it alphabetically. This feature may help the searcher to recognize the term he really needs to use (in this case, perhaps, FLEXIBILITY) and also will compensate for certain spelling errors.

Clearly, a vocabulary-display capability of this type is an essential feature of an on-line system, whether the data base to be searched uses a controlled or an uncontrolled vocabulary. Not only can such a feature be used to verify the existence of a term, but it may lead the searcher to an alternative, more appropriate term than the one he began with, to the extent that alphabetic proximity will bring related terms together. The on-line system may even give the searcher the capability of "paging" up or down the alphabetic display. (He could, in fact, view the entire vocabulary of the system in this way, although this activity would be a most inefficient and costly use of on-line connect time.)

It is important when a vocabulary is displayed on-line in this way that the user be able to select from the display without the need to enter terms at the keyboard. Selection of terms from the list by use of identifying line numbers saves the searcher's time and reduces the probability of error.

A simple alphabetic listing of terms is of little use in the formulation of a comprehensive search strategy. The searcher needs to be able to view terms that are more clearly semantically related. For any term entered at the terminal, the system should be able to display all the terms that the vocabulary shows to be related paradigmatically and syntagmatically. There are a number of forms in which such a display could be presented. It could be a conventional thesaurus display showing, for the starting term, the terms that are broader hierarchically (BT), those that are narrower (NT), and those that are related in a nonhierarchical way (i.e., the related terms or RTs). Exhibit 34 is an example. Again, the searcher should be able to select any term from this display without having to enter it in full. Perhaps even better than the thesaurus display is a display in the form of a hierarchical classification, as in the example in Exhibit 32. In MEDLINE, such a display is generated in response to the command TREE. The display in Exhibit 32 would be formed in response to the command TREE TUBERCULOSIS.

1	SHELLS	
2	BT	STRUCTURES
3	NT	ANISOTROPIC SHELLS
4		AXISYMMETRIC SHELLS
5		CONICAL SHELLS
6		CYLINDRICAL SHELLS
7		ELLIPSOIDAL SHELLS
8		HELICAL SHELLS
9		INTERSECTING SHELLS
10		NONHOMOGENEOUS SHELLS
11		NONLINEAR SHELLS
12		ORTHOTROPIC SHELLS
13		SHALLOW SHELLS
14		SHELLS OF REVOLUTION
15		TOROIDAL SHELLS
16	RT	PRESSURE VESSELS
17		SHELL THEORY

Exhibit 34   Thesaurus entry displayed on-line.

Not only should the on-line system be able to display term hierarchies, it should also allow the searcher to incorporate an entire hierarchy of terms into a search strategy by some simple command. In MEDLINE, this is achieved through the EXPLODE command. In the case of a display of the type shown in Exhibit 34, the complete hierarchy of terms can be incorporated by use of all appropriate numbers (in this example, perhaps, 1, 3–15).

14 *Identifiers and Checklists*

The descriptors organized within a thesaurus tend to be nouns or noun phrases but may not include very many names. Nevertheless, in many subject fields, names of people, places, organizations, or objects will also be needed to represent the subject matter of documents. Rather than greatly expanding the hierarchical structure of the thesaurus, names can be controlled in a separate vocabulary tool resembling the name authority files commonly used in library cataloging practice. The names treated in this way are frequently referred to as *identifiers,* and the list used to control them may have some cross-references but no real "structure."

Examples of the types of terms treated as identifiers in various information services include names of weapons and other equipment (in defense-related systems); proper names (e.g., authors or historical characters); names of geographic regions; names of chemical compounds; and names of institutions (e.g., companies, libraries).

Of course, not all names are to be treated as identifiers in all thesauri. A political science thesaurus will need names of countries and groups of countries as an integral part of the thesaurus structure. But a thesaurus in education, on the other hand, has less need for geographic descriptors; names of countries can be handled through the identifier list. In fact, in a subject area in which such names will only occasionally be needed, it is perhaps best to adopt some existing authority for the names. In the United States, the source for geographic descriptors is the publications of the Board on Geographic Names.

For a thesaurus on English literature, names of authors will be needed, but it is impractical to try to include all authors in the thesaurus structure. It is sufficient to include names of only major authors as descriptors and treat the others as identifiers. In this case, a rather obscure nineteenth-century essayist might be indexed under relevant descriptors—ESSAYISTS and NINETEENTH CENTURY—as well as under his name from the identifier list.

CHECKLISTS

If a vocabulary is sufficiently specialized (and therefore small), it might be reproduced in toto on a few large sheets of paper. Such conciseness has certain advantages. Terms can be looked up quickly and easily. The entire vocabulary can be scanned in a glance or two, allowing the indexer to consider the relevance of virtually every term to each document. A very small controlled vocabulary in a highly specialized area is best presented this way. The U.S. Patent Office has developed some small retrieval systems restricted to one or several classes in the patent art. Specialized vocabularies have been devised that are small enough to be printed on one or two sheets. Exhibit 35 illustrates such a vocabulary on chemical testing. The entire vocabulary can be easily scanned, preventing the indexer from overlooking an important term and eliminating the need for him to type terms or to write them down. In this case, multiple copies of the term list are available, and a patent is indexed merely by circling the appropriate terms or their codes on a copy of the list. All subsequent processing is clerical. A microthesaurus developed for the Air Pollution Technical Information Center, as described by Tancredi and

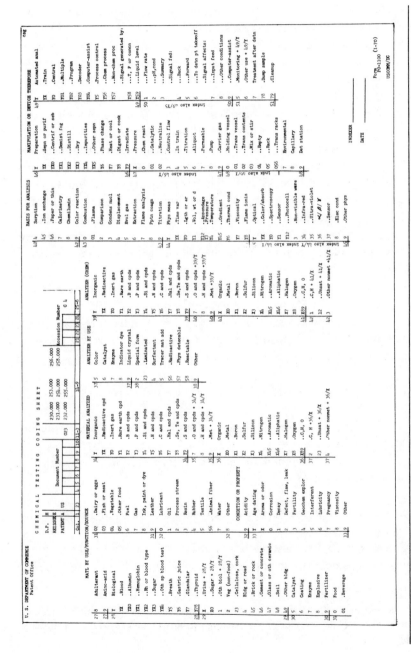

Exhibit 35   U.S. Patent Office vocabulary on chemical testing.

Nichols (1968), was also designed for use by circling of terms. A portion of this microthesaurus is illustrated in Exhibit 36.

A large vocabulary cannot be presented in this way in its entirety, but portions of it can be. If certain classes of terms are potentially relevant to most documents in a system, it is efficient and economical to preprint these on an indexing form and allow the indexer to check them when they are applicable. This practice, which is followed by the National Library of Medicine, reminds the indexer that these terms must be assigned when appropriate and reduces the amount of writing he must do. A MEDLARS indexing form (Exhibit 37)* contains "check tags" for such items as age, sex, and type of study. Terms from this group *must* be assigned to all documents for which they are relevant. The indexer assigns check tags by checking the appropriate box. These terms are treated in this way because they are potentially applicable to virtually all articles in the biomedical field.

In some systems, a form has been designed to help indexers structure their work in terms of the system's syntax. Exhibit 38 shows such a form as it was used with links and role indicators (explained in Chapter 15) in the SHARP (Ships Analysis and Retrieval Project) system of the Bureau of Ships. Note several features:

1. Each row of the coding sheet can be used to represent a single link.

2. Descriptors can be entered in columns to indicate the role indicators that apply to them.

3. The form is designed for ease of interpretation by a clerk for input to the system.

Such forms greatly facilitate the application of links and roles to the indexing process.

Caless (1969) has described a similar form used to index documents on seismology via the *Universal Decimal Classification* (*UDC*)

---

*At the end of 1983, the National Library of Medicine was converting to indexing on-line, so the paper version of the indexing form will be replaced by an on-line display.

BK-65	BIOMEDICAL TECHNIQUES & MEASUREMENT
BK-66	ABSENTEEISM
BK-67	ATTACK RATES
BK-68	BIOCLIMATOLOGY
BK-69	EPIDEMIOLOGY
BK-70	GENETICS
BK-71	HEALTH STATISTICS
BK-72	HEMATOLOGY
BK-73	BLOOD CHEMISTRY
BK-74	BLOOD GAS ANALYSIS
BK-75	CARBOXYHEMOGLOBIN
BK-76	HEMOGLOBIN INTERACTIONS
BK-77	IMMUNOLOGY
BK-78	ANTIBODIES
BK-79	ANTIGENS
BK-80	LIFE SPAN
BK-81	MORBIDITY
BK-82	MORTALITY
BK-83	OCCUPATIONAL HEALTH
BK-84	OUTPATIENT VISITS
BK-85	PATHOLOGICAL TECHNIQUES
BK-86	RADIOLOGICAL HEALTH
BL-48	TISSUE CULTURES
BK-87	TREATMENT & AIDS
BK-88	ARTIFICIAL RESPIRATION
BK-89	BREATHING EXERCISES
BK-90	DIAGNOSIS
BK-91	AUTOPSY
BK-92	BIO-ASSAY
BK-93	BIOPSY
BK-94	SKIN TESTS
BK-95	DRUGS
BK-96	ANTIDOTES
BK-97	BRONCHODILATORS
BK-99	INHALATION THERAPY
BL-00	MEDICAL FACILITIES
BL-02	PHYSICAL THERAPY
BL-03	RADIOGRAPHY
BL-04	SURGERY
BL-05	VETERINARY MEDICINE
BK-22	URINALYSIS

BL-06	BODY CONSTITUENTS & PARTS
BL-07	BODY FLUIDS
BL-08	BONES
BL-13	CELLS
BL-14	BLOOD CELLS
GR-41	LEUKOCYTES
BL-17	LYMPHOCYTES
BL-15	CHROMOSOMES
BL-16	CILIA
BL-18	SPERMATOZOA
BL-09	CIRCULATORY SYSTEM
BL-10	BLOOD VESSELS
BL-11	HEART
BL-19	DIGESTIVE SYSTEM
BL-20	ESOPHAGUS
BL-21	INTESTINES
BL-22	LIVER
BL-23	MOUTH
BL-24	STOMACH
BL-25	ENZYMES
BL-46	EPITHELIUM
BL-26	EXCRETIONS
BL-27	EYES
BL-28	GLANDS
BL-29	HISTAMINES
BL-30	HORMONES
BL-31	KIDNEYS
BL-32	LIPIDS
BL-33	MEMBRANES
BL-34	NERVOUS SYSTEM
GY-29	NUCLEIC ACIDS
BL-35	PROTEINS
BL-36	AMINO ACIDS
BL-37	RESPIRATORY SYSTEM
BL-38	BRONCHI
BL-39	LARYNX
BL-40	LUNGS
BL-41	ALVEOLI
BL-42	NOSTRILS
BL-43	SINUSES
BL-44	TRACHEA
BL-45	SKIN
BL-46	EPITHELIUM
BL-47	TISSUES

BL-49	BODY PROCESSES & FUNCTIONS
BL-50	ADAPTATION
BL-52	BLOOD PRESSURE
BL-53	CELL GROWTH
BL-54	CELL METABOLISM
BL-55	DIGESTION
BL-56	INGESTION
BL-57	INHIBITION
BL-58	METABOLISM
BL-59	PULSE RATE
BL-60	REPRODUCTION
BL-61	RESPIRATORY FUNCTIONS
BL-62	BREATHING
BL-63	COMPLIANCE
GY-51	DEPOSITION
GY-98	LUNG CLEARANCE
BL-64	OXYGEN CONSUMPTION
BL-65	PULMONARY FUNCTION
BL-66	OXYGEN DIFFUSION
BL-67	PULMONARY RESISTANCE
BL-68	VENTILATION (PULMONARY)
BL-69	RETENTION
BL-71	SYNERGISM
BL-72	THRESHOLDS
BL-73	TOXIC TOLERANCES

BL-74	DISEASES & DISORDERS
BL-75	ALLERGIES
BL-76	ANEMIA
BL-77	ANOXIA
BL-79	ASPHYXIATION
Y-71	BERYLLIOSIS
BL-80	BLINDNESS
BL-81	CANCER
BL-82	BRONCHIAL
BL-83	LEUKEMIA
BL-84	LUNG
BL-85	SKIN
BL-86	TRACHEAL
Y-78	CARCINOGENS
BL-87	CARDIOVASCULAR DISEASES
BL-88	ERYTHEMA
BL-89	EYE IRRITATION
BL-90	FLUOROSIS
BL-91	HEADACHE
BL-92	HEALTH IMPAIRMENT
BL-93	HYPERSENSITIVITY
BL-94	HYPERVENTILATION
BL-95	HYPOXIA
BL-96	INFECTIOUS DISEASES
BL-97	LACHRYMATION
BL-98	METAL POISONING
BL-99	MUTATIONS
GR-00	NAUSEA
GR-01	ORGANIC DISEASES
GR-02	RESPIRATORY DISEASES
GR-03	ADENOVIRUS INFECTIONS
GR-04	ASTHMA
GR-05	BRONCHITIS
GR-06	BRONCHOCONSTRICTION
GR-07	BRONCHOPNEUMONIA
GR-08	COMMON COLD
GR-09	COUGH
GR-10	EMPHYSEMA
GR-11	HAYFEVER
GR-12	INFLUENZA
GR-13	LARYNGITIS
GR-14	PLEURISY
GR-15	PNEUMOCONIOSIS
P-84	ANTHRACOSIS
BL-78	ASBESTOSIS
S-72	BYSSINOSIS
S-84	FARMER'S LUNG
GR-18	SILICOSIS
GR-16	PNEUMONIA
GR-17	PULMONARY EDEMA
GR-19	TUBERCULOSIS
GR-20	STERILIZATION
GR-21	TUMORS

Exhibit 36 Section of microthesaurus of the Air Pollution Technical Information Center. Reprinted from Tancredi and Nichols (1968), copyright John Wiley & Sons, Inc., by permission of the publisher.

① C	⑧ PAGINATION	⑨ LANGUAGE ENG. ___ ___ ___	ANONYMOUS A □	⑰ REFS	⑮ SUBJECT NAME
	⑩ AUTHOR DATA				

⑬ TITLE *(Eng or Transl)*

⑭ TITLE *(Vernac or Translit)*

⑲	⑳	J □ CATS	V □ HUMAN	f □ 15th CENT	⑫ AUTHOR
A □ HIST ART	A □ PREGN	K □ CATTLE	W □ MALE	g □ 16th CENT	□ AFFIL
B □ HIST BIOG	B □ INF NEW (to 1 mo)	L □ CHICK EMBRYO	X □ FEMALE	h □ 17th CENT	
C □ BIOG OBIT	C □ INF (1–23 mo)	M □ DOGS	Y □ IN VITRO	i □ 18th CENT	⑫ AUTHOR
G □ MONOGR	D □ CHILD PRE (2–5)	O □ GUINEA PIGS	Z □ CASE REPT	j □ 19th CENT	□ ABST
H □ ENG ABST	E □ CHILD (6–12)	P □ HAMSTERS	b □ COMP STUDY	k □ 20th CENT	
	F □ ADOLESC (13–18)	Q □ MICE	c □ ANCIENT	l □ NIH/PHS SUP	⑳ NIH/PHS GRANT NO.
	G □ ADULT (19–44)	S □ RABBITS	d □ MEDIEVAL	m □ OTHER US GOVT SUP	
	H □ MID AGE (45–64)	T □ RATS	e □ MODERN	n □ NON-US GOVT SUP	
	I □ AGED (65 +)	U □ ANIMAL			

㉑

1
2
3
4
5
6
7
8
9
10
11
12
13
14
15
16
17
18
19
20
21
22
23
24
25
26
27
28
29
30
31

NIH-1416
Rev. 6-80

INDEXED CITATION FORM

GPO : 1983 0 – 411-962

Exhibit 37 MEDLARS indexing form.

BUSHIPS TECH. LIBRARY-PROJECT SHARP
Doc. Subj. Processing Sheet (Rev. 8-63)

NOTE: (1) Record the link identification before each phrase.
(2) Record the role number after each term.

DOCUMENT ACCESSION NUMBER:

DOCUMENT SECURITY CLASSIFICATION:

- - - - - - - - - - Detach here - - - - - - - - - - Detach here - - - - - - - - - - Detach here - - - - - - - - - -

BUSHIPS TECH. LIBRARY-PROJECT SHARP.   Document Coding Sheet (Rev. 8-63).

ROLE 8 Primary Topics Principal Subjects	ROLE 1 Inputs	ROLE 2 Outputs	ROLE 3 Undesirables Unnecessaries	ROLE 4 Present, Possible, and Later Uses	ROLE 5 Media; Adverbs; Adjectives Geog. Loc's	ROLE 6 Independent Variables Causes	ROLE 7 Dependent Variables Effects	ROLE 9 Passive Recipients Location	ROLE 10 Means of Accomplishment	Sec. Class	ROLE 0 Accession Number (Bib Data)	Linkage	Card No.	Subcard No.
1-7	8-14	15-21	22-28	29-35	36-42	43-49	50-56	57-63	64-70	71	72-77	78	79	80
1													1	
2													1	
3													1	
4													1	
5													1	
6													1	
7													1	
8													1	
9													1	
10													1	
11													1	

Exhibit 38   Indexing form used in SHARP system of the Bureau of Ships.

	THING	MATERIALS	PROCESSES	OPERATIONS	AGENTS	KINDS	PARTS	PROPERTIES
1	Earthquakes					Shallow		
2	Aftershocks							
3								
4								
5								
6								
7								

	PLACE	TIME	VIEWPOINT	FORM	LANGUAGE
1	California				
2		Short-Term			
3					
4					
5					
6					
7					

Exhibit 39 Form used in indexing documents on seismology using the *Universal Decimal Classification*. Reprinted from Caless (1969).

(Exhibit 39). Rows represent conceptual links, and columns list the major facets, although not in the exact order in which they are to be cited. The indexer should ask himself if each facet is present in the document being indexed. If it is, he should account for it by entering the appropriate term in the matrix. The form is intended to aid the intellectual analysis of a document and to help in the structuring of a correct UDC number. In the exhibit, the particular document describes shallow-depth earthquakes related to California aftershock sequences of short duration. In entering his conceptual analysis, the indexer has linked "shallow" with "earthquakes" and "short term" with "aftershocks" and "California." From this form, the full UDC number is constructed using the facet sequence *thing, kind, part, material, processes, properties, operations, agents.* The full number resulting from this analysis is 550.348.436.098,23: 550.348.433 (#AFTER) (794) "403."

The more indexing is reduced to a check-off type of operation, the more consistent it is likely to be. Such an approach, however, is only possible in highly specialized areas with very small vocabularies. It is less likely to have great advantages when indexers are operating directly at on-line terminals.

15 *The Influence of Vocabulary on the Performance of a Retrieval System*

Before addressing the effect of vocabulary on a retrieval system's performance, two things must be considered: the criteria by which performance can be evaluated and the procedures by which an evaluation can be conducted. These matters are discussed in detail in Lancaster (1979) and are reviewed only briefly here.

USER REQUIREMENTS

To evaluate the *effectiveness* of a retrieval system, one must determine how well it meets the needs of its users. In general, any operation can be evaluated in terms of quality, time, and cost, and there are always trade-offs among these criteria. In the retrieval environment, the following performance criteria are important:

1. *Quality*
   a. The coverage of the data base.
   b. The ability of the system to retrieve relevant documents from this data base in response to a subject request. This is

usually known as *recall* and may be expressed quantitative-
ly by means of a *recall ratio*.

c. The ability to hold back nonrelevant documents at the
    same time, which is usually known as *precision* and may be
    expressed quantitatively by a *precision ratio*.

d. Form and format of output for easiest and most convenient
    use.

2. *Effort*—The amount of effort involved in use of the system.
    Eventually, this is reduced to the *cost* of using the system.

3. *Response time.*

All users of a retrieval system have one fundamental requirement
in common: They expect the system to be able to retrieve one or
more documents that contribute to the satisfaction of their information need (*relevant documents*). All users are presumed to have an
information need; otherwise they would not have approached the
system. Actually, this "fundamental requirement" is a slight oversim-
plification. In some rare situations, the user wants the system to retrieve nothing (i.e., when the user believes and hopes nothing exists,
such as in certain patent-searching situations). If nothing exists, the
system behaves perfectly if it retrieves nothing.

In most situations, however, the user wants and expects the system to retrieve relevant documents. It is possible to express quantita-
tively, by a recall ratio, the degree of system success in retrieving
relevant literature from its data base. The recall ratio is defined as

$$\frac{\text{the number of relevant documents retrieved by the system}}{\text{the total number of relevant documents contained in the system}} \times 100$$

Suppose that for a particular subject request made to some retrieval
system, one can establish that there are only 10 relevant documents
in the entire data base. If an actual search retrieves seven of these,
the recall ratio is $7/10 \times 100$ or 70 percent.

The recall ratio is a very important measure of the success of a
search, but it is not the only measure. In fact, alone it is somewhat
meaningless; one can always get 100-percent recall for any search in
any system if one is prepared to search broadly enough and to retrieve a sufficiently large portion of the collection. An information re-

trieval system is essentially a filter, and, therefore, it should be capable of letting through what is wanted while withholding what is not. The recall ratio expresses the ability of the system to let through what is wanted, but a companion measure that will express the ability of the system to withhold what is not wanted is also needed. One such measure is the precision ratio, which is defined as

$$\frac{\text{the number of relevant documents retrieved by the system}}{\text{the total number of documents retrieved by the system}} \times 100$$

Returning to the hypothetical search, one may find that the system retrieved a total of 50 items, 7 of them relevant and 43 not. The precision ratio for this search is thus 7/50, or 14 percent. Therefore, the search has operated at 70-percent recall and 14-percent precision. These two measures, used jointly, indicate the filtering capacity of the system and, together, give a good picture of system effectiveness.

The precision ratio measures the efficiency with which the system is able to achieve a particular recall ratio. Clearly, achievement of 70-percent recall at a precision of 7/14 (50 percent) indicates greater efficiency than the attainment of the same recall at 7/50 (14 percent) precision or 7/100 (7 percent) precision; greater filtering capacity has been brought into play. In a sense, the precision ratio can be regarded as a measure of the effort required from the user to achieve a particular recall ratio. This effort is expended after the search results have been delivered by the system in order to separate the relevant items from the irrelevant ones. Obviously, it takes longer to select 7 relevant items from 100 (7-percent precision) than it does to select 7 from 50 (14-percent precision). Viewed in this light, the precision ratio is a valid and useful measure of search efficiency.

Recall and precision tend to vary inversely in searching; that is, whatever one does to improve recall (by broadening a search) will usually reduce precision, and whatever one does to improve precision (by searching more stringently) will reduce recall. In fact, if one conducts a search or a whole group of searches at varying strategy levels from very broad to very stringent, a series of performance points can be derived that would form a curve resembling that shown in Exhibit 40.

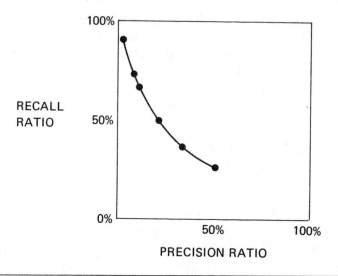

Exhibit 40　Typical performance curve when recall is plotted against precision.

Although the vocabulary of a retrieval system has no effect on the coverage of the system, it may affect the amount of user effort needed to exploit the system and indirectly affect response time. It certainly has a very direct influence on system recall and precision capabilities.

EVALUATION PROCEDURES

The complete results of a search in a retrieval system can be presented in the form of a 2 × 2 table, as shown in Exhibit 41. In evaluating a retrieval system, one must put values into this table for a representative set of requests (searches). Three of these values are directly observable: the total collection size $(a + b + c + d)$, the total number of items retrieved $(a + b)$, and the total not retrieved $(c + d)$. The other values must be established, or at least estimated, through an evaluation program. Assume that a search has been conducted

USER RELEVANCE JUDGMENT

		RELEVANT	NOT RELEVANT	TOTAL
SYSTEM RELEVANCE PREDICTION	RETRIEVED	*a* Hits	*b* Noise	*a + b*
	NOT RETRIEVED	*c* Misses	*d* Correctly Rejected	*c + d*
	TOTAL	*a + c*	*b + d*	*a + b + c + d* (Total Collection)

Exhibit 41   2 × 2 contingency table for search results.

and has retrieved a number of documents or document surrogates $(a + b)$. These are presented to the requester, who is asked to indicate which items he considers relevant (a) and which he considers irrelevant (b). Preferably he should be asked to judge relevance on some type of scale ("major relevance," "minor relevance," and "no relevance" should suffice). Although the topic of relevance has generated much literature and heated discussion, and although a great many factors influence a requester's relevance decisions, when evaluating an operating system in its entirety, one must accept that a relevant document is one that contributes to the satisfaction of the user's information need (sometimes referred to as a "pertinent" item) and an "irrelevant" document is one that does not. Therefore, relevance assessments are value judgments placed on documents by individuals with information needs.

Once the requester has assessed relevance, a precision ratio $(a/a + b)$ is derived for the search. In practical application, these relevance assessments should be recorded by the requester on assessment forms. The requester should also be asked to indicate reasons for his various judgments—that is, why one document is of major relevance, a second of no relevance, and a third of minor relevance. These recorded reasons will be extremely useful in the analysis of system performance.

There are still two values missing from the 2×2 table, c and d. These are difficult to determine, but they are needed to establish a recall ratio. There is only one way to arrive at these values absolutely (and thereby derive a "true" recall figure), and that is by having the requester examine all the nonretrieved items $(c + d)$ and decide which are relevant (c) and which are not (d). If this were possible, one could establish an absolute value for c and thus derive an absolute recall ratio $(a/a + c)$. In the evaluation of experimental or small prototype systems, this is sometimes possible. In most operating systems, however, $c + d$ will be a very large portion of the entire collection, making it unreasonable to expect the requester to examine all these items or even a large number of them. Moreover, $c + d$ will usually be so large (in relation to c) that one cannot even use conventional random sampling procedures; in other words, an impossibly large sample would need to be drawn from $c + d$ to achieve any expectation of finding even one relevant document.

In evaluating a retrieval system of any size, one may just as well abandon the idea of trying to establish true recall and be satisfied with the best possible *recall estimate*. Probably the most reasonable method of doing this is that of Lancaster (1968) (see Exhibit 42), justified statistically by Shumway (1968).

For any particular subject request posed to the collection, I, there will be a set of documents, A, that the requester would judge relevant

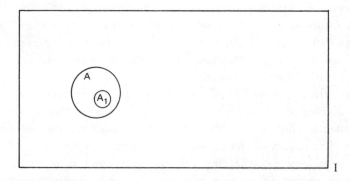

Exhibit 42   Method of estimating recall by extrapolation from hit rate for known population, A_1, to hit rate for unknown population, A.

if he saw them. If one knew A and what portion of it was retrieved by a search in the collection, one could establish absolute recall. But one cannot establish the composition of A in a system of any significant size; however, one *can* find a portion of A, the subset A_1, and base a recall estimate on the proportion of A_1 retrieved by a search in the system. The subset A_1 is a group of documents *contained in the data base of the system* and judged to be relevant by the requester but found by methods extraneous to the system to be evaluated. For example, A_1 can be composed of relevant documents known to the requester at the time he first approaches the system and makes his request. Alternatively, it can be composed of documents found by the evaluator through outside sources (e.g., other information centers or published indexes), submitted to the requester for his assessment and judged relevant by him. The subset can also comprise items partly from the first source and partly from the second. For instance, a scientist comes to an information system and makes a subject request, at which time he already knows two relevant items. The evaluator does a parallel search in another source and finds 12 "possibly relevant" items. Of these, eight are judged relevant by the requester. The evaluator now has a group of 10 documents known to be relevant to the request (the two the requester knew originally and the eight found subsequently). Assuming that all 10 appear in the data base of the system, a *recall base* of 10 relevant items, the subset A_1, has been established. When the results of the search actually conducted in the system are checked, one finds that 7 of the 10 items were retrieved and 3 were not. Thus, the recall estimate is $7/10 \times 100$, or 70 percent. If A_1 is a representative sample of A, it is then reasonable to assume that the "hit rate" (recall ratio) for the entire set A will approximate the hit rate for the subset A_1.

The recall and precision ratios are valuable measures of effectiveness and can be used as indicators of how the system performs under various conditions or modes of operation. Nevertheless, the figures do not explain why the system behaves as it does. To determine this, one must apply a high level of intellectual analysis. Since evaluation is essentially a diagnostic (and eventually therapeutic) procedure, one is particularly concerned with the identification of sources of system failure. The system failures of most interest are failures to retrieve relevant documents (*recall failures*) and failures to screen out irrelevant documents (*precision failures*). Failure analysis is, in fact, the most important aspect of evaluation because eventually it will suggest ways to improve the system. It involves the examination of documents, indexing records, request statements, search strategies, completed relevance assessment forms, and whatever further information can be obtained from users participating in the study. On the basis of all these records, the precise reasons that various failures occur in the system can be determined.

The principal sources of failure fall within the four major subsystems of a complete retrieval system: the indexing subsystem, the vocabulary subsystem, the searching subsystem, and the user-system interface. Although each is extremely important, this book is about vocabulary control (or lack of it), and, therefore, the remainder of the chapter concentrates about the vocabulary as a source of system failure and the influence of the vocabulary on the performance of a retrieval system.

VOCABULARY FAILURES

Retrieval failures due to the system vocabulary primarily stem from lack of specificity in the vocabulary or ambiguous and spurious relationships between terms. Lack of specificity is by far the more important. Consider a technical information system including documents on metallurgical engineering. Some of the documents in the collection deal with arc welding using argon as a shielding gas (i.e., argon arc welding). The vocabulary of the system is not sufficiently specific to allow an indexer to identify this class of documents uniquely. Instead, he must index them under the more general term SHIELDED ARC WELDING. In other words, the class "argon arc welding" is subsumed under the broader class "shielded arc welding" and thus loses its separate identity. Consequently, when asked to conduct a search on the precise topic "argon arc welding," the searcher will be unable to retrieve this class of documents as a unique entity; he can only retrieve the broader class of "shielded arc welding" (Exhibit 43). It is unlikely that a search on argon arc welding will

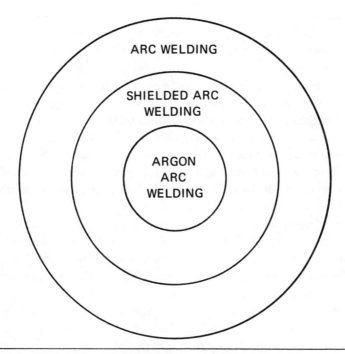

Exhibit 43   Levels of specificity in document classes.

achieve a very high precision since not everything in the class "shielded arc welding" is relevant to argon arc welding. Thus, the inability of the vocabulary to express the precise concept of the request will lead inevitably to precision failure. If the vocabulary were even less specific—for example, if ARC WELDING were the narrowest term—precision would be further reduced.

What effect will this lack of specificity have on the recall ratio of a search on argon arc welding? It need have no deleterious effect, providing indexers and searchers know unequivocally that documents on argon arc welding must always be indexed, and thus found, under the term SHIELDED ARC WELDING. It is extremely important that the vocabulary make this fact explicit to indexers and searchers by means of a *see* or *use* reference. Without such explicit instruction, different indexers probably will index documents on argon arc welding in various ways, leading to inconsistency in the indexing of the precise topic and causing the subject matter to become dispersed. Furthermore, if one begins a search on a subject and the vocabulary does not state explicitly where to look, the searcher may not think of the right terms to use. If the indexing has been inconsistent, the searcher may think of some, but not all, of the headings under which documents have been indexed, and recall failures will occur.

Lack of specificity will always cause precision failures, but it need not cause recall failures so long as the appropriate references are included in the entry vocabulary. If no specific term exists and no references are made from it, both recall and precision failures are likely to occur in a search on the specific topic.

The specificity of the vocabulary is the principal factor affecting the precision capabilities of a retrieval system. Indexing and searching can only be as specific as the language of the system. Nevertheless, there is some tendency for a highly specific vocabulary to reduce recall at the same time it improves precision. The problem is that consistent indexing becomes increasingly difficult the larger the number of terms and, hence, the finer the shades of meaning the vocabulary can express. The more shades of meaning possible, the more subject expertise may be required of indexers and searchers. For example, all indexers can agree that a particular document deals with welding, but there may be less agreement that it is about arc welding, and even less that it is on shielded arc welding. The non-specific vocabulary improves indexing consistency and, in terms of recall, simplifies the searching task. With a broad vocabulary, one can be reasonably sure that everything on argon arc welding has been indexed under WELDING. With a highly specific vocabulary, one may find that some documents are indexed under ARGON ARC WELDING, some under SHIELDED ARC WELDING (either because the indexer did not recognize the fact that argon was used as a shielding gas or because the document in question discusses several types of shielded arc welding and was indexed at the generic term rather than under the specific term), some under ARC WELDING (where the indexer did not recognize the fact that a shielding gas, namely argon, was involved, or where the indexer did not recognize a synonym for shielded arc welding, e.g., "submerged arc"), and even some under GAS WELDING (on the grounds that argon is a gas). Obviously, if the searcher sticks rigidly to the term ARGON ARC WELDING, he might miss some relevant documents.

In summary, a highly specific vocabulary will allow high precision but may cause low recall, whereas a nonspecific vocabulary is likely to allow high recall but will certainly yield low precision.

The situation is illustrated simplistically in Exhibit 44. A specific vocabulary allows one to place a document into many small classes,

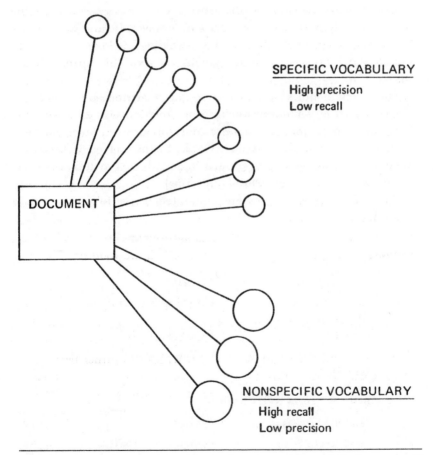

SPECIFIC VOCABULARY

High precision
Low recall

DOCUMENT

NONSPECIFIC VOCABULARY

High recall
Low precision

Exhibit 44   Relation of specific and nonspecific vocabularies to recall and precision.

enabling a search in small classes and the achievement of high precision, but complicating the search when one must expand to achieve
high recall. The nonspecific vocabulary facilitates the generic search
and minimizes indexing inaccuracies, thus improving recall, but it
lacks the facility for high precision. All in all, it is better to err on the
side of specificity. When high recall is essential, the scope of search
strategies can be broadened (e.g., by retrieving everything on any
type of shielded arc welding or any type of arc welding), thus com-
pensating for indexing inaccuracies and for the fact that general
reports may also discuss specific aspects. One cannot compensate for
lack of specificity to improve precision, however. If "argon arc welding" is subsumed under "shielded arc welding," it loses its separate
identity, and no search strategy will retrieve this specific class
uniquely.

The second major source of system failure attributable to vocabulary is caused by ambiguous or spurious relationships among terms.
There are two distinct types: false coordinations and incorrect term
relationships. Both occur because words, by themselves, lack syntax.
Index terms assigned to a document frequently lack syntax, especially if these terms are single words (uniterms).

The two types of failures are illustrated in the following simple
examples:

1. **False Coordination**

Document Indexing	*Request*
ALUMINUM	Cleaning of aluminum
CLEANING	
COPPER	*Search Strategy*
ULTRASONIC	ALUMINUM *and* CLEANING
WELDING	

2. **Incorrect Term Relationship**

Document Indexing	*Request*
COMPUTERS	Design of computers
DESIGN	*Search Strategy*
AIRCRAFT	COMPUTERS *and* DESIGN

In the first example, the document is retrieved in response to a search on cleaning of aluminum, but it turns out to be completely irrelevant to this topic. In fact, it discusses the fabrication of various electronic components, including the welding of aluminum and the cleaning of copper parts by ultrasonics. There is no direct relationship between the index terms CLEANING and ALUMINUM. This is a false coordination: The two terms causing retrieval are essentially unrelated in the document. Similar false coordinations could occur in response to searches on other legitimate topics, including "welding of copper" and "ultrasonic welding." In a system without syntax, the more index terms assigned, the greater the likelihood that false coordination will occur. This type of failure is especially prevalent in uniterm and natural-language systems. It is less prevalent in systems in which the vocabulary is more pre-coordinate (and hence more specific) and more carefully controlled. False coordination can be avoided by linking related terms together and separating these linked terms from others unrelated to them:

ALUMINUM	A
CLEANING	B
COPPER	B
ULTRASONICS	B
WELDING	A

Here, a letter code has been used to group together the terms that are related and to separate them from terms that are not. For a document to be retrieved in such a system, it must not only contain the terms searched on but must contain them in the same link. Several potential false coordinations can be avoided by this simple device, including

ALUMINUM *and* COPPER (searcher looking for an aluminum-copper alloy or the coating of one metal on a substrate of the other)
ALUMINUM *and* ULTRASONICS
ALUMINUM *and* CLEANING
COPPER *and* WELDING

The second example—incorrect term relationship—is rather different. Here, the document is retrieved in response to a request relating to the design of computers. It is not relevant. It deals not with the design of computers but with the design of aircraft using the computer as a tool in the design function. This is an incorrect term relationship: The two terms causing retrieval are indeed directly related, but they are not related in the way that the requester wants them related. Again, incorrect term relationships are most prevalent in uniterm systems. They occur less frequently where more pre-coordinate vocabularies are used. For example, the precision failure would not have occurred had the more specific index term COMPUT-ER DESIGN (or AIRCRAFT DESIGN) existed in the vocabulary.

Incorrect term relationships cannot be avoided by a simple linking device. In the example given, for instance, both the words COM-PUTER and DESIGN would appear in the same link since they are directly related. Incorrect term relationships can only be avoided by the use of devices that indicate relationships between terms.

One way to resolve this ambiguity in a post-coordinate system is by the use of roles or role indicators. A role indicator is a symbol added to a descriptor to indicate the relationship the descriptor bears to the other descriptors used in indexing a particular document. The role is a true syntactical device, and one can devise a set of roles to solve the problems arising in a particular document collection. For example, to solve the "computer design" problem, only two roles are needed. Let *4* represent the role "object of action, patient, recipient" and *2* the role "tool, agent, means of accomplishment." When the document on *design of aircraft with computers* is indexed, it is assigned descriptors and roles as follows:

DESIGN
AIRCRAFT (*4*)
COMPUTERS (*2*)

But a search for documents on *design of computers* will use the strategy

COMPUTERS (*4*) *and* DESIGN

Although the strategy matches the irrelevant document at the term level, it does not match it at the term-role level; the irrelevant citation is thus correctly rejected.

This type of device increases the specificity of the vocabulary and makes it possible to express fine shades of meaning. Consequently, indexing consistency is reduced, and, although precision is likely to improve, it becomes increasingly difficult to achieve a high recall. Moreover, the use of links and roles requires greater intellectual effort from indexers and increases costs significantly.

The vocabulary will also have less-direct effects on the indexing and searching functions. Its structure is likely to profoundly impact the searching operation: The more highly structured it is and the more relationships it can display, the more useful it will be in the construction of search strategies. If the vocabulary does not bring together all related terms (by hierarchical organization, cross-reference structure, or both) and the searcher does not think of all terms relevant to a particular topic (which will most likely be the case), search failures will result. For example, in a particular thesaurus, FAILURE is shown to be related to FATIGUE and to have as narrower terms FRACTURE and RUPTURE. A search on failure of structural panels, however, might not be completely successful on this group of terms alone. Reports on failure of structural parts will frequently use the terminology INSTABILITY or STABILITY rather than FAILURE. The term STABILITY (which includes INSTABILITY) also appears in the vocabulary and has, in fact, been used in indexing to express the notion of structural stability. The searcher is guided by the thesaurus and uses only FAILURE, FATIGUE, and RUPTURE. Recall failures occur because the searcher was not guided to the term STABILITY.

The vocabulary also exerts a strong influence on the indexing process. Again, the structure of the vocabulary should aid the indexer in choosing the most appropriate terms. The reference or hierarchical structure of the vocabulary is important in this respect. It should lead the indexer who thinks first of ARC WELDING to the subordinate terms such as SHIELDED ARC WELDING and ARGON ARC WELDING, allowing him to choose these more specific descriptors where appropriate. Similarly, an explicitly stated relationship between STA-BILITY and FAILURE should aid the indexer in term selection. Term definitions and scope notes are also important in the selection of terms.

See or *use* references are particularly valuable in ensuring indexing consistency and accuracy of searching. Such references should be made both from synonymous expressions and from specific terms that are not used as descriptors in the system. If there is no reference from ARGON ARC WELDING to SHIELDED ARC WELDING, there is no guarantee that an indexer will know how to express the specific concept or that a searcher will know where to look for it.

In summary, the specificity of the vocabulary is its most important characteristic. Vocabulary specificity directly controls the level of precision one can attain in searching because it controls the size of the classes into which documents are placed. *The size of the classes defined by a vocabulary is much more important than the arrangement of these classes.* Consider the two displays presented in Exhibit 45. Under A is a set of class labels arranged in a hierarchical display, as they would appear in a classification scheme or a classified catalog. Under B is the same set of labels arranged in a strictly alphabetic order, as they would appear in a thesaurus or alphabetic subject catalog. Both schemes are identical in the specificity with which they can index the literature on vision disorders. Providing system B supplies references showing BT/NT/RT relationships to help indexers and searchers choose the most appropriate terms, both systems will offer identical retrieval capabilities; that is, both can obtain the same recall and precision figures for a particular set of requests. The fact that the two systems arrange the classes, or their labels, in different sequences is unimportant.

THE CONTROLLED VOCABULARY IN INDEXING

An index language exists primarily to

1. Allow an indexer to represent the subject matter of documents in a consistent way

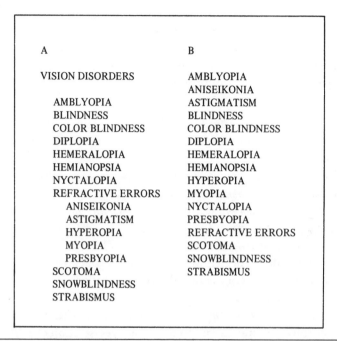

A	B
VISION DISORDERS	AMBLYOPIA
	ANISEIKONIA
AMBLYOPIA	ASTIGMATISM
BLINDNESS	BLINDNESS
COLOR BLINDNESS	COLOR BLINDNESS
DIPLOPIA	DIPLOPIA
HEMERALOPIA	HEMERALOPIA
HEMIANOPSIA	HEMIANOPSIA
NYCTALOPIA	HYPEROPIA
REFRACTIVE ERRORS	MYOPIA
ANISEIKONIA	NYCTALOPIA
ASTIGMATISM	PRESBYOPIA
HYPEROPIA	REFRACTIVE ERRORS
MYOPIA	SCOTOMA
PRESBYOPIA	SNOWBLINDNESS
SCOTOMA	STRABISMUS
SNOWBLINDNESS	
STRABISMUS	

Exhibit 45   The same set of class labels arranged in a classified sequence (A) and alphabetically (B).

2. Bring the vocabulary used by the searcher into coincidence with the vocabulary used by the indexer

3. Provide means whereby a searcher can modulate a search strategy to attain comprehensive or selective results as user needs dictate

In considering the role of the controlled vocabulary in the indexing process, it is necessary to recognize that subject indexing entails two distinct steps: the analysis of subject content (i.e., "conceptual analysis" or "content analysis") and the translation of this conceptual analysis into terms selected from some vocabulary.

Content analysis involves determining a document's subject matter and, even more important, deciding who is likely to use it and for what purpose (i.e., anticipating requests for which this document might provide a relevant response). The process of conceptual analysis is intellectually distinct from that of translation, even though the activities may virtually occur simultaneously. Conceptual analysis is not influenced by the system vocabulary (or at least should not be).

At the time of indexing, various errors or defects can occur that will adversely affect the performance of the retrieval system. Essentially, there are five types of problems:

1. *Conceptual analysis failure*—The indexer fails to understand the subject matter of the document and misinterprets its content in his conceptual analysis.

2. *Translation failure*—The indexer recognizes what the document is about but chooses the wrong terms to express it.

3. *Error of omission*—The indexer omits an important aspect of the document in his conceptual analysis.

4. *Lack of specificity in the vocabulary*—The indexer recognizes what a document is specifically about in his conceptual analysis but is forced to index it more generally because of lack of specific terms in the system vocabulary.

5. *Lack of specificity in indexing*—The indexer uses vocabulary terms that are general in relation to the precise subject matter discussed in a document, even though more specific terms are available in the vocabulary.

Strictly speaking, only the fourth problem is directly caused by limitations of the vocabulary. Nevertheless, the controlled vocabulary may contribute, at least indirectly, to some of the indexing failures, and it is worth considering them in this light.

Errors 1 and 2, although theoretically distinct, are in practice impossible to distinguish; it is not possible to determine exactly why an indexer assigns the term X to a document when the term Y is correct. Is it because he failed to understand the subject of the document or because he failed to understand the distinction between X and Y? Regardless, the end result is the same—an incorrect term is assigned. This type of error can result in either a recall failure or a precision failure, depending on the type of search conducted. If term X is assigned when Y should be, the document will be incorrectly retrieved in a search on X (precision failure) and missed in a search on Y (recall failure).

The controlled vocabulary does not contribute directly to these failures. They are due either to lack of subject knowledge or to carelessness. Nevertheless, the controlled vocabulary may help to minimize failures of this kind. Presumably, careful term definition and adequate cross-referencing will reduce problems of incorrect term assignment. This is particularly true if descriptors that are somewhat related are carefully distinguished by scope notes. For example,

COILS
(Compact windings of conductors to form inductors. For coils producing magnetic fields for the conversion of electrical into mechanical energy, see SOLENOIDS.)

Related term references also should help the indexer to select the most appropriate term to represent a topic. For example, he may think first of ELECTROMAGNETIC PUMPS but is led on by the vocabulary (RT or *see also*) to LIQUID METAL PUMPS, which he realizes better describes the subject matter. The entry vocabulary also will play an important part in guiding the indexer to the most appropriate descriptors. In fact, the richer the entry vocabulary, the less subject knowledge the indexer need have.

Indexing errors involving incorrect term assignments are relatively rare. More likely is the complete omission of an important aspect by the indexer. In the evaluation of MEDLARS by Lancaster (1968), it was found that 10 percent of all recall failures were due to the omission of an important term in indexing. Most of these were caused by carelessness, and the system vocabulary has no influence on them. Some omissions, however, may occur as a direct result of an inadequate entry vocabulary. They happen simply because the indexer does not know how a particular topic is to be indexed; there is no descriptor for this topic in the system, and the entry vocabulary fails to indicate how it should be indexed. For example, one aspect of a medical article deals with equational division. There is no "equational division" descriptor in the system vocabulary, and the indexer does not know how to deal with the subject. He therefore takes the easy way out and omits it entirely. An adequate entry vocabulary might have avoided this omission by providing an appropriate instruction to the indexer:

Equational Division *use* MEIOSIS

A full entry vocabulary will not, of course, eliminate all errors of indexer omission, but it may reduce these errors considerably.

In studying causes of failure in a retrieval system, it is important to distinguish lack of specificity in the vocabulary from lack of specificity in indexing. The former implies that no specific term is available in the system to describe some precise concept, and the indexer is thus forced to use a more general term. Lack of vocabulary specificity is likely to be a significant cause of precision failures in all retrieval systems using a controlled vocabulary. It was responsible for 18 percent of the precision failures discovered in the MEDLARS evaluation.

Lack of specificity in indexing is another matter. In this situation, an appropriate specific term is available in the vocabulary but the indexer, for some reason, uses a more general term; for example, he assigns POLYSACCHARIDES to a document that deals specifically with lipopolysaccharides, even though the precise term exists in the vocabulary. This type of error is relatively rare, and it is usually an error of indexer carelessness. The index language will contribute to these errors, however, if it fails to present the true hierarchical structure of the vocabulary. If the indexer looks under the term POLYSACCHARIDES, he must be led to the more specific term LIPOPOLYSACCHARIDES by a cross-reference, a graphic display, or a classified arrangement. If the vocabulary fails to do this, it contributes to nonspecific indexing.

One expects that a controlled vocabulary will promote consistency in indexing. Actually, this will be true only after indexers have learned the particular nuances of a vocabulary and the rules and protocols associated with its use. Until they gain such familiarity, two indexers may be more consistent with each other when using uncontrolled terms extracted from the text of the documents.

The nature of the controlled vocabulary also influences consistency. The more specific the vocabulary (and, thus, the finer the shades of meaning it can express), the more difficult it may be to use consistently. A highly "suggestive" (as opposed to "prescriptive") vocabulary also may reduce consistency.

THE CONTROLLED VOCABULARY IN SEARCHING

Vocabulary has prescriptive and suggestive roles to play in the search process. It prescribes the language the searcher must use by directing him from nonaccepted to accepted terms. The entry vocabulary bears the burden of this activity. This prescriptive function brings the vocabulary of the searcher into coincidence with the vocabulary of the indexer. In other words, the controlled vocabulary must relate its own terminology to variant expressions occurring in the literature and in requests made to the system.

The suggestive role in searching is played by the organization of the vocabulary: its faceted structure, its hierarchy, and its network of cross-references. It must help the searcher construct the best possible strategy in terms of a user's needs (high recall, high precision, or some compromise between the two). In particular, it should prevent a searcher from missing relevant documents through failure to bring together semantically related terms. In Lancaster's evaluation of MEDLARS, it was found that 21.5 percent of all recall failures were attributable to the search analyst's inability to think of all possible approaches to retrieval. In some cases, one might conclude that the searcher lacked ingenuity or perseverance in the construction of his strategy; but, in other instances, the vocabulary was at fault because it did not provide enough assistance to the searcher by bringing together all related terms.

The more help the vocabulary gives in displaying possibly useful relationships among terms, the lighter the intellectual load on the searcher and the less likely he is to overlook alternative approaches to retrieval. Most controlled vocabularies are reasonably good at presenting formal hierarchical relationships among terms, but some fail in the presentation of valid relationships that cut across the hierarchical structure of the vocabulary.

THE VOCABULARY IN USER-SYSTEM INTERACTION

A very important problem plaguing most information systems is user-system interaction. Users interact with the system to make their needs known. A search can only be conducted for a user after his needs have been clearly stated. This stage of the complete retrieval process is critical. If a user submits a request that inadequately represents his real information need, the subsequent search is largely doomed to failure, however adequate the indexing, vocabulary, and search strategies. Unfortunately, it is frequently difficult for a user to be explicit in his request, and the system must help him as much as possible.

The MEDLARS evaluation indicated fairly conclusively that the requests that best represent information needs are usually those that the requester phrases in his own natural-language terms. These requests are not constrained by the logic and language of the system. They should be recorded in writing by the requester, preferably on a well-designed search request form. It was discovered that requests resulting from an interview between the user and a librarian or information specialist tend to be further removed from the actual information need. Apparently, this is because an unconscious distortion may take place in a face-to-face interview. This is particularly true if the information specialist tries to get the requester to use the language of the system in formulating his request, thereby placing a linguistic constraint on the user that is highly undesirable. As a result, the user may settle for less than what he really wants. In the situation where the user records his request in writing in his own terms, he is unconstrained by the logic and language of the system; hence, he is much more likely to ask for what he really wants than for what he feels the system can supply.

Furthermore, if requests are always made in terms selected from the controlled vocabulary, there is little opportunity to improve the vocabulary by making it more responsive to user requirements. In other words, one is given no evidence that the vocabulary needs to be more specific. Suppose the term WELDING exists in a vocabulary but that there are no terms for specific types of welding and the user must always phrase his request in controlled-vocabulary terms. One knows that many users request searches on welding of various metals or products, and searches are evaluated on this basis. It may be overlooked, however, that many requesters are really interested only in specific welding processes—shielded arc welding, argon arc welding, resistance welding, spot welding—and that many of the searches conducted are unsatisfactory to the users because they produce very low precision. It is important that the request statement record the precise topic in which the user is interested *even when the vocabulary of the system will not allow searching at this precise level.* If a requester is seeking information on nephrogenic diabetes insipidus, this is how his request should be recorded, even if the vocabulary only includes the general term DIABETES. How else can one discover inadequacies in the vocabulary, and how else can the vocabulary be developed to the level of specificity required to satisfy the majority of demands placed on the system?

Searching, like indexing, involves both conceptual analysis and translation steps. The requester should be concerned with the conceptual analysis stage. Only when an adequate conceptual analysis of an information need has been recorded should the searcher consider how best to translate this into the controlled terms of the system. Natural-language search systems have certain advantages in this respect because they do not impose constraints on the user's vocabulary.

16 *Evaluation of Thesauri*

A thesaurus can be superficially evaluated merely by examining it. For example, one can check certain aspects of its completeness: Is there an adequate introduction indicating its scope and explaining any unique features? Are alternative displays present (at least complementary alphabetic and hierarchical components)? At a more sophisticated level, are the BT/NT and RT relationships used correctly? Are terms that are unusual or ambiguous explained by their context, by qualifiers, or by scope notes? One can also check that all relationships properly reciprocate, although with computer processing, it seems highly unlikely that they would not.

A subject expert could further evaluate the thesaurus by checking to see if various topics are represented and if the terms that represent them are sufficiently specific. This test could also be performed by taking a random sample of articles or abstracts and checking to determine if key terms appear in the thesaurus.

It is possible to confirm that the thesaurus adheres to international standards in terms of singular/plural conventions, acceptable word forms, direct entry, and other matters of consistency. Aesthetic aspects of layout and typography can also be considered.

Beyond this, various statistical tests for the evaluation of thesauri have been proposed and applied. For example, Kochen and Tagliacozzo (1968) evaluated a number of controlled vocabularies in terms of a *connectedness ratio* and an *accessibility measure.* The connectedness ratio is the ratio of cross-referenced terms (i.e., terms linked to at least one other term—e.g., by BT, NT, or RT) to total terms in the vocabulary. The accessibility measure is the mean number of references received by the descriptors in a vocabulary. For example, an accessibility measure of 2.923 implies that, on the average, each term in the vocabulary is referred to by almost three other terms. These measures indicate the extent to which linkage (i.e., cross-referencing) occurs among the terms of a vocabulary. Higher figures presumably imply a more useful thesaurus.

These types of measures, based essentially on counting, have been carried much further by the Bureau Marcel Van Dijk (1976). The connectedness ratio is referred to as *connectivity* and defined as $(b - a)/b$, where a is the number of descriptors in the vocabulary that are isolated (i.e., not linked to any other) and b is the total number of descriptors in the vocabulary. The closer to unity, the better the thesaurus. The Kochen and Tagliacozzo accessibility measure becomes an *enrichment ratio.* A value between 2 and 5 is recommended; it is suggested that too many references per descriptor (i.e., substantially more than 5) will be more of a hindrance than a help.

Various new measures also were suggested, including

1. The *equivalence ratio,* which is the ratio of nondescriptors to descriptors in the vocabulary, really a measure of the richness of the entry vocabulary. The authors of the Bureau Marcel Van Dijk report recommend that this value exceed 1, that is, that there be more entry terms than descriptors.

2. The *reciprocity ratio,* which is the extent to which BT, NT, and RT relationships are reciprocated.

3. *Definition,* which is represented by the equation $(b - a)/b$, where a is the number of descriptors that are possibly ambiguous because they lack scope notes, qualifiers, or hierarchical relationships

to put them in context and *b* is the total number of descriptors in the vocabulary.

4. *Flexibility*, which is the proportion of words in multiword descriptors that appear in the vocabulary as descriptors or nondescriptors. A value of 0.6 or higher is recommended.

5. *Pre-coordination level*, which is the mean number of words per descriptor. It is recommended that this value be in the range 1.5–2.0 for English and French thesauri and 1.1–1.2 for German thesauri.

6. The *size of term groups* (i.e., the groups that comprise the categorized list of a thesaurus). Thirty to forty terms per group is recommended.

Some of these measures are ingenious, but others seem trivial (reciprocity ratio) and even arbitrary (flexibility). The values suggested are almost totally arbitrary. They were derived by collecting some thesauri presumed to be "good" and doing the various counts on these.

Of course, it is impossible to evaluate a thesaurus except under conditions of actual use. The acid test is whether the terms are sufficiently specific to adequately represent the subject matter of documents and requests, how much syntactic ambiguity exists in the data base, and how helpful the thesaurus is in suggesting all terms needed to adequately perform a particular search.

17 Natural-language Searching and the Post-controlled Vocabulary

Because the terminology of information retrieval is not always precise and consistent, it is necessary to define some terms before proceeding any further. Exhibit 46 illustrates different ways of implementing natural-language systems in information retrieval. The term *natural language* means nothing more than the language of common discourse (e.g., as used by authors in a particular subject field). In a natural-language retrieval system, the subject matter of documents and of information needs is represented by an open-ended vocabulary of words and phrases commonly used in the field. The key term here is *open-ended*. The antonym of "natural language" is "controlled vocabulary," that is, some restricted set of terms that must be used by indexers and searchers. A controlled vocabulary is a subset of the natural language of a field. It need be nothing more than this; in other words, it can be as simple as a list of acceptable terms. More commonly, however, it will have some structure, as in the case of classification schemes, thesauri, and lists of subject headings. In information retrieval, then, a natural-language system is one

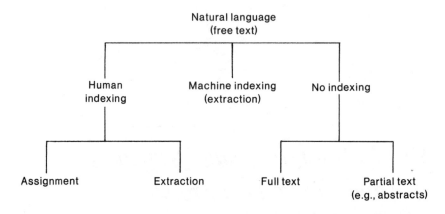

Exhibit 46   Various possibilities in implementing natural-language systems.

in which no control is imposed on the vocabulary used to operate the system. As shown in Exhibit 46, "free text" is sometimes used as a synonym for natural language, although, strictly speaking, the term implies the use of words and phrases exactly as they occur in documents and thus can be considered more restrictive.

As shown in the diagram, a natural-language system can be based on human indexing, machine indexing, or no indexing at all. When humans index with natural language, they are likely to do so by extracting words and phrases from the text of documents. This is indexing by extraction or "derivative" indexing. The assignment of additional terms not appearing in the text also could occur. For example, an indexer might decide that the word *aerodynamics* should apply to a particular document, even though it might not appear in the document. Natural-language indexing by computer ("machine indexing" in Exhibit 46) is always extraction indexing. Although it is possible to program a computer to assign terms to documents, the limited set of terms that the computer could be programmed for would constitute a controlled vocabulary.

This chapter deals with systems that operate without "indexing" in the conventional sense. The implication is that some portion of the text of a document is stored in machine-readable form and that the data base thus created can be searched using combinations of words and phrases appearing in the text. In some systems the full text of documents is searchable, but usually only part of the text is stored. This might be the title, an abstract, or some other section presumed to be rich in content-indicative words (e.g., a conclusions or summary section).

CONTROLLED VOCABULARY VERSUS NATURAL LANGUAGE

Natural-language systems offer one distinct advantage over controlled-vocabulary systems. Because they use an unrestricted vocabulary, they tend to allow greater specificity in retrieval. In fact, the more specific an information need, the more likely it is that the natural-language system will produce better results than the controlled-vocabulary system. For example, in a "pure" controlled-vocabulary system (i.e., one having no natural-language component), a search on "air pollution in Rio de Janeiro" might have to be broadened to "air pollution in Brazil" if the descriptor BRAZIL exists in the thesaurus but names of individual cities do not.

Controlled vocabularies have advantages, too. A controlled vocabulary serves three principal functions: It tends to reduce semantic ambiguities, to promote consistency in the representation of subject matter, and to facilitate the conduct of comprehensive searches. The first function is achieved by distinguishing among the various meanings of homographs, the second through the control of synonymous and nearly synonymous expressions, and the third by some superimposed structure that links semantically related terms.

In the implementation of retrieval systems, a possible trade-off exists between input and output costs or effort. Controlled-vocabulary systems impose cost and effort at the time of input, whereas natural-language systems shift this cost and effort to output (i.e., to the searching of the data base). An experienced searcher can develop a strategy that will compensate for the lack of vocabulary control at input. In essence, he is using the strategy to achieve the same ends that a controlled vocabulary would be designed to achieve.

The homograph problem is the most trivial; it is more theoretical than actual. Homographs are usually only ambiguous when they stand alone. In information retrieval, however, one rarely uses words standing alone. Thus, the word *seals* could refer to an aquatic animal or to devices used to close containers, but possible ambiguities will probably be considerably reduced by the context of the data base. In an applied mechanics data base, the probability that "seals" would refer to aquatic animals is almost nil. Given that both meanings occur in a data base (e.g., an index to newspapers or magazines), possible ambiguity is reduced, if not eliminated entirely, through the context provided by the search strategy. A search on the breeding habits of seals, combining the word "seals" with such words as "breeding" and "reproduction," almost eliminates the possibility of retrieving items on closures. No special procedures are necessary to deal with homography in natural-language systems.

In dealing with synonymy in a natural-language system, one must use the search strategy to accomplish what is already built into a controlled-vocabulary system. Thus, a thesaurus may include the reference "triangular wings *use* delta wings." In searching for airfoils of this configuration in a natural-language system, the user must specify triangular or delta. A natural-language search on delta wings might yield the same outcome as a controlled-vocabulary search. The only disadvantage of the former method is that the searcher must be able to recognize "delta" and "triangular" as synonymous in this context.

Here, the natural-language system offers no real advantages, since the two words are exactly synonymous. In controlled vocabularies, however, near-synonyms, as well as true synonyms, may be merged. In this situation, natural language offers the advantage of being able to distinguish the fine shades of meaning that the controlled vocabulary obscures. For example, a thesaurus may include the reference "nutrition *use* diet." The vocabulary builders have decided that, within the context of a particular data base, these terms are sufficiently related in meaning that the distinction is not worth maintaining. To perform a comprehensive search on "what people eat," one would need only search on the descriptor "diet," whereas with natural language one would at least have to use "diet or nutrition." The controlled vocabulary is more convenient: It gives the searcher one place to look, instead of two or more, and reduces the possibility that a search will be incomplete. Nevertheless, something may be lost. By using both terms as alternatives, the searcher of a natural-language system may achieve essentially the same result that the controlled-vocabulary system achieves by conflating the near synonyms. Yet, the natural-language system allows one to maintain the distinction between the two terms when it is useful to do so.

The following example illustrates that a natural-language system is more flexible than a controlled-vocabulary system. Suppose that in a particular data base there are 100 abstracts dealing with the subject of "nourishment" and that the word "diet" occurs in 50 of these and the word "nutrition" in the other 50. A natural-language system essentially puts the documents into two classes — those including the word "diet" and those using the word "nutrition" (Exhibit 47a). The controlled-vocabulary system, on the other hand, treats the two words as synonyms and puts all 100 documents into a single class (Exhibit 47b). The controlled-vocabulary system makes it more convenient to retrieve the entire set. By using "diet or nutrition," however, the natural-language searcher builds the same class that the thesaurus did (Exhibit 47c) but without destroying the separate identities of the two subclasses. Thus, in the natural-language system, one can achieve with a minimum of ingenuity what the controlled-vocabulary system achieves and even more, since one can still distinguish between the two subclasses when necessary (e.g., when distinguishing food intake in general from health aspects of food intake).

The third function of the controlled vocabulary, and probably the most important, is to facilitate the conduct of comprehensive searches. Consider the subject of South America. A thesaurus may explicitly draw our attention to all the terms necessary to achieve a comprehensive search, as follows:

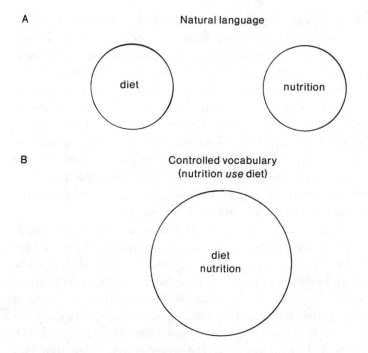

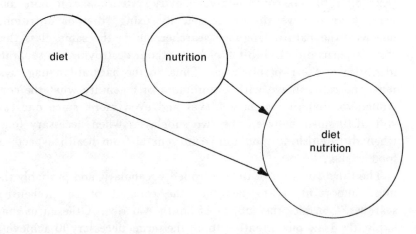

Exhibit 47   Example of the flexibility of a natural-language system.

```
SOUTH AMERICA
    BT   AMERICA
    NT   ARGENTINA
         BOLIVIA
         BRAZIL
         CHILE
         COLOMBIA
         ECUADOR
         FALKLAND ISLANDS
         FRENCH GUIANA
         GUYANA
         PARAGUAY
         PERU
         SURINAM
         URUGUAY
         VENEZUELA
    RT   ORGANIZATION OF AMERICAN STATES
```

At the very least, the thesaurus tells us that to achieve a comprehensive search on this subject, one must use not only the general term SOUTH AMERICA but also the range of individual countries (NTs). But a computerized system may facilitate this search in other ways. For example, as with MEDLINE, one may be able to "explode" the entire hierarchy so that all the necessary terms (in this case, SOUTH AMERICA and its NTs) are brought into the strategy in one fell swoop. Alternatively, some systems may "post-up" so that the term SOUTH AMERICA carries the postings for documents indexed under individual countries. (This is not recommended unless the system can distinguish documents on South America in general from those on specific countries.) A third alternative is for the system to display the thesaurus entry on-line and allow the searcher to select all necessary terms from this display without having to enter them at the keyboard.

Let us assume that there is a direct equivalence between a set of abstracts and the use of a controlled vocabulary by indexers (e.g., the word "Bolivia" occurs in all abstracts of documents to which the descriptor "Bolivia" is assigned) and that the level of specificity of the controlled vocabulary is such that one can specify the country in the thesaurus but not a particular location within a country. For a search on an individual country, the two systems are identical in all respects; it makes no difference whether one searches on the word "Bolivia" or the descriptor "Bolivia." The controlled-vocabulary system offers advantages for a broad search on all of South America. The natural-language searcher must think of all the necessary country names, as well as the general term "South America," and must enter them all in some way. Nevertheless, although inconvenient, this can be done; a comprehensive search is as feasible in the natural-language situation as it is in the controlled-vocabulary system. For a search more specific than the thesaurus allows, natural language wins hands down. Only with the natural-language system would one be able to restrict a search to "La Paz."

To take this further, suppose the thesaurus includes only "South America" but not names of individual countries. The controlled-vocabulary system allows only the generic search, but natural language permits searches on individual countries, locations within countries, and, with somewhat more difficulty, at the generic level. Once again, the natural-language system has greater flexibility than the controlled-vocabulary system.

This discussion has been overly simplistic. The examples used are unusually favorable to the natural-language system. For example, simple synonyms (one word for one word) are assumed (whereas synonymy is often much more complex [e.g., a single word may be synonymous with a phrase]) and other assumptions (e.g., about the existence of content-indicative words in abstracts) have also been made. On the other hand, some of the advantages of natural language have been glossed over. For example, it has greater redundancy: An abstract may contain the names of three cities, indicating involvement of Brazil; the searcher need only hit on one of these. The controlled-vocabulary situation tends to be less redundant. Finally, a very crude natural-language system, one with no searching aids, has been assumed. In reality, a natural-language system may help the searcher with various devices and aids. Some favorable assumptions have been made about the controlled-vocabulary system, too. More-or-less perfect indexing has been assumed (e.g., the descriptor "Bolivia" is assigned every time it should be assigned), whereas human indexing rarely approaches perfection.

SEARCHING AIDS

Information retrieval via natural language predated computerized systems. But purely manual systems are not really suited to natural language because of the large number of words (and thus cards) that may need to be manipulated to perform a search approaching completeness. Computers were first applied to natural-language searching at a significant level in the field of law in the late 1950s and early 1960s. Even the earliest of these systems developed various aids to assist the searcher.

The most primitive aid allowed by today's software is probably the alphabetic display (or printout) of the "significant" words occurring in the data base, with an indication of how frequently each one occurs.

Some type of word-distance indicator (metric operator) is also common. The ability to specify how close two words must be is particularly useful in the searching of full-text data bases where words occurring in different paragraphs may not be directly related at all.

Perhaps the most powerful aid to natural-language searching is the ability to search on parts of words, that is, to truncate or perform word-fragment searching. The value of word-fragment searching has been described by Williams (1972). The most flexible software allows searching on any fragment: right truncation (e.g., all words beginning with "condens"), left truncation (all words ending with "mycin"), "infix" truncation (the beginning and end of a word are specified but the middle is not), or any possible combination of these (e.g., all words including the character string "magnet," wherever it appears). Although potentially useful in all fields, word-fragment searching seems most valuable in science and technology, where the language tends to be more predictable. In a sense, this capability allows one to compensate for lack of a controlled vocabulary by building useful classes of words into a strategy. Thus, searching on the stem "condens" will presumably allow retrieval of a group

of documents having something to do with condensers and conden-
sation; searching on the suffix "mycin" will produce documents dealing with antibiotics; and searching on "tri. . .cobaltate" (infix
unspecified) will retrieve a related family of chemical compounds.

Word-fragment searching achieves some of the capabilities of the
conventional thesaurus but does so at the time of output rather than
imposing control at the input stage. For example, the ability to
search on the suffixes "biotics or illin or mycin or cycline or myxin"
goes a long way toward equivalency with a conventional thesaurus
entry "antibiotics" that leads to a list of narrower antibiotics terms.
The conventional thesaurus is a pre-controlled vocabulary, whereas
the building of word or word-fragment classes into a search strategy
is a kind of post-controlling process.

THE POST-CONTROLLED VOCABULARY

The earliest system developed to search large bodies of legal text (at
the University of Pittsburgh Health Law Center) used a kind of thesaurus to aid the search process. This was merely a compilation of
words with similar meanings, resembling *Roget's Thesaurus* more
than the thesaurus structure commonly used in information retrieval. Even without any significant degree of "structure," such a thesaurus could be an extremely valuable searching aid; words with
similar meanings are potentially substitutable in a search, and such
a tool relieves individual searchers from having to think of all the
words that might express a particular idea. Investing in the construction of such a searching aid allows significant economies in a system
in which large numbers of searches are performed. This simple type
of thesaurus is a kind of controlled vocabulary, with the control applied at output rather than input. It is a post-controlled vocabulary.

The properties of the post-controlled vocabulary can be further illustrated with an example. Consider a public affairs data base that
is indexed with a thesaurus. The thesaurus includes the term AIR-
LINES, so it is possible to perform a broad search on this subject. It is
not possible, however, to limit a search to a particular airline, since

specific names do not appear in the thesaurus. Thus, it would be impossible to restrict a search to "financial conditions of Varig"; the best one might do is to retrieve everything on the financial conditions of airlines. The general search tends to be easy in the pre-controlled vocabulary situation, but certain highly specific searches may be virtually impossible.

In contrast, consider an alternative public affairs data base that dispenses with indexing but allows searches on titles and abstracts. Retrieving items on Varig or Swissair will likely be easy. More difficult would be the general search on airlines. To perform a comprehensive search, one would need to go far beyond the use of the word "airlines" and would need such synonyms as "air carriers" and names of individual companies. The search strategy might look like "airlines or air carriers or Varig or Swissair or Lufthansa or...," perhaps a very long list. What the searcher is doing is creating part of a post-controlled thesaurus. Regrettably, in present information services, such thesaurus entries are rarely retained and stored once they have been created and used. Within a large network, much duplication of effort takes place. "Airlines" may appear as a facet of many searches performed during a year, and the work of building the search strategies of varying degrees of completeness will be repeated time and time again. How much more sensible to store it in retrievable form for future use.

A true post-controlled vocabulary consists of tables with names and identifying numbers that can be called up and consulted by users of natural-language data bases within some on-line network. Thus, the searcher could retrieve the "airlines" entry, the "financial affairs" entry, and so on. The tables can be viewed on-line and terms selected from them. Alternatively, the entire table can be incorporated into a search strategy by its identifying number. Such tables need not be restricted to words but may incorporate word fragments. Thus, a surgery table might look like "surg..., operat..., section...,...section,...otomy,...ectomy,...plasty," and so on. The vocabulary can also be given some minimal structure by cross-referencing of related tables.

A number of controlled experiments have consistently shown that natural-language searching can outperform controlled-vocabulary searching (Cleverdon et al., 1966; Aitchison et al., 1970; Lancaster et al., 1972; Cleverdon, 1977). The natural-language systems used in these experiments had only minimal searching aids. A post-controlled vocabulary system can offer all the advantages of natural language with many of the attributes of the pre-controlled vocabulary. Such a system should generally perform significantly better than one based solely on a pre-controlled vocabulary. To return to an earlier example, one could search for individual airlines with ease or use the "airlines" table to form the class defined by "airlines" in the conventional thesaurus.

One of the beauties of natural language is that it is data base-independent. Thus, an "airlines" table would be equally applicable to all data bases in the English language. One could visualize a natural-language thesaurus that would be applicable to several hundred data bases offered by some on-line vendor or within an on-line network. In principle, there is no reason why such tools could not be made multilingual, for use in international networks.

CONSTRUCTING THE POST-CONTROLLED VOCABULARY

Despite the fact that natural-language searching is becoming commonplace in the on-line environment and is likely to increase in importance as more text becomes accessible on-line, very little work has been done on the concept of the post-controlled vocabulary. In fact, in some ways, the natural-language systems of today offer less aid to the searcher than those of 20 years ago. Since the time of experienced on-line searchers is valuable and on-line connect time is by no means cheap, post-controlled vocabularies offer the possibility of improving the quality of searching while introducing significant economies.

The basic element of a post-controlled vocabulary was introduced by searchers at the National Library of Medicine almost 20 years ago. Parts of search strategies that were difficult to construct were stored for future use. Because these fragments tended to cut across the structure of the hierarchical trees of *Medical Subject Headings,* they were referred to as "hedges." Thus, one might have an "oral manifestations" hedge—a list of terms, in a logical OR relationship, that collectively covers oral manifestations and that can be plugged into a wide range of search strategies (e.g., oral manifestations of arthritis). Similar hedges or "search facets" have been built for use with the Educational Resources Information Center (ERIC) data base (Markey and Atherton, 1978). Conceptually, such hedges are similar to the thesaurus entries of a post-controlled vocabulary, although in the original MEDLARS (National Library of Medicine's Medical Literature Analysis and Retrieval System) hedges were restricted to terms selected from a conventional pre-controlled vocabulary.

"Stored searches" have also been used in information retrieval systems (see, e.g., Cook et al., 1971). These differ from the post-controlled vocabulary concept in that they store complete search strategies rather than fragments of strategies. Other tools vaguely resembling the post-controlled vocabulary have also been produced—for example, *Agricultural Terms* (1978), based on the data base of the National Agricultural Library, and the *Guide to the Vocabulary of Biological Literature,* issued by Biological Abstracts (see Lefever et al., 1972). These tools tend to be restricted to the consolidation of words having common roots rather than to synonyms and near-synonyms and to "conceptual groups" of semantically related terms. None of these is a complete post-controlled vocabulary as discussed in this chapter.

An approximation of the post-controlled vocabulary approach has been described by Semturs (1978), who discusses the Thesaurus and Linguistics Integrated System of IBM's STAIRS (STAIRS/TLS). Algorithms can automatically expand search words by including common inflections of these words. Exceptions can be handled by stored tables, and a variety of thesauri, including multilingual thesauri, can be accommodated. Semturs deals mostly with the capabilities of the software and is vague on the extent to which these capabilities have actually been applied to data base searching.

The closest tool to the post-controlled vocabulary is the TERM data base implemented by Bibliographic Retrieval Services (BRS) and described by Knapp (1983). TERM is a data base of tables, representing concepts, that include both controlled terms and free-text terms needed to perform searches in a variety of data bases in the social and behavioral sciences. A sample table is displayed in Exhibit 48. The title (TI) of the table is POVERTY AREAS. This term is used to retrieve items on this topic in ERIC (ER), in data bases indexed by *Medical Subject Headings* (ME) and in the PsycINFO (PS) data base (in which a related term is GHETTOS). In Sociological Abstracts (SO), possible terms are SLUM, GHETTO, and APPALACHIA, whereas a narrower ERIC term (EN) is SLUMS. Finally, a detailed list of related free-text (FT) terms, useful for a search on this subject in any English-language data base, is given.

A strategy can be developed on the TERM data base and saved and executed on the bibliographic data bases at a later time. As of May 1985, some 4,500 concepts were already represented, and growth to 8,000 is planned.

A post-controlled vocabulary in a particular subject field can be built by human intellectual effort in much the same way as a conventional thesaurus. The task might be simplified considerably by machine manipulation of the words occurring in relevant data bases so

---

TI	POVERTY AREAS.
ER	POVERTY-AREAS+.
ME	POVERTY-AREAS*.
PS	POVERTY-AREAS. CONSIDER ALSO: GHETTOS.
SO	CONSIDER: SLUM. GHETTO. APPALACHIA.
EN	SLUMS.
FT	POVERTY AREAS. SKID ROW. BOWERY. SLUM. INNER CITY. POOR NEIGHBORHOODS. MILIEU OF POVERTY. DEPRESSED AREAS. SLUMS. GHETTOS. GHETTO. GHETTOES. APPALACHIA. LOW INCOME AREAS. GHETTOIZATION. STREET CORNER DISTRICT. ETHNIC NEIGHBORHOOD. BLACK NEIGHBORHOOD. BLACK COMMUNITY. SEGREGATED NEIGHBORHOOD. DISADVANTAGED AREA. BLACK SCHOOL DISTRICTS. MINORITY NEIGHBORHOOD. REDLINED AREAS. REDLINING.

Exhibit 48 Sample table from the BRS/TERM data base. Reprinted by permission of Bibliographic Retrieval Services, Inc.

that various levels of "statistical association" are derived. Perhaps it would be more sensible, however, to collect and edit the "search fragments" actually entered by users of some on-line systems (any list of terms entered in an OR relationship would be a candidate), thus producing a kind of "growing thesaurus" as visualized by Reisner (1966), but with some editorial control imposed to avoid complete anarchy.

THE FUTURE OF VOCABULARY CONTROL

It seems certain that natural language will become the norm in information retrieval and that the use of conventional controlled vocabularies will decline. There are numerous reasons for this, including the escalating costs of human intellectual processing, the rapidly declining costs of computer storage, the increasing amount of text becoming accessible in machine-readable form (including electronic mail and the full text of journals and newspapers), and the gradual reduction in dependence on the skilled intermediary in on-line searching. In the long term, we may well have large on-line systems operating effectively on the basis of questions posed in unrestricted narrative form (e.g., Salton, 1971; Doszkocs and Rapp, 1979), with all the inner workings of the system being "transparent" to the user (i.e., the user receives responses to his question but is not necessarily aware of how these results were achieved). For now, however, it is doubtful that such transparent systems could outperform the human searcher given effective searching aids, and it may be a long time before they do so. Meanwhile, it seems reasonable to conclude that the development of post-controlled vocabularies offers considerable promise for improving the effectiveness and cost-effectiveness of searching within on-line networks. Indeed, this approach deserves more attention than it has so far received.

18 *Hybrid Systems*

The term *hybrid* in this context refers to information retrieval systems operating on a combination of controlled terms and natural language. These include systems in which both sets of terms are assigned by human indexers and systems in which a data base can be searched on a combination of humanly assigned controlled terms and words occurring in titles and abstracts.

Since the early days of computer-based systems in the 1950s, there has been an evident trend toward simplification in information retrieval. It has become more widely recognized that it is possible to operate systems effectively with a minimal level of vocabulary control or with none at all. As an illustration of this trend, let us consider an actual case history involving a large information processing agency in the United States.

The Central Intelligence Agency made a deliberate move away from a highly sophisticated system based on a large, carefully controlled vocabulary (a classification scheme including various relational indicators) to one of lesser sophistication, in which three separate vocabulary components are involved in the indexing and retrieval operations:

1. A small controlled vocabulary of approximately 250 broad subject codes
2. A list of codes representing geographic areas (area codes)
3. Keywords or phrases occurring in the titles or texts of documents

In indexing a document, the analyst assigns subject codes and area codes necessary to represent adequately the broad subject matter and the countries involved. He also marks up the title of the document to indicate words or phrases that might be useful for retrieval purposes ("keywords"). If the title is insufficiently descriptive, the indexer will expand it by adding, parenthetically, additional descriptive words or phrases contained in the text of the document or otherwise illustrative of its content or type.

This indexing represents a significant economy over indexing that used the large, carefully controlled vocabulary for two reasons:

1. The subject codes are sufficiently broad that they can be assigned without much difficulty by an indexer not having a high level of education or subject expertise.
2. The number of subject codes is small enough that the indexer can retain most by memory and avoid having to constantly look up codes in a vocabulary listing.

For items received as hard copy, indexing is done on the document; that is, the indexer writes subject codes and area codes on the face of the document and marks up the title to indicate keywords, adding additional words to the title if necessary. No indexing forms are completed; the input typist works directly from the document. Indexing is fast. In fact, a good indexer may index one hundred or more items a day. For items received "electrically," some machine-aided indexing occurs. The indexer reviews the document on-line; checks the computer-assigned terms; and adds, modifies, or deletes as necessary.

Searching is conducted by trained search analysts on combinations of keywords, subject codes, and area codes. Although any one of these on its own is relatively crude, the joint use of a keyword (to give specificity) and a subject or area code (to give context) is an extremely powerful device. For example, the keyword PLANTS may mean something entirely different when coordinated with a subject code relating to agriculture than when coordinated with a subject code relating to some industry. Likewise, the keyword STRIKE associated with the area code for Lebanon may indicate a military operation; when it is coordinated with the area code for England, on the other hand, it is more likely to signify a labor dispute. Moreover, the joint use of broad subject codes, area codes, and keywords is extremely effective in illustrating relationships, even when these relationships are not explicitly specified. For instance, area code New Zealand, area code England, and keyword LAMB are very likely to represent a document discussing some aspect of export of lamb from New Zealand to England.

Keywords are uncontrolled in this system. The indexer may assign any word or phrase he wishes. The searcher is supplied with various searching aids, including a complete list of keywords with an indication of the number of times each one has been used, and lists showing the number of times each keyword has co-occurred with each subject code and vice versa. The result is a crude classification of keywords that is nevertheless extremely useful in searching. For example, under the broad code for metal industry appears a complete list of industry-related keywords. This is an interesting example of one system operating effectively with a minimum of vocabulary control. In fact, the system works on a combination of a small controlled vocabulary of broad descriptors used in association with a very large uncontrolled vocabulary of natural-language expressions occurring in documents, particularly document titles.

A very similar approach (i.e., one using two-level searching — broad subject codes plus specific keywords or descriptors) has been described by Uhlmann (1967) and by Holst (1966). The system, in the field of nuclear science, used a thesaurus having three parts:

1. A group of broad subject categories, derived from those used by *Nuclear Science Abstracts*, with intercategory cross-references.

2. An alphabetic list of terms without any cross-reference structure.

3. An association list showing statistics on co-occurrence (in indexing) of terms and categories. This is a searching aid.

In this system, a document cannot be indexed by terms alone. Terms must be accompanied by one or more of the subject categories:

Document	*Category*	*Terms*
"Influence of irradiation on corrosion behavior of Zircaloy"	0905 RADIATION EFFECTS ON MATERIALS	CORROSION ZIRCALOY
"Influence of corrosion on radiation effects on Zircaloy"	0902 CORROSION	RADIATION EFFECTS ZIRCALOY

Note how the joint use of broad subject categories and specific terms enables the unambiguous and economical expression of complex relationships.

Perez (1982) has discussed the advantages of using a limited controlled vocabulary in conjunction with the full text of newspapers. He refers to this as a form of "text enhancement."

Many of the data bases that are now accessible through on-line networks can be searched on combinations of controlled terms and keywords or phrases occurring in titles or abstracts, the latter permitting greater specificity. This combination is still powerful.

19 *Compatibility and Convertibility* *

In searching several data bases to satisfy a particular information need, it would seem desirable (at least on the surface) to use a single set of terms throughout. Merging of data bases would also be greatly facilitated if vocabularies were identical or at least compatible. Neelameghan (1979) has stated this very concisely:

> To facilitate the integration and collaborative functioning of the information systems developed in different contexts, if would be helpful if the "languages" used for representation of subjects in the different systems are syntactically consistent, compatible with each other, and inter-convertible at a reasonable cost. (p. 166)

---

*Chapters 19 and 20 are based substantially on contributions made by the author to the Unesco report *Compatibility Issues Affecting Information Systems and Services* and are reproduced here with the permission of Unesco, Division of the General Information Programme.

He goes on to point to two major approaches to achieving these goals:

> 1. To use the same or very nearly the same information storage and retrieval language in all the information systems, and
> 2. To use an intermediate language or switching language through or by which one moves from one information system to another. (p. 168)

The library community has long used common vocabularies, including such tools as the *Dewey Decimal Classification (DDC)*, the *Universal Decimal Classification (UDC)*, and the *Library of Congress Classification* (for arranging books and other physical objects) and standard lists of subject headings (for organization of entries in alphabetic subject catalogs). These tools are most applicable to the general, multitopical library and are useful in achieving compatibility in the arrangement of many libraries of this type. It is relatively easy to accept a common vocabulary at this macrolevel. General libraries, almost by definition, involve compromises; they provide access to all subjects at a general level but fail to provide the detailed level of access needed by any one field of specialization. A general medical library may not be organized optimally for one whose specialty is neurology, and even a neurology library may not be organized optimally for the specialist in epilepsy.

Adoption of a completely standardized vocabulary for all specialist fields, where detailed indexing of the contents of, say, science journals is involved, seems completely impractical. It is true that the *UDC* has been used for such detailed subject indexing but, as Shemakin and Kulik (1970) have pointed out,

> The *UDC*. . .was created primarily as a hierarchical, pre-coordination system intended for manual retrieval. The results of the most recent research into the use of the *UDC* in the coordinate-indexing mode in automated [information retrieval systems] do not seem to offer much promise. (p. 36)

Moreover, the procedures that exist for keeping the *UDC* up-to-date are cumbersome and diffuse, making indexers reluctant to rely on this tool for microlevel indexing.

Information centers in the same subject field might be willing to use the same vocabulary, although this could mean the generation of bilingual or multilingual thesauri. Nevertheless, little commonality of vocabularies exists — hence, our present preoccupation with achieving compatibility.

VOCABULARY COMPATIBILITY

Perhaps somewhat surprisingly, controlled vocabularies tend to promote internal consistency within information systems but reduce intersystem compatibility. Systems based on natural language are inherently more compatible than those using controlled vocabularies. Consider, for example, two data bases in the biological sciences, each consisting of bibliographic citations and abstracts in English. Given technical compatibility in encoding conventions and record formats, these data bases are easily merged. More important, however, a single search strategy can be used to interrogate the merged file because the terminology used in one set of abstracts, being essentially the language of scientific discourse, should not differ substantially from that used in the other.

Suppose, on the other hand, that each data base is indexed with a different thesaurus. Given technical compatibility, the two files can again be merged, but they cannot be searched by an identical strategy, because a single concept might be quite differently represented in the two vocabularies.

Take the case of two information centers operating in the same subject field and wishing to share resources, either by exchanging data bases or by allowing each other direct on-line access. Assume that both operate in English-speaking countries. For resource sharing (but not necessarily for other purposes), it would be desirable that both use the same controlled vocabulary (which could, perhaps, be the *Universal Decimal Classification*) or that both use natural language to represent the subject matter of documents. If both use a different controlled vocabulary (e.g., different thesauri), the situation is more complicated. The data bases could still be merged, but each would need to be searched using its own set of terms. Moreover, it would be impossible to generate common outputs such as printed bibliographies arranged by identical descriptors.

For some reason, each center wants to continue using its present vocabulary and is unwilling to accept the cost and inconvenience of changing to that of the other agency. Thus, if center A wishes to incorporate records from center B and to produce common outputs, it will be necessary to convert ("map") B's vocabulary to A's. This means that for each term in B's vocabulary, the nearest equivalent term in A's vocabulary must be determined and recorded. If the table of equivalents were stored in machine-readable form by A, it would be possible to automatically convert B's records so that their subject matter is represented in the same terms as A's. The situation can be depicted diagrammatically as

This will allow A to use B's records, but it will not allow B to use A's records. Mapping of B to A is not quite the same as mapping of A to B. Presumably, A will have some terms that do not appear in B, and no equivalency relationships will be known for these terms if B is mapped to A but the reverse mapping is not performed. If each center wishes to make use of the other's records, reciprocal mapping must be carried out: A must be mapped to B and B to A, which can be represented as

Standards, by promoting the structural compatibility of vocabularies, facilitate the conversion of one vocabulary to another. Thus, two thesauri following the ISO standards for thesaurus construction are likely to be more easily reconciled than two built on different principles. Moreover, such standards promote compatibility in a more general way: Once he has become familiar with one thesaurus, it should be easy for a user of information services to convert to another thesaurus constructed according to the same conventions.

But structural compatibility is not the only consideration. Sokolov (1977), for example, deals with the matter as follows:

Thesaurus compatibility means not only that the design and internal structure are uniform but also—and much more importantly—that they have the same working decisions concerning the formulation of keywords and descriptors, the creation of conditional equivalence classes, and the determination of paradigmatic relations. Ideal compatibility (obviously unattainable) would mean descriptor blocks could be mechanically exchanged between different thesauri. A practical approximation to this ideal would be the assimilation of parts of one thesaurus by another without much change in the paradigmatic structure of the latter. Only if thesauri are compatible can search patterns expressed in descriptor language be exchanged between different information systems. (p. 22)

The situation becomes increasingly complex as more and more centers attempt to interchange records in some way. Let us say there are four such centers. Assuming that complete reciprocity is desired, this could be achieved by mapping each vocabulary to the others, which can be depicted as

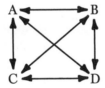

This is an expensive proposition, since it requires 12 separate mapping operations.

There is an alternative, namely, the construction of a neutral "switching" language that can be used to convert from any one vocabulary to another:

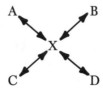

Here, X represents the switching language or "intermediate lexicon." Equivalencies must be established between each component

vocabulary and this neutral switching language. Within an on-line network, this would allow a user of B to interrogate the data bases of A, C, and D, as well as B, using only B's vocabulary. Through the switching language, this will be converted to any one of the other vocabularies. To search C's data base via B's vocabulary, the path would be:

$$B \longrightarrow X \longrightarrow C$$

In other words, B's terms are converted to X and, through X as an intermediate lexicon, into C's terms.

With four centers, possible savings are not large, since eight mappings (X to A, B, C, and D reciprocally) are still necessary. Clearly, the more centers that wish to cooperate, the more likely it is that this approach will prove economical, compared with bilateral vocabulary-to-vocabulary mappings.

The ease with which one vocabulary can be translated to another depends on several factors. The most obvious is the extent of overlap in the subject matter. To use a somewhat absurd example, one would not expect a very satisfactory mapping between a vocabulary in engineering and one in medicine simply because they have very few terms, or even concepts, in common. Another important factor is specificity. If vocabulary A is large and highly specific, it may map rather easily to a smaller and less-specific vocabulary, B. The reverse will not be true: Mapping the very broad vocabulary to the highly specific one is likely to be less than satisfactory. A third factor is degree of pre-coordination in the terms (Levy, 1967). The more alike the two vocabularies are in this respect, the easier the conversion is likely to be. A vocabulary consisting mostly of single-word descriptors is unlikely to map readily to one having many compound (pre-coordinated) descriptors, such as TURBOJET ENGINE NOISE. Finally, the extent to which the vocabularies are "structured," with hierarchical, synonymous, and other relationships clearly displayed, will affect the ease with which a human is able to detect useful equivalencies between the two (see, for example, Wersig, 1979). Gopinath and Prasad (1976) have produced a useful study of the extent of structural compatibility between thesauri and classification schemes.

Some of the problems involved in mapping one vocabulary to another have been explicated by Neville (1970), who refers to the process as "vocabulary reconciliation." Neville recognizes various levels of correspondence between terms in two vocabularies, including

1. *Exact correspondence*—This includes singular/plural variations. Thus, AIRFIELD and AIRFIELDS are considered identical. Also included are exactly synonymous terms in different languages. FLUGPLÄTZE, for example, is considered to correspond exactly to AIRFIELDS.

2. *Synonymy*—UNDERGROUND STRUCTURES, BURIED STRUCTURES, and SUBSURFACE STRUCTURES are synonymous. Sometimes, such synonyms are identified explicitly through a cross-reference appearing in one of the thesauri. The reference Underground structures *use* SUBSURFACE STRUCTURES, for example, indicates that these terms are considered synonymous, at least by the compilers of one particular thesaurus.

3. *Specific to broader term*—The term SNOWDRIFTS, for example, appearing in vocabulary B, may need to be mapped to the more generic term SNOW in vocabulary A.

4. *Term mapping at different levels of pre-coordination*—For example, the term FROST PENETRATION in one vocabulary is considered equivalent to two terms, FROST and PENETRATION, in a second. In a more complex and less obvious example, the term STIFFNESS METHODS in A may be taken as equivalent to the terms STRUCTURAL ANALYSIS and DISPLACEMENT in B.

5. *Antonyms*—The term CONTRACTION may be considered equivalent to EXPANSION in one vocabulary or to EXPANSION/CONTRACTION in another.

6. *Semantic factoring*—This is the most complex situation. The term THERMOMETER in thesaurus A can only be translated into three uniterms, TEMPERATURE, MEASUREMENT, and INSTRUMENT, in thesaurus B.

Smith (1974) also has addressed the problems of human mapping from one vocabulary to another and has reduced the process to a series of rules. The problems of thesaurus reconciliation in the social sciences are dealt with by Sager et al. (1981).

Glushkov et al. (1978) distinguish between semantic compatibility and structural compatibility of index languages. Semantic compatibility implies the ability to represent the same body of knowledge. Two vocabularies in the field of irrigation can be expected to have a high level of semantic compatibility. Structural compatibility refers to the similarity of the vocabularies according to such internal factors as the types of terms they use. Two vocabularies that use subject headings followed by subheadings would show some level of structural compatibility. Clearly, there is no direct relationship between semantic compatibility and structural compatibility. A pair of languages may have structural compatibility but virtually no semantic overlap.

Glushkov and his colleagues go on to further divide the two forms of compatibility. Semantic compatibility can be reduced to lexical, paradigmatic, and syntagmatic compatibility; that is, compatibility in the representation of objects, in hierarchical relations recognized, and in nonhierarchical relations recognized, respectively. Structural compatibility can be reduced to morphological compatibility (similarity in the structure of terms) and syntactic compatibility (similarity with respect to the structure of groups of terms).

The convertibility of one vocabulary to another (including the convertibility of bibliographic classification schemes) has been studied for many years. In the early 1960s, several related investigations sought to determine how easy it would be to convert the indexing language used by one agency of the United States government to that used by another agency. If the vocabularies of several agencies could be harmonized (e.g., by creating a master table of equivalents among them), the processing of reports produced by these agencies could be integrated and combined subject bibliographies generated. This work was performed by the Datatrol Corporation and is discussed in reports by Hammond (1965), Hammond and Rosenborg (1962, 1964), Painter (1963), Jaster (1963), and Datatrol Corporation (1963).

The results achieved in these related studies are subject to different interpretations. In general, the Datatrol investigators were optimistic and claimed that their experiments had revealed that useful tables of equivalents among indexing vocabularies could be prepared. Painter was more cautious. She maintained that, although many of the terms in a relatively specialized vocabulary could be mapped to the vocabulary of a larger and more diverse agency, the reverse was not true: Only a small percentage of the terms in the diverse vocabulary had equivalents in the more specialized vocabulary. Painter concluded that the specialized vocabulary could usefully be mapped to the more general vocabulary, but not vice versa. This conclusion may have little to do with the size of the vocabulary (in numbers of terms): The specialized vocabulary involved included more than 13,000 terms, whereas the more diverse vocabulary (covering virtually all of science and technology) included around 7,000.

Painter also pointed to the practical problems associated with performing a useful conversion—in particular, the effect of indexing error or lack of consistency on the convertibility of indexing records of one agency into those of a second agency. She claimed that the variable quality of indexing might greatly reduce the utility of any such conversion. For example, term x in vocabulary A may be judged equivalent to term y in vocabulary B. If x is only assigned to 72 percent of the documents to which it should be assigned, however, many records that should receive the term y (in a conversion from system A to system B) will not receive it. Likewise, errors in B's indexing would cause the same imperfections in a conversion from B to A. If a combined bibliography were generated, the entries appearing under x/y might be many fewer than they should be.

The intellectual task of converting one vocabulary to another can be both time-consuming and tiresome. Given that both vocabularies exist in machine-readable form, however, it is possible that at least some of the conversion can be done automatically. Wall and Barnes (1969), for example, produced a mapping algorithm that would identify exact matches, some variant spellings, and some variations in word forms; also, under certain conditions, it would effect mapping on the basis of the cross-references and hierarchical structure of the vocabularies. Some examples of the types of automatic mapping possible are

1. *Exact match*	CALORIMETRY to CALORIMETRY
2. *Variant spellings*	ELECTRO OSMOSIS *to* ELECTROOSMOSIS HAEMOGLOBIN *to* HEMOGLOBIN
3. *Word forms*	ELECTRIC MOTORS *to* ELECTRICAL MOTORS
4. *Inversions*	DISEASES, HUMAN *to* HUMAN DISEASES
5. *Via cross-references*	ABATTOIRS *to* SLAUGHTERHOUSES (where one vocabulary contains a reference ABATTOIRS *use* SLAUGHTERHOUSES)
6. *Via hierarchy*	CAROTID SINUS *to* ARTERIES (where the hierarchy in the mapped-from vocabulary indicates that CAROTID SINUS is immediately subordinate to ARTERIES)

The algorithm will not do all of the conversion automatically, but it can greatly reduce the number of intellectual decisions that must be made. Wall and Barnes found that the more alike (compatible) two vocabularies were in structure, the more conversion could be performed automatically. They could automatically map 76 percent of a sample of *Medical Subject Headings,* the vocabulary of the National Library of Medicine, to the *Agricultural/Biological Vocabulary* of the National Agricultural Library, because both were structured vocabularies somewhat similar in format and with a surprisingly high level of subject matter overlap. In contrast, only 11-percent success was achieved in converting an uncontrolled vocabulary to the *Agricultural/Biological Vocabulary* and even less in mapping Library of Congress subject headings to this vocabulary. It should be noted that Wall and Barnes did not actually implement the algorithm by computer but performed the entire study through a simulation.

The more vocabularies involved, the more conversion may be possible automatically. To take a simple example, if vocabulary A includes the term *x*, vocabulary B the reference *y use x*, and vocabulary C the term *y* (but not *x*), it is reasonable to infer that term *x* in vocabulary A is equivalent to term *y* in vocabulary C. No such inference could be made if vocabulary B had not been processed.

THE INTERMEDIATE LEXICON

The intermediate lexicon (Coates, 1970) is nothing more than a switching language. In fact, within a network of information centers, such a device is conceptually similar to an automatic switchboard within a telecommunications network. The situation can be represented as follows:

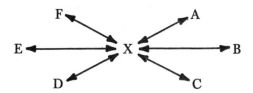

where A–F are information centers and X is the switching language. If the network works properly (e.g., in an on-line environment), each center should be able to search the data base of any other center using its own vocabulary. Thus, a user could sit at a terminal in center A and enter terms from A's vocabulary. The terms would be converted to the codes of X and switched to the appropriate terms in, say, D's vocabulary. To use a concrete example, A's user enters TUMORS, which is converted to the intermediate lexicon (X) code,

17904, and switched from this to NEOPLASMS, the equivalent term in D:

TUMORS ──────────▶ 17904 ──────────▶ NEOPLASMS

Clearly, for this to happen, the vocabulary of each center must be mapped to the switching language. Also, a reasonable level of commonality in subject matter must exist among the centers; otherwise there would be little point in the activity and little chance of convertibility from one vocabulary to another.

In the example TUMORS to NEOPLASMS, the two terms can be considered reasonably synonymous. Some of the transformations will involve identity (JET ENGINES to JET ENGINES), some near-identity (MOUSE to MICE, TIRES to TYRES, ELECTRIC UTILITIES to ELECTRICAL UTILITIES), and some specific-to-general conversions (STREPTOMYCIN to ANTIBIOTICS). Some, of course, may be extremely general. For example, FOURIER SERIES may map to MATHEMATICAL ANALYSIS.

The major problems with such mapping are

1. Vast differences in the degree of pre-coordination among vocabularies (one uses mostly single-word terms; a second uses more complex, multiword terms)

2. The general-to-specific situation (one can map FOURIER SERIES to MATHEMATICAL ANALYSIS, but how should the reverse be handled—if vocabulary B has only the general term MATHEMATICAL ANALYSIS and A has many specific mathematics terms, how does one map from B to A?)

3. Complete absence of a category of terms in one vocabulary (one vocabulary has specific mathematical analysis terms, such as FOURIER SERIES, whereas another has no mathematical terms whatsoever)

The first problem, while difficult, is tractable. For example, JET ENGINE NOISE in A may need to be mapped to JETS and ENGINES and NOISE in vocabulary B. The second problem can also be solved by a one-to-many mapping; that is, ANTIBIOTICS can be mapped to a whole group of terms in a second vocabulary:

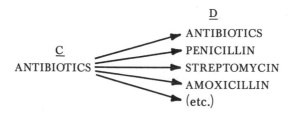

In this case, entry of the term ANTIBIOTICS in system C will cause the entire group of antibiotics terms in D to be introduced, in an OR relationship, into the strategy. The last problem can only be handled satisfactorily by tampering with one of the vocabularies (in the example given, by introducing at least the term MATHEMATICS or MATHEMATICAL ANALYSIS to the vocabulary in which this concept is lacking).

The intermediate lexicon can be used in a multilingual environment. Indeed, this is potentially one of its most useful applications. An English thesaurus may map more readily to a French thesaurus, similar in subject matter, structure, level of specificity, and degree of pre-coordination, than it will convert to another English vocabulary having quite dissimilar structural characteristics.

Preliminary work on the concept of the intermediate lexicon was conducted in France by Gardin (1969). Since then, it has been more fully tested in England in the field of library and information science, as reported by Horsnell (1974, 1975) and Horsnell and Merrett (1978). These investigators claim that "retrieval performance from indexes constructed from switched indexing is comparable to the retrieval performance from indexes constructed from normal indexing." The implication of this claim is that, when search strategies in A's vocabulary are applied to a data base consisting of items supplied by center A and also of items supplied by center D (D's vocabulary switched to A's), no significant difference will be detected in retrieval performance when the two subsets are compared. Readers must conclude for themselves whether this point is proved definitively.

Neville (1970) also was concerned with developing a concordance between several vocabularies in the same general subject area and a "supra-thesaurus" consisting of code numbers to represent all the concepts appearing in the various vocabularies. The procedures used for reconciliation may involve the extensive addition of cross-references to each thesaurus. Some additional terms may also need to be added, but these are kept to a minimum. No existing index terms, in any vocabulary, are deleted.

Assuming the need to reconcile four vocabularies, A, B, C, and D, one can begin by taking A as the "source thesaurus." Each term in A is given a unique code, and equivalent terms in B, C, and D are located and assigned the same code. Thesaurus B then becomes the source thesaurus and new terms (not already encountered in the processing of A) are given codes and reconciled with the other thesauri. The remaining vocabularies, C and D, are handled similarly. Presumably, one takes the largest thesaurus as first source. As one moves to the smaller thesauri successively, the amount of new reconciliation needed will be progressively reduced.

Beling and Wersig (1977) have discussed a wider notion of an "intermediary language" to interconnect a multitude of information systems within the Federal Republic of Germany. Included in their conceptual model is a Bundes-Thesaurussystem, which has a number of subsystems designed to achieve compatibility without imposing undesirable restrictions on the operations of the component information centers. In justifying their approach, the authors claim that "the time of the large universal systems has gone and the time of more complex intermediary systems mediating between a multiplicity of individual need-oriented systems is approaching" (p. 120).

Somewhat related to the intermediate lexicon are the procedures used within the TITUS II system of the Institut Textile de France (Ducrot, 1974), which operates in German, English, French, and Spanish. A key element is the ability to automatically translate sentences in abstracts from one language to another. This is possible because a multilingual textile vocabulary was prepared and because abstractors are required to use a pre-established set of 18 sentence structures ("skeleton sentences"). The procedures resemble the concept of the intermediate lexicon in that sentences (in whatever language) input to the computer are first translated into a "swivel language" and from this neutral language into any target language.

The subject of multilingual processing is discussed in more detail in Chapter 20. The long-term objective of automatic translation applied to information services is to develop an approach that is simple and inexpensive enough to permit translation on demand at the time of system output. For example, a Spanish user of a data base will receive abstracts in Spanish (whatever language they were originally written in), but the translation is performed in "real time" when the user's search is completed.

Diener and Tsuffis (1977) have discussed some of the factors to be considered in deciding whether to establish an intermediate lexicon among a group of agencies. In addition, they describe a method for testing the feasibility of an intermediate lexicon before extensive resources are committed to its development. By examining records representing documents indexed by several agencies, similarity of terminology can be established and problems likely to occur in the reconciliation of the vocabularies can be identified. In essence, the method they recommend entails the establishment of a limited lexicon based on documents common to several data bases. This takes indexing policies and protocols into account and is not quite the same as the reconciliation of vocabularies qua vocabularies, divorced from concern as to how these tools are applied in practice.

INTEGRATED VOCABULARY APPROACH

The intermediate lexicon is still a theoretical approach in that no such tool has yet been fully implemented. In an on-line search environment, an alternative is to provide the user with a composite or integrated vocabulary, the terms drawn from all of the data bases processed by a particular information facility. The purpose is a little different from that of the intermediate lexicon in that equivalencies among vocabularies (synonymy or near-synonymy) are not established. Nevertheless, the approach has certain advantages, not the least of which is the guidance it may give on which data base is most likely to be responsive to a particular information need. The integrated vocabulary has already been implemented by the major on-line service centers in the United States.

DIALINDEX (DIALOG Information Retrieval Service) and CROSS (Bibliographic Retrieval Services) are files of all the searchable terms appearing in the many data bases of bibliographic records accessible through these services. In response to a term entered by a user on-line, such a tool will show which data bases the term occurs in and how frequently it occurs in each. Thus, a user can determine which data base seems to include the most information on a particular topic. DIALINDEX and CROSS allow searching on word stems and also permit Boolean combinations of terms to be entered. For example, it is possible to enter a combination such as IRRIGATION and BRACKISH WATER and get a count, for each data base, of how frequently these terms appear together.

The System Development Corporation's DATABASE INDEX is similar in purpose to DIALINDEX and CROSS, as is the QUESTINDEX feature of the European Space Agency's information retrieval system.

One approach to vocabulary merging that does seek term equivalencies has been mentioned by Butler and Brandhorst (1980). The Women's Educational Equity Communications Network (WEECN) extracts from many machine-readable data bases those bibliographic references that deal with equal opportunity for women in education. Thus, a *tertiary data base* on this subject is compiled. A "vocabulary guide," which is essentially an alphabetic display, in a single sequence, of all terms related to WEECN's interests that appear in each of five data bases, is prepared. For each term, synonyms, near-synonyms, and otherwise-related terms from all vocabularies are displayed, as in the following example:

FEAR (MeSH)[*]
   RT   CONFLICT (ERIC)
         CONFLICT (PA)[†]
         CONFLICT (SSIE)[††]
         CONFLICT (TEST)[§]
         FEAR (ERIC)
         FEAR (SSIE)
         FEAR (TEST)
         PSYCHOLOGICAL PATTERNS (ERIC)
         STRESS (PSYCHOLOGY) (TEST)
         STRESS-BEHAVIORAL ASPECTS (SSIE)

This shows that the term FEAR in MeSH appears explicitly in three of the other vocabularies and is "related to" the term CONFLICT in four of the vocabularies, to PSYCHOLOGICAL PATTERNS in one vocabulary, and to variants of STRESS in two others. A vocabulary guide of this kind, although loosely structured, has a number of possible uses. It can facilitate the searching of the original data bases, as well as of the derived (tertiary) data base, and can be used to aid the conversion of terms from any of the five data bases to the preferred vocabulary, that of ERIC.

Work on the construction of a more sophisticated type of integrated vocabulary, known as the Vocabulary Switching System (VSS), has been performed at the Battelle Columbus Laboratories (Niehoff, 1976, 1980; Niehoff et al., 1979, 1980). The original objective was to create a conversion guide or "synonym table" that would permit on-line switching from one energy-related data base to another. Experiments were conducted by extracting energy-related terms from 10 data bases and establishing equivalencies among them. As in the work described by Wall and Barnes (1969), it was discovered that a

---

[*]MeSH: Medical Subject Headings.
[†]PA: Psychological Abstracts.
[††]SSIE: Smithsonian Science Information Exchange.
[§]TEST: Thesaurus of Engineering and Scientific Terms.

significant amount of the reconciliation could be performed automatically when the terms were manipulated by computer. The conversion guide constructed in this way could be used to generate a display through which the on-line searcher could identify appropriate
terms. A user could, for example, enter the term LIME, which would
generate a display looking somewhat as follows:

Data bases	A	B	C	D	E	F
Terms	LIME	LIME		CALCIUM OXIDES	LIME	CALCIUM OXIDES

This indicates that LIME is a searchable term in A, B, and E; that the
equivalent term is CALCIUM OXIDES in D and F; and that the concept seems not to appear in data base C. The same display would be
generated if CALCIUM OXIDES were entered by the user. As an alternative application, however, the equivalents could be automatically
and "transparently" substituted. This means, for example, that the
term LIME would be used to search A, B, and E, but that CALCIUM
OXIDES could be substituted, by computer lookup, for the interrogation of D and F.

The work performed at Battelle permits a searcher to choose any
of several predefined switching strategies or to construct his own
strategy to achieve different levels of matching between a term entered and the available corpus of terms in a particular data base.
Switching strategies, either predefined or user-defined, frequently
execute several of the following functions in some combination:
exact match, singular/plural match, stem match (e.g., WELDING and
WELDABILITY), synonym match, word match (e.g., find all terms in
which the word *magnetic* occurs), broader term match, narrower term
match, and related term match. In the latest version of the programs, the display generated includes a record of the type of match
that led to the terms shown for each data base (see Exhibit 49). Presumably, to obtain high precision of search results, one would select
a fairly exact matching strategy. To improve recall, however, one
would relax the matching requirements.

In later work at Battelle (Niehoff, 1980; Niehoff et al., 1980), the

```
PLEASE ENTER SEARCH TERM OR VSS COMMAND
    ?MEMORY

SWITCH SUCCESSFUL
```

TERM TYPE	VOCAB	TERM
YOUR TERM	ERIC	MEMORY
YOUR TERM	PSYCH	MEMORY
REL PHRAS	ERIC	MEMORIZING
RELATED	ERIC	COGNITIVE PROCESSES
RELATED	PSYCH	COGNITIVE PROCESSES
RELATED	ERIC	CUES
RELATED	PSYCH	CUES
RELATED	PSYCH	FORGETTING
RELATED	PSYCH	HUMAN INFORMATION STORAGE
RELATED	PSYCH	LEARNING/
RELATED	ERIC	LEARNING
RELATED	PSYCH	MEMORY DISORDERS
RELATED	PSYCH	RELEARNING
RELATED	ERIC	RETENTION
RELATED	PSYCH	RETENTION
RELATED	ERIC	ROTE LEARNING
RELATED	PSYCH	ROTE LEARNING
RELATED	ERIC	LEARNING PROCESSES
RELATED	ERIC	MNEMONICS
RELATED	ERIC	RECALL (PSYCHOLOGICAL)
RELATED	ERIC	RECOGNITION
RELATED	ERIC	VISUALIZATION
WD MATCH	ERIC	COMPUTER STORAGE DEVICES*
WD MATCH	ERIC	KINESTHETIC PERCEPTION*
WD MATCH	PSYCH	KINESTHETIC PERCEPTION*
WD MATCH	PSYCH	MEMORY FOR DESIGNS TEST
WD MATCH	PSYCH	SHORT TERM MEMORY
WD MATCH	PSYCH	MEMORY TRACE
WD MATCH	PSYCH	MEMORY DECAY

Exhibit 49 Example of display generated by VSS when the term *memory* is input. For two data bases, ERIC and PSYCH, exact matches, word variants, related terms, and word matches ("memory" as a component of other terms) are shown. The terms marked * are brought in through thesaurus cross-references from "memory." Reprinted by permission of Battelle Columbus Laboratories.

scope of the project was expanded to other subject areas, encompassing 15 vocabularies in science and technology, the social sciences, and business. An on-line integrated vocabulary of nearly 90 million characters has been built and tested in an experimental setting. The investigators claim that the approach used is as relevant in a multilingual setting as it is in a monolingual setting (one of the vocabularies worked with is an English/Spanish/Portuguese vocabulary on ferrous metals). They have also discovered varying degrees of vocabulary compatibility in different subject areas, social science vocabularies being more compatible than those in other areas. The approach adopted by Battelle has yet to be implemented in a real information service setting. Testing of the approach was completed in 1983, and the results are reported by Niehoff and Mack (1984).

The integrated vocabulary is different from the intermediate lexicon approach because no neutral switching language has been created. Within an on-line network, however, the end results of the two approaches may not be too different, since vocabulary equivalencies are established in both procedures. Dahlberg (1981b) has referred to a similar method as a "compatibility matrix."

Somewhat related to the work of Niehoff are the investigations reported by Williams and Preece (1977) on an automatic "data base selector." By storing a merged vocabulary drawn from many data bases and developing an appropriate algorithm, such a device can be used to test a rough search strategy before a particular data base is selected for interrogation. Based on the frequency with which terms occur in these data bases, the selector can point to the data base (or data bases) offering the best possibility of satisfying a particular information need.

MICROTHESAURI

The term *microthesaurus* has no universally accepted definition. It is frequently used loosely to refer to a rather small and specialized thesaurus. In its original application, however, a microthesaurus was a specialized subset of terms extracted from, and therefore compatible with, a larger thesaurus, and this restricted usage is certainly preferable. A microthesaurus can therefore be defined as a specialized vocabulary that maps to some broader thesaurus and is entirely included within the hierarchical structure of that thesaurus.

Consider a network of specialized information centers in, say, agriculture. The hub of the network is a coordinating center maintaining a general thesaurus and a general data base in the agricultural sciences. Each center operates in a specialized subject field: irrigation, dairy sciences, cacao, rice culture, and so on. Each produces its own specialized data base and printed bibliography. The coordinating unit produces a general index in agriculture.

The problem is that the satellite centers need to index their specialized literatures with much greater specificity than the coordinating center. In the general data base, some of the terms contributed by the specialized centers should appear at a higher level of specificity. The coordinating center needs a complete but rather general vocabulary covering all of agriculture. Each satellite needs a highly specific vocabulary for its field of specialization but also needs to draw on less-specific terms from other areas of agriculture that impinge on its own specialized area.

This is an ideal situation for the use of microthesauri. Each satellite develops a highly specific vocabulary for its specialty that maps to the general thesaurus, fitting entirely within its hierarchical structure. In indexing its collection, the satellite uses its microthesaurus and draws more general agricultural terms from the parent thesaurus. The indexing of the satellites is completely compatible with the needs of the general data base: Machine-readable records from each can be merged by the coordinating unit, specialized terms being automatically mapped to the appropriate general terms (e.g., CHAROLAIS might be converted to BEEF CATTLE). In this situation, the vocabularies of all specialized centers are compatible—compatibility being attained through the structure of the parent thesaurus—but mapping is only one way (i.e., from the specific vocabularies to the general).

An example of the integration of two thesauri, one specialized and one general, so that one becomes a satellite thesaurus of the other, is found in Hammond (1969). The integration of a "base" thesaurus in chemistry, with supplementary special thesauri, is discussed by Bauer (1967). Neicu (1975) has referred to the need to make satellite thesauri oriented to specific subject areas compatible with the Romanian national thesaurus and to develop standards to promote this compatibility.

Soergel (1972) pointed to the need for a "core classification" from which "extended schemes" could be developed for specific applications. He later (1974) expanded this into the notion of a universal source thesaurus, from which others could be derived. Recently, the British Standards Institution (BSI) produced something resembling such a tool; its *ROOT Thesaurus* (1981; see also Dextre and Clarke, 1981) is intended as a comprehensive indexing and searching tool in the field of technology. *ROOT* contains some 11,800 descriptors plus an additional 5,500 entry terms. In fact, it is more of a thesaurofacet than a conventional thesaurus, combining the features of a faceted classification scheme with those of a thesaurus. *ROOT* is available in both printed and machine-readable form. Because it has BSI behind it, it is reasonable to suppose that it will be kept current. The reason for its mention here is that the compilers claim that the tool can form a base for specialized thesauri developed by other agencies. To quote from a BSI brochure on *ROOT:*

The combination of a logical structure and computer generation system means specialized thesauri can be produced quickly and easily, to suit your particular requirements. All you have to do is select and expand the desired schedules, take extracts from other supporting areas and discard any irrelevant sections. The computer will then do the rest to provide you with a custom-made thesaurus at minimum cost.

Several microthesauri developed from *ROOT* would be compatible with each other as well as with the parent tool.

Although they are not microthesauri as such, a number of specialized vocabularies have been built to complement a more general controlled vocabulary. The SfB system, in the field of building construction, is an example of a specialized classification scheme designed to complement and be compatible with *UDC* (Giertz, 1979).

Sokolov et al. (1978) have described and tested procedures for the formulation of a group of interrelated thesauri fitting within the conceptual structure of a "universal paradigm." The faceted approach adopted recognizes three levels of subject access: a *universal paradigm* of facets common to all thesauri whatever the subject; *type paradigms*, which extend the universal paradigms into broad subject areas such as transportation; and *specific paradigms*, which extend the type paradigms to a greater level of detail—for example, navigation as a subset of transportation. If this were carried to its logical conclusion, one could presumably create a cohesive structure of interlocking thesauri, at various levels of specificity, suitable for application in a multifaceted national information program. Different levels of microthesauri would exist within the complete structure. Sokolov et al. describe the construction of two mutually compatible thesauri at the lowest level of the structure, one on navigation and one on seaports. On a more theoretical level, Vitukhnovskaya (1976) has discussed principles involved in constructing a whole system of compatible thesauri.

The *ROOT Thesaurus* could conceivably serve as the superstructure of a national information system, the various specialized vocabularies being developed to fit within this superstructure. The entire system might comprise three, four, or five levels, as in the following example:

> Multidisciplinary superstructure
> Science and technology
> Energy
> Renewable energy sources
> Solar energy

Thesauri would exist at each level. Thus, the thesaurus on solar energy (suitable for use in a solar energy research institute) would be a microthesaurus of the energy thesaurus, and so on. Since the entire structure would be interlocking, terms from higher generic levels could readily be selected by any specialized center (e.g., the solar energy institute might need to draw some general terms from, say, social science and medicine).

Plante et al. (1977) have described a French macrothesaurus from which various subject-related editions can be derived. The *Macrothe-*

saurus des Sciences et Techniques covers mathematics; the physical sciences; biomedicine; the earth and space sciences; industry; agriculture; and some aspects of economics, law, and geography.

Unfortunately, most existing index languages have been developed completely independently; although they may conform to common guidelines in their structure, they have not been integrated or interconnected with a common superstructure. Of course, the polythematic thesauri needed to provide the superstructure have not previously been available; at least, thesauri that might have performed such a function (e.g., the monumental *Thesaurus of Engineering and Scientific Terms* in the United States) were not developed in a form suitable for such application and have not had much influence in this regard.

Referring to the current situation in the Soviet Union, Shemakin and Kulik (1970) have pointed to the inefficiencies associated with the continued proliferation of specialized thesauri that are not interlocked within a single superstructure:

The problem of creating this fundamental thesaurus and general compatibility principles is becoming more acute in that at present various branch thesauruses are being more and more actively developed. If these are not placed under some sort of supervision—and the means of this supervision should be the polytechnical thesaurus—then when the various ministerial [informational retrieval systems] develop their own autonomous thesauruses and index their document collections using them, organizational and technical difficulties will arise as the result of the necessity of adjusting these available thesauruses to the normative terminology and the necessity of reindexing the existing document files. (p. 40)

This section has described the development of specialized vocabularies to fit within an existing superstructure. The reverse procedure, building a superstructure to encompass existing vocabularies, will now be discussed.

THE MACROVOCABULARY

The macrothesaurus approach (see Wolff-Terroine, 1979) is conceptually similar to that of the microthesaurus, but the method of implementation is virtually reversed. The idea is simply to create a kind of generic superstructure of terms that will subsume a group of thesauri, or other types of vocabularies, in diverse subject fields. In fact, when this approach was first proposed as a means of interconnecting several vocabularies used by government agencies in the United States, it was referred to as a "common subsumption scheme." The subsumption scheme was, in fact, developed under the auspices of the Committee on Scientific and Technical Information (COSATI), U.S. Federal Council for Science and Technology (*COSATI Subject Category List*, 1964). The list is used to arrange the *Government Reports Announcements* of the National Technical Information Service, the major bibliography of technical reports within the United States. It has been used to "partition" the terms in several thesauri (e.g., the *Thesaurus of Engineering and Scientific Terms*) into broad subject categories.

The Broad System of Ordering, or BSO (1978), developed as an element of the UNISIST program, is the most obvious manifestation of the macrovocabulary approach. As reported by Toman and Lloyd (1979), the BSO was conceived as a tool to allow the interconnection of information systems, services, and centers using diverse index languages; to permit the consistent representation of subject fields and subfields at a generic level; and to categorize information centers and other sources of information, thus permitting the establishment of a world register or referral center. Essentially, then, the BSO was intended primarily as a switching language (but only as a general superstructure rather than the more specific switching approach embodied in the intermediate lexicon), although other potential applications also were recognized, including the broad organization of multidisciplinary publications, data bases, and, possibly, libraries.

The BSO exists in the form of a classification scheme, with notations, containing slightly more than 4,000 terms. The justification for including a term was *institutional warrant* (Coates, 1979); that is, a term was included if it was known to represent at least one "organized information source" (e.g., information service or center, abstracting or indexing service, university department).

The merits and demerits of the Broad System of Ordering have been widely discussed in the literature (Wellisch, 1979; Foskett, 1979; Vickery and McIlwaine, 1979; Perreault, 1979; Soergel, 1979;

USSR State Committee for Science and Technology, 1979; Dahlberg, 1980; Coates, 1981). Many of the criticisms relate to minor structural features, more relevant to the ordering of physical artifacts (e.g., books on library shelves) than to the indexing of machine-readable records. More important is an understanding of the limitations of the scheme in terms of its possible applications.

The BSO does have potential uses. It could be used to organize a small multidisciplinary library or to segment a multidisciplinary data base, such as the French PASCAL. It would certainly be valuable for the categorization of information sources within a general referral center (although not specific enough to support the activities of a specialized referral system such as INFOTERRA) and perhaps for categorizing the contents of data bases within a large on-line network. It could also be used to switch broad categories of records between machine-readable data bases (e.g., "metals industry" records appearing in a biomedical data base could be transmitted to an information center serving this industry), but only if each data base tagged its records with BSO codes, as well as its own index terms, or if its own vocabulary were mapped to BSO (either requirement being rather expensive to implement). Because of its lack of specificity, the BSO is unsuitable as a means of converting the detailed indexing of one agency into the detailed indexing of another. For the same reason, it would not serve the network purpose of allowing a vocabulary-specific search strategy to be converted into the vocabulary of another data base. Thus, it cannot perform the function of an intermediate lexicon as defined earlier. (Vilenskaya, 1977, distinguishes between intermediary languages and switching languages. She would regard BSO as a switching language but not as an intermediary language.)

There are other potential uses that appear not to have been explored. Suppose, for example, that journal publishers assigned BSO codes to all articles published and that these codes were carried in a general machine-readable file (such as the three major data bases of the Institute for Scientific Information, covering the sciences, social sciences, and humanities). The general file could then be used to "feed" the more specialized indexing/abstracting services, thus obviating the need to define the scope of these services almost exclusively in terms of a limited set of journal titles and facilitating access to the more fugitive literature appearing in unlikely sources, and even to "feed" specialized information centers on an interest profile basis.

Another possibility, given that records in various data bases include BSO codes as well as their own index terms, is to use the superstructure to suggest useful search terms to retrieve information on particular subjects from a variety of data bases. Research on this approach was conducted almost 20 years ago in an effort to achieve some compatibility or convertibility in the handling of technical reports within the United States. The idea is simply to develop, for each of the broad terms from the superstructure, a profile of the terms from a specific data base that are associated most frequently with the broad code. For example, Exhibit 50, taken from Hammond (1965), shows two term profiles for the subject category HEAT TRANSFER, one taken from the data base of the National Aeronautics and Space Administration (NASA) and one from that of the Defense Documentation Center (DDC). Such a display could be used, for example, within an on-line network to bring to the attention of a DDC user the NASA terms relevant to a search on heat transfer (or vice versa). Although experiments along these lines have been conducted, this approach appears not to have been implemented in an operational setting.

Whether any of these uses materializes is largely dependent on Unesco's ability to conceive and promote innovative applications of the BSO and its willingness to commit resources to keep the system up-to-date. At this time, no actual applications of the scheme have been identified, although experiments have been conducted on the use of the scheme in referral activities.

In the development of its National Technical Information System, the Soviet Union seems to be favoring what is essentially a macrothesaurus approach. Pershikov (1977) refers to the need to make interfacing subsystems compatible with the parent system at the vocabulary level as well as in hardware, formats, computer programs, and technical procedures. The interfacing subsystems are automated scientific and technical information systems of all-union, republican, regional, and specialized information agencies. The situ-

TERM PROFILES

			DDC					NASA

1935 HEAT TRANSFER					**1100 HEAT TRANSFER**			
264	92	702	Ablation		237	56	550	Ablation
1578	119	511	Aerodynamic Characteristics		175	58	598	Aerodynamic*Heating
519	57	502	Aerodynamic Configurations		109	53	635	Boiling
525	226	817	Aerodynamic Heating		666	201	714	Boundary*Layer
722	77	528	Air		261	52	518	Conduction
541	103	640	Atmosphere Entry		252	120	716	Convection
291	79	658	Blunt Bodies		450	109	622	Cooling*/Noun/
331	54	554	Bodies of Revolution		198	53	561	Enthalpy
49	26	620	Boiling		304	61	535	Flatness, *Flat
783	209	754	Boundary Layer		2537	350	659	Flow*/Noun/
1007	90	514	Combustion		615	86	513	Fluid*/Noun/
253	51	576	Compressible Flow		19	12	509	Free*Convection
360	60	568	Conical Bodies		1811	170	505	Gas*/Noun/
215	119	780	Convection		1214	334	754	Heat*/Noun/
21	13	563	Cook-off		98	41	591	Heat*Flux
128	64	706	Coolants		127	116	786	Heat*Test
591	196	773	Cooling		481	99	589	Heating, *Heated
900	115	597	Cylindrical Bodies		691	138	619	Hypersonics
196	56	629	Enthalpy		392	127	675	Laminar
10	9	563	Film Boiling		626	85	507	Layer
27	15	567	Film Cooling		86	42	612	Mass*Transfer
20	10	511	Flat Plate Models		799	98	503	Nozzle*/Noun/
975	142	637	Fluid Flow		22	17	570	Nucleate
476	79	595	Fluid Mechanics		23	17	565	Nusselt*Number
208	34	506	Fluids		651	89	513	Plate
444	66	562	Friction		594	83	509	Point*/Noun/
1208	244	736	Gas Flow		64	34	600	Prandtl*Number
1673	178	613	Gases		43	26	587	Radiative
366	55	544	Heat		267	67	576	Reynolds*Number
226	118	773	Heat Exchangers		240	48	510	Skin
502	66	544	Heating		295	107	672	Stagnation
62	17	500	Hemispherical Shells		2834	261	547	Temperature*/Noun/
1820	132	514	High Temperature Research		140	62	640	Temperature*Distribution
451	109	676	Hypersonic Characteristics		34	17	520	Temperature*Profile
437	126	712	Hypersonic Flow		1255	154	550	Thermal*/See*Also*Thermo-, *Heat/
217	43	556	Hypersonic Wind Tunnels		187	40	501	Thermocouple
300	68	620	Hypervelocity Vehicles		677	309	808	Transfer*/Noun/
429	169	778	Laminar Boundary Layer		362	82	583	Turbulent
26	13	540	Liquid Cooled		448	70	511	Viscosity
169	47	607	Liquid Metals		419	82	562	Wall*/Noun/
514	65	537	Liquids		50	34	628	Wall*Temperature
168	31	513	Mach Number					
7383	369	534	Mathematical Analysis					
167	39	567	Nose Cones					
25	18	615	Nucleate Boiling					
214	43	558	Pipes					
3041	222	570	Pressure					
31	15	552	Radiators					
28	12	514	Reactor Coolants					
523	85	600	Reentry Vehicles					
179	38	552	Reynolds Number					
414	61	552	Rocket Motor Nozzles					
950	83	502	Rocket Motors					
428	53	513	Shock Tubes					

Exhibit 50 Term profiles for the broad category HEAT TRANSFER in two vocabularies. The 1935 and 1100 refer to the frequency with which the parent term has been used in indexing. Numbers in the three columns represent, respectively, how frequently the specific term has been used in indexing, how frequently it has been used with the parent term, and an "association factor" reflecting the frequency of co-occurrence of specific term and parent term. Reproduced from Hammond (1965).

ation can be handled by an information retrieval language having two levels: a classification level in the form of a subject heading authority for topical areas and a descriptor level in the form of a set of descriptor languages corresponding to the various topical areas. The subject heading authority is used to organize resource files and to distribute requests among the topical subdivisions (i.e., act as a macrothesaurus), and the descriptor languages are used for indexing and retrieval of documents in a precise subject area.

The need is further discussed by Chernyi (1978):

> We believe that a single information system of subject headings for the National Information System must be a collection or composite of the systems of subject headings of VINITI (for published scientific documents), the AUSTIC* System (for unpublished scientific documents), and the system of subject headings of all specialized information systems. For convenience all these systems should be equipped with an alphabetical subject index to link them as well as a UDC index. (p. 71)

In France, the macrothesaurus approach was once seen as the solution to linking various specialized information centers and to achieving some measure of compatibility among the vocabularies of these centers. According to Michel (1982), the approach has been abandoned. It was found difficult to implement because of the problems of polyhierarchy (i.e., topics falling legitimately into various hierarchies).

ALGORITHMIC APPROACHES

The methods so far discussed relate primarily to the mapping of one vocabulary to another. Related work has been performed at the data base level. The situation arises in the construction of a tertiary data base—one derived by drawing records from other data bases; it can be illustrated as follows:

---

*AUSTIC is the All-Union Scientific and Technical Information Center. Its subject headings are used for categorizing unpublished reports on research and development projects carried out in the Soviet Union.

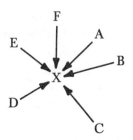

Suppose, for example, that X is a tertiary data base on solar energy, drawing its bibliographic records from the existing data bases A–F, covering energy in general, physics, engineering, and so on. Given that A–F exist in machine-readable form, a "profile of interest" for X can be matched against A–F on a regular basis, in much the same way that a user interest profile is matched against data bases in selective dissemination of information (SDI) systems. Thus, A–F continually feed the tertiary data base X.

In theory, this process could be carried further so that when records are transferred into X, the appropriate index terms from the X vocabulary are automatically assigned. This could be achieved by developing a complete set of mappings between the vocabularies of A–F and the vocabulary of X. This is an expensive proposition, however. An alternative is to seek means of assigning X terms automatically in some other way. This field of research is a branch of automatic indexing or automatic classification—subjects that have extensive literatures in their own right (see, e.g., Stevens, 1980; Sparck Jones, 1974; and Fangmeyer, 1974). The topic is touched on further in Chapter 21. Research on automatic classification has been performed with the goal of establishing "automatic data base translation and mapping procedures." For example, Cahn and Herr (1978) have described techniques for automatically classifying documents in a tertiary data base in the energy field. In essence, index terms/text phrases in the records are used to predict to which category a particular record should be assigned. The terms/phrases used as "predictors" of a category are those occurring frequently in records that human indexers have assigned to that category. Thus, the process tries to achieve algorithmically what the human classifier does intellectually. This type of mapping should be regarded as purely experimental at the present time.

Another area of related research has to do with the automatic linking of synonymous or semantically related terms within a particular data base. The main reason for this is to suggest possibly relevant terms to a user of the data base (e.g., a searcher at an on-line terminal might enter a particular group of terms and the "system" uses these leads to draw him to other terms or to add further search terms automatically). The pioneering work in this area was Stiles's "associative indexing" (Stiles, 1961; Salisbury and Stiles, 1969), but many similar techniques have been developed. The most recent, and in many ways the most sophisticated, is a natural-language interface developed for use with MEDLARS (Doszkocs, 1978; Doszkocs and Rapp, 1979).

OTHER ASPECTS OF TERMINOLOGICAL COMPATIBILITY

Terminological compatibility in general (unlike compatibility among index languages) is somewhat tangential to the main thrust of this chapter. Nevertheless, it is important to mention that the standardization of terminology, including some degree of international harmonization, is an area of increasing interest and activity.

This type of standardization has traditionally been promoted through the use of technical dictionaries and glossaries. Multilingual versions of these tools assist translators and promote consistency in translation. Such tools, however, are expensive to produce and tend to become obsolete very quickly.

An alternative, and one of growing importance, is the *terminology data bank,* which De Besse (1977) refers to as "A kind of living multilingual electronic dictionary containing hundreds of thousands of technical and scientific terms together with the appropriate terminological information" (p. 133). In the last few years, many such data banks have been set up, mostly by governmental agencies but some within private industry. Several can be accessed on-line. Schulz (1977) describes the TEAM system developed to aid translation activities at Siemens AG; Paré (1976), a French/English data bank at the University of Montreal; and Felber (1977), the use of terminology banks and other methods of achieving harmonization of technical terminology within the countries of the Council for Mutual Economic Assistance (CMEA). Perhaps the most important terminological data bank is Eurodicautom, a multilingual source of terminology operated within the European Community and accessible on-line (Goetschalckx, 1977a,b). A more complete discussion of this subject can be found in *Terminological Data Banks* (1980), which contains several papers detailing the problems involved in the exchange of terminological data, including international exchange. Design factors are discussed by Morton (1978).

The single most obvious manifestation of international concern for the standardization of terminology was the establishment in Vienna in 1971 of the International Information Centre for Terminology (INFOTERM), an integral component of the UNISIST program that is affiliated with the Austrian Standards Institute (Felber et al., 1982). INFOTERM's goal is to coordinate terminological activities worldwide through

collecting relevant publications in all languages; preparing bibliographies of terminological publications; maintaining information on libraries having relevant collections; disseminating information on terminological publications; providing advisory services, particularly to institutions in developing countries; organizing meetings; and promoting the interconnection of terminology data banks.

Through INFOTERM's initiative, a loosely structured network of centers involved in terminological work, known as TermNet, has existed since 1979, and plans are being made for the reciprocal exchange of data in machine-readable form. According to Riggs (1979), 16 terminology banks were known to be in existence during 1977.

Beling (1977) has pointed out that the development of a true network of terminological data banks, linked through telecommunications, is impeded by lack of compatibility in the content and data structures used in the various centers. He describes the characteristics of MATER (Magnetic Tape Exchange for Terminological/Lexicographical Records), a magnetic tape interchange format for terminological/lexicographical data, serving the same function for terminological data banks that UNIMARC does for bibliographic data bases. MATER was drafted by the German Institute for Standardization (DIN); it was later elaborated as an international standard, ISO/DP 6156. Work is now proceeding at INFOTERM on the identification of mandatory and optional data elements for terminological records (Felber, 1980, 1981).

The Unesco project INTERCONCEPT, launched in 1977, has as a major goal the establishment of a bank of terms — with definitions — in the social sciences (Dahlberg, 1981a; Vasarhelyi, 1980).

A good picture of the present status of work on the standardization of terminology can be found in *Terminologies for the Eighties* (1982) and *Theoretical and Methodological Problems of Terminology* (1981), both publications of INFOTERM.

PROBLEMS OF ACHIEVING COMPATIBILITY

Several reconciliation problems were identified earlier: wide differences between vocabularies in degree of specificity, differences in degree of pre-coordination, and complete absence of a needed concept in a particular vocabulary. There are other problems associated with the use of computer processing to achieve some level of reconciliation automatically. The most obvious is that in different vocabularies, a term may have quite different usages (e.g., STRIKES could relate to a labor dispute in one and to a military operation in another) or, alternatively, a slightly different nuance. For example, Kirtland et al. (1980) cite the difference between the term BUDGETING in a general sense, perhaps related to personal finances, and BUDGETING specifically restricted to a formal activity performed by some business or government organization, and Smith (1974) cites the difference in scope between ELASTICITY in an engineering thesaurus and the same term in a medical thesaurus.

It seems obvious that, given the desire to reconcile controlled vocabularies, the whole process would be considerably simplified if more organizations followed the same conventions. Two thesauri following the ISO *Guidelines for the Establishment and Development of Monolingual Thesauri* (ISO 2788-1974), or following a compatible national standard (the U.S. standard, ANSI Z39.19-1974 — *Guidelines for Thesaurus Structure, Construction and Use*—is, in almost all respects, fully compatible with the ISO standard), are much more likely to be readily convertible than two vocabularies constructed on different principles or following different standards. Nevertheless, although the standards do promote consistency in several important respects (e.g., by requiring direct entry rather than inversion and by establishing singular/plural conventions), they fail to grapple successfully with at least two of the most important characteristics of vocabularies—the appropriate level of specificity and the degree of pre-coordination. Variations in these characteristics are among the greatest barriers to the convertibility of vocabularies.

The specificity problem, in fact, is not amenable to solution through standardization, since it is unreasonable to expect that any organization would want to develop every term hierarchy to the same level of specificity. The pre-coordination problem is somewhat more tractable, but universally acceptable and fully explicit guidelines on this matter have not yet been produced (see, for example, Jones, 1981).

An additional problem relates to updating. To maintain its utility, a vocabulary needs to be kept current. This is not necessarily an easy task. Currency would seem to be especially important in the case of a switching language. But the problems of updating are compounded when input from a whole group of information centers is involved. It is not enough to build a switching language; a mechanism must exist for keeping it up-to-date at all times (Foskett, 1979).

The problems of vocabulary convertibility are frequently underestimated. Although it may be possible to convert vocabulary A to vocabulary B, in practical application this transformation may be fraught with danger. Unfortunately, it is insufficient to consider the vocabularies of systems A and B without also considering the underlying indexing policies and protocols of the two organizations (i.e., how these vocabularies are applied in practice). To take a simple example, in one system the term OPHTHALMOLOGY may be used very generally to include all aspects of diagnosis and treatment of eye diseases. In a second system, however, the term might be used exclusively to represent the profession of ophthalmology. Interconversion of these vocabularies, at the surface level, could produce some very strange results were the indexing records of center A converted to those of B.

The problem is likely to be especially acute in any automated mapping operation. Suppose that a mapping algorithm converts FUNGAL DISEASES in A to what appears to be the closest equivalent term in B, FUNGI. Assuming that both data bases are biomedical, such a mapping seems reasonable at first glance. On the other hand, system B, by convention, always represents fungal diseases by the joint use of FUNGI and the term DISEASES. If the indexing of system A is converted to that of B, via vocabulary reconciliation and without taking indexing conventions into account, inconsistencies and inaccuracies will inevitably occur.

A related problem is that of variations in the exhaustivity of indexing in different organizations. Center A may index with an average of 3 terms, whereas B may use an average of 10. Although it may be possible and useful to convert B's indexing to A's —

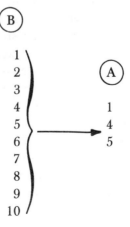

since mapping from specific to general will usually be involved, the reverse procedure may be much more difficult.

Even spelling errors among index terms could affect the convertibility of data bases if they occurred frequently. In a study of 3,600 terms drawn from 11 data bases, Bourne (1977) discovered that, although misspellings in index terms were less than 0.5 percent in one source, they reached almost 23 percent in another. With inaccuracies as high as 23 percent, mapping from one vocabulary to another could be a haphazard process when terms are derived from the bibliographic records. As Zamora (1980) has pointed out, however, automatic recognition and correction of spelling errors may be possible.

The reconciliation of vocabularies by an intermediate lexicon or in some other way seems feasible. Whether such reconciliation will allow the merging of data bases or the exploitation of a variety of data bases in a network situation is debatable. The achievement of a more useful level of convertibility among data bases—taking indexing policies into account—is much more difficult and costly than vocabulary conversion. Moreover, it is not fully attainable because the policies and protocols of a particular organization may not be completely and explicitly stated. Thus, it is hardly surprising that, although research on vocabulary convertibility has proceeded for at least 20 years, actual implementations of conversion or switching projects in a real information service environment are practically nonexistent.

It seems justifiable to conclude that the flurry of relatively uncoordinated activity in information systems development evident over the last 20 years has resulted in an undesirable proliferation of overlapping vocabularies. Unfortunately, when a new information service is created, the tendency is to develop a new vocabulary rather than to adopt or adapt one already existing in the same general subject area. Consequently, when organizations become more serious about coordination, the sharing of resources, or the establishment of a network, a terminological barrier is immediately encountered: The different vocabularies already in use need to be reconciled.

This does not mean that there will always be an existing vocabulary that meets local requirements. Nevertheless, the continued proliferation of thesauri raises the question of whether all newly established vocabularies are really necessary or whether needs could have been met by adopting or adapting some existing tools.

Although the desirability of vocabulary compatibility has been assumed throughout this discussion, not everyone accepts this assumption. Gaaze-Rapoport (1978), for example, takes a completely different view:

When discussing problems associated with IRL's [information retrieval languages] one often speaks about so-called compatibility of IRL's and sometimes it is even required that the unified system of IRL's include only compatible languages. It seems to us that such stress on compatibility is unwarranted and in essence disorients both the developers and users of information service systems. Actually, by compatibility of languages is meant the possibility of reading a text written in one language by means of another language without a translator or translating program. This is possible only in the case of complete coincidence of the vocabulary and grammar of both languages, i.e., when actually there is one language, or when one of the languages is an expansion of the other, i.e., its vocabulary and grammar contain as a part the vocabulary and grammar of the narrower sublanguage. In this case the texts written in the narrower language (sublanguage) can be regarded also as texts of the broader supralanguage (but not vice versa). In all other cases there is no compatibility and it does not make sense to speak about it, and one must simply master both languages. It is senseless to speak, for example, about the compatibility of Russian and English languages or Chinese and Hindi languages. Analogously, it is senseless to speak about the compatibility of artificial languages, for example ALGOL and APL. Therefore, talks about the compatibility requirement create the illusion that such compatibility is possible in principle, and, therefore, they are harmful. . . .

Thus, in our opinion, the problem consists not in attempts to create a system of compatible information retrieval systems, which are doomed to failure beforehand, but in the rational use of the entire rich set of different IRL's and in selecting such a subset from this set which best meets the requirements of the specific subject field or specific problems facing a particular local information system. (p. 46)

Gaaze-Rapoport is correct in reminding us that compatibility should not be the overriding consideration in selecting an index language for a particular application. There seems little point in achieving compatibility with other organizations at the expense of using a tool less than ideal for the purpose intended. Nevertheless, he does

adopt a very narrow view of compatibility, according to which microthesauri would be considered compatible with their parent thesaurus but the other approaches discussed in this chapter would not
be regarded as "achievement of compatibility." Clearly, this chapter
takes a wider view of compatibility by including convertibility and
by considering compatibility factors (e.g., structural compatibility)
affecting convertibility.

20 *Multilingual Aspects*

The technological developments that facilitate cooperation among information services in general make it increasingly possible for such cooperation to take place on an international level. One impediment to effective global information transfer, however, is the large number of national languages in use.*

Languages, like empires, rise and fall. Greek and Latin no longer exert much worldwide influence. Earlier in the twentieth century, German was the major language in the sciences (Hulme, 1923). Today this position is occupied by English (Narin and Carpenter, 1975). A scientist who reads English with ease is thus in a favored position vis-à-vis his colleagues who do not. This advantage is even more pronounced in relation to formal information services: The indexing and abstracting services, especially those in machine-readable form, are mostly produced by English-speaking countries. Iljon

---

*Another impediment is the multiplicity of scripts, but this is outside the scope of this book.

(1977b) reports that of 337 data bases in use in Europe in 1976, 76 percent used English as a carrier language and 99 percent of the use of all data bases was achieved through the medium of English. The worldwide adoption of English as the lingua franca of scholarly communication, however, is not an acceptable solution to the "language barrier" problem, for political and nationalistic reasons if no other.

The ability to handle publications in many languages and to accommodate several languages in the design of information services is becoming more important as truly international systems become operational. One example can be found in the activities of the Commission of the European Communities. Not only are several languages involved, but this multilingualism is mandated by law. Means of solving concomitant problems are wide ranging: expansion and improvement of language teaching, research on terminology, development of terminology banks, publication of multilingual glossaries and thesauri, refinement of machine translation procedures, and so on (*Overcoming the Language Barrier,* 1977).

Language differences may become more of a barrier to effective information transfer in the future than they have been in the past. As Price (1963) pointed out more than two decades ago, the pace of progress in science and technology has already begun to slow in the most developed countries. In parts of the developing world, on the other hand, a rapid acceleration is evident in scientific and technological achievement. Although many of the researchers from these countries still choose to publish abroad in journals perceived to be more prestigious (most of which are in English), it seems only a matter of time before the literature of science (and of scholarship in general) becomes scattered over more languages than ever before. Goetschalckx (1977b) has suggested that the proliferation of "significant" languages may force us to seek different approaches in information handling, perhaps even the adoption of some artificial language:

At the theoretical level, it is not unreasonable to consider the usefulness of a universal intermediate language, whether it be a numerical language, esperanto, or something else. When the developing countries take their place, there will be needs out of all proportion to the intellectual and linguistic capital needed to cope with the work of human translation alone. (p. 146)

Multilingual processing in documentation activities can be considered at several levels, including access to bibliographic records (in printed or machine-readable data bases) of foreign-language literature and intellectual access to the content of the actual documents. Significant improvements in intellectual access have occurred over the last 30 years. More material is translated than ever before (some periodicals are regularly translated cover-to-cover); translation is facilitated by improved glossaries and other aids; and national and international translation centers maintain records of translations, announce these translations, and offer copies for sale.

Multilingual access to bibliographic records can be broken down to at least three levels: translation of titles, translation of index terms, and translation of abstracts. Several indexing and abstracting services include titles in the original language and in translated form, but data bases containing index terms in more than one language are rare. The French data base PASCAL (accessible on-line as PASCALINE) does have some subfiles in which keywords appear in English and French, allowing searches to be performed in either language.

In general, however, a data base indexed by terms selected from language A can only be searched by terms in language B if A's terms are humanly translated into B's terms or if A's terms are automatically translated into B's, possibly through a multilingual glossary or thesaurus.

Bilingual and multilingual controlled vocabularies are not new. Muench (1971), for example, described the development of a bilingual (English/Spanish) index to six such vocabularies in the field of biomedicine. The National Library of Medicine's *Medical Subject Headings* now exists in several languages, allowing MEDLINE to be interrogated in languages other than English.

Notable multilingual thesauri include one developed by the French Road Research Laboratory for use by the road research laboratories of OECD (Organization for Economic Co-operation and Development) member countries (Van Dijk, 1966), and the trilingual

Metallurgy Thesaurus (Rolling, 1979), used by the Commission of the European Communities. Iljon (1977a) describes the development of three multilingual thesauri in the field of agriculture, also within the Commission.

The compilation of multilingual thesauri has been made easier by the appearance of the *UNISIST Guidelines for the Establishment and Development of Multilingual Thesauri* (1980)* and the development of computer programs to manipulate such thesauri (Rolling, 1979). But although guidelines reduce the problems, they do not eliminate them. Some of the problems of constructing a multilingual thesaurus are discussed and illustrated by Pigur (1979) and by Bykova and Muzrukov (1970), with special reference to translation to and from Russian.

The *UNISIST Guidelines* recognize three possible approaches to the construction of multilingual thesauri:

1. Begin from scratch and collect terms from all the languages involved, seeking equivalencies after the terms are collected.
2. Take an existing thesaurus in one language and translate it into the other languages.
3. Take two or more existing thesauri, in different languages, and merge them.

The last approach is considered the most difficult by the authors of the guidelines. Schuck (1977), after describing problems encountered in translating an English thesaurus into German, concludes that it would be easier and more efficient to collect terms from both languages and to organize these simultaneously.

Whichever method is used, the major problem faced is finding equivalencies among terms in the various languages. Some terms may translate exactly from one language to another, whereas others will not. In some cases, a term in one language needs to be translated into two or more terms in a second language. The French *gros betail*, for example, has no exact equivalent in English. It really translates into *cattle* and *horses*. On the other hand, the French word *mouton* could translate into either *sheep* or *mutton*. The *UNISIST Guidelines*

---

*Now available as an international standard (ISO 5964).

suggest that it will occasionally be necessary to coin a phrase to establish equivalency. For example, *steam cracking,* an accepted term in English, has no direct equivalent in French. It could, however, be represented as *vapocraquage.* Phrases coined in this way should almost certainly be given a scope note.

German presents special problems because it contains many compounds that can only be translated into rather lengthy phrases in most other languages. For example, the word *Expertengutachten* really translates into "written report of expert opinion," and *Schwerbeschaedigter* into "seriously injured person." Some German words, indeed, seem to defy translation into English; try, for example, to translate *Schwerpunktstreik* into anything concise and intelligible in English. Schuck (1977) discusses problems encountered in translating from English to German.

The *UNISIST Guidelines* present many sound suggestions for handling these various problems and should be studied by anyone contemplating the construction of a multilingual thesaurus. One important aspect, dealt with in the international standard derived from the guidelines, is that of display. A number of possibilities exist. The terms can be put into broad subject categories and, within each, arranged alphabetically by one of the languages, as shown in Exhibit 51. Permuted word indexes in each of the languages (Exhibit 52) would be useful supplements to such a display. A thesaurofacet may be an ideal way to handle the multilingual situation: Equivalents in the various languages can be grouped under the "neutral" notation, with alphabetic supplements supplied in each language.

An alternative approach, strictly alphabetic, is shown in Exhibits 53 and 54. Here a bilingual thesaurus appears in two parts, a French/English version and an English/French version.

The most ingenious form of display uses transparent overlays designed to allow the terms of one language to be superimposed over the terms of another. Exhibit 55, for example, shows a French display that is equivalent to the English display given in Exhibit 21. These are designed to be superimposable. The method is used in the thesaurus developed for the road research laboratories of OECD member countries (Van Dijk, 1966), as well as in the multilingual *Metallurgy Thesaurus* (Rolling, 1979), from which Exhibits 21 and 55 are taken.

```
10200  COMMUNICATION STRUCTURE

   10210

   COMMUNICATION CHANNEL / CANAL DE COMMUNICATION / CANAL DE COMUNICACIÓN
       RT  COMMUNICATION SYSTEM / SYSTEME DE COMMUNICATION / SISTEMA DE COMUNICACIÓN

   COMMUNICATION STRUCTURE / STRUCTURE DE COMMUNICATION / ESTRUCTURA DE COMUNICACIÓN
       USE  COMMUNICATION SYSTEM / SYSTEME DE COMMUNICATION / SISTEMA DE COMUNICACIÓN

   COMMUNICATION SYSTEM / SYSTEME DE COMMUNICATION / SISTEMA DE COMUNICACIÓN
       SN  Use in connection with the whole of the elements implied in information
           transfer (transmitter, receiver, channel, code, etc.) and with types of
           ordering / Désigne l'ensemble des éléments impliqués dans la transmission
           de l'information (émetteur, récepteur, canal, code, etc.) et les modalités
           de leur agencement / Indica el conjunto de elementos que necesita la trans-
           ferencia de información (emisor, receptor, canal, código, etc.) y las
           modalidades de su arreglo.
       UF  COMMUNICATION STRUCTURE / STRUCTURE DE COMMUNICATION / ESTRUCTURA DE
           COMUNICACIÓN
       NT  ONE-WAY COMMUNICATION / COMMUNICATION UNIDIRECTIONNELLE / COMUNICACIÓN
           UNILATERAL
           POINT-TO-POINT COMMUNICATION / COMMUNICATION DE POINT A POINT / COMUNICACIÓN
           DE PUNTO A PUNTO
           TWO-WAY COMMUNICATION / COMMUNICATION BIDIRECTIONNELLE / COMUNICACIÓN
           RECIPROCA
       RT  COMMUNICATION / COMMUNICATION / COMUNICACIÓN
           COMMUNICATION CHANNEL / CANAL DE COMMUNICATION / CANAL DE COMUNICACIÓN

   MEDIATION / MEDIATION / MEDIACIÓN
       RT  VICARIOUS EXPERIENCE / EXPERIENCE VICARIALE / EXPERIENCIA VICARIAL

   NETWORK / RESEAU / RED
       RT  NETWORK ANALYSIS / ANALYSE DE RESEAU / ANÁLISIS DE REDES

   ONE-WAY COMMUNICATION / COMMUNICATION UNIDIRECTIONNELLE / COMUNICACIÓN UNILATERAL
       BT  COMMUNICATION SYSTEM / SYSTEME DE COMMUNICATION / SISTEMA DE COMUNICACIÓN

   POINT-TO-POINT COMMUNICATION / COMMUNICATION DE POINT A POINT / COMUNICACIÓN DE
   PUNTO A PUNTO
       BT  COMMUNICATION SYSTEM / SYSTEME DE COMMUNICATION / SISTEMA DE COMUNICACIÓN

   TELECONFERENCING / CONVERSATION A DISTANCE / CONVERSACIÓN A DISTANCIA
       RT  DISTANCE / DISTANCE / DISTANCIA
           TWO-WAY COMMUNICATION / COMMUNICATION BIDIRECTIONNELLE / COMUNICACIÓN RECIPROCA

   TWO-WAY COMMUNICATION / COMMUNICATION BIDIRECTIONNELLE / COMUNICACIÓN RECIPROCA
       BT  COMMUNICATION SYSTEM / SYSTEME DE COMMUNICATION / SISTEMA DE COMUNICACIÓN
       RT  TELECONFERENCING / CONVERSATION A DISTANCE / CONVERSACIÓN A DISTANCIA
```

Exhibit 51   Displaying a multilingual thesaurus. Reproduced from Viet (1975) by permission of Unesco.

Van Slype (1977) has analyzed 10 multilingual thesauri and produced data reflecting the quantitative criteria described in Chapter 16.

One result of increasing activity in international information systems has been a resurgence of interest in machine or machine-aided

		PERSUASION		
36620		PERSUASION		
36500		PERVERSION		
10712		PHILOSOPHY		
25320	PICTURE	PHONE	USE	VIDEOPHONE
23000		PHONOGRAPH	USE	RECORD PLAYER
22000		PHOTO ARCHIVES		
22000		PHOTO JOURNALISM	USE	NEWS PICTURE
30310		PHOTO-NOVEL		
21130		PHOTOCOMPOSITION		
22000		PHOTOCOPY		
22000		PHOTOGRAPH		
22000		PHOTOGRAPH LIBRARY	USE	PHOTO ARCHIVES
22000		PHOTOGRAPHER		
22000		PHOTOGRAPHY		
10713		PHYSICAL SCIENCES		
10713		PHYSICS		
30200		PICTURE		
24210	MOTION	PICTURE	USE	FILM
22000	NEWS	PICTURE		
25320		PICTURE PHONE	USE	VIDEOPHONE
24230	ANAMORPHIC	PICTURES		
10742		PILOT PROJECT		
25440		PIRATE STATION		
35240		PLAN		
32230	DEVELOPMENT	PLAN		
35240		PLANNING		
34300	COMMUNICATION	PLANNING		
32230	DEVELOPMENT	PLANNING		
33240	EDUCATIONAL	PLANNING		
37540	FAMILY	PLANNING		
35240	LOCAL	PLANNING		
35240	NATIONAL	PLANNING		
35240	REGIONAL	PLANNING		
37400	SOCIAL	PLANNING		
23000	RECORD	PLAYER		
30320		PLOT		
31200	CULTURAL	PLURALISM		
21220		POCKET BOOK	USE	PAPERBACK
30310		POETRY		
10210		POINT-TO-POINT COMMUNICATION		
34300	COMMUNICATION	POLICY		
31500	CULTURAL	POLICY		
32230	DEVELOPMENT	POLICY		
32230	ECONOMIC	POLICY		
21370	EDITORIAL	POLICY		

Exhibit 52   Permuted word index from thesaurus illustrated in Exhibit 51. Reproduced from Viet (1975) by permission of Unesco.

CONFLITS FRONTALIERS
  BORDER CLASHES
     RT   CONTESTATIONS DE FRONTIERE
         BORDER DISPUTES

CONFRONTATIONS
  CONFRONTATIONS
     RT   CONNAISSANCE TOUCHANT L'ADVERSAIRE
         ADVERSARY'S PERCEPTIONS

CONNAISSANCE TOUCHANT L'ADVERSAIRE
  ADVERSARY'S PERCEPTIONS
     BT   THEORIE DES RELATIONS ETRANGERES
         FOREIGN RELATIONS THEORY
     RT   CONFRONTATIONS
         CONFRONTATIONS

CONSEIL EXECUTIF
  EXECUTIVE COUNCIL
     RT   CHEF D'ETAT
         CHIEF OF STATE

CONSUL SUPPLEANT
  ACTING CONSULS
    PERSONNES HABILITEES A AGIR EN QUALITE
    DE CONSUL DURANT L'ABSENCE DE CE DERNIER
     RT   AGENTS CONSULAIRES
         CONSULAR OFFICERS

CONTESTATIONS DE FRONTIERE
  BORDER DISPUTES
    DISPUTES ENTRE ETATS RESULTANT
    DE DIFFICULTES FRONTALIERES
     UF   CONTESTATIONS FRONTALIERES
         BOUNDARY DISPUTES
     NT   REVENDICATIONS FRONTALIERES
         BOUNDARY CLAIMS
     RT   CONFLITS FRONTALIERS
         BORDER CLASHES
         FRONTIERES DE FACTO
          DE FACTO BOUNDARIES
         INCIDENTS DE FRONTIERE
         BORDER INCIDENTS
         PROBLEMS DE FRONTIERE
         BORDER PROBLEMS
         RECTIFICATIONS DE FRONTIERES
         BOUNDARY ADJUSTMENTS

Exhibit 53   French/English thesaurus format. Reproduced by permission of Infodata Systems Inc.

```
AMBASSADOR AT LARGE
   AMBASSADEUR ITINERANT

AMBASSADOR DESIGNATE
   AMBASSADEUR DESIGNE
   A PERSON NAMED BUT NOT YET
   ACCREDITED AS AMBASSADOR
      BT    AMBASSADORS
               AMBASSADEURS
               CHARGE D'AFFAIRS
                  CHARGE D'AFFAIRS
               DIPLOMATIC TITLES
                  TITRES DIPLOMATIQUES
      RT    DIPLOMATIC APPOINTMENTS
               NOMINATIONS DIPLOMATIQUES

AMBASSADORS
   AMBASSADEURS
   THE PERSONAL REPRESENTATIVE OF A
   CHIEF OF STATE. AMBASSADORS NORMALLY
   ARE ACCREDITATED TO ANOTHER CHIEF OF
   STATE
      UF    CHIEFS OF MISSION
               CHEFS DE MISSION
               DIPLOMATIC MISSION CHIEFS
                  CHEFS DE MISSION DIPLOMATIQUE
      BT    CHARGE D'AFFAIRS
               CHARGE D'AFFAIRES
               DIPLOMATIC TITLES
                  TITRES DIPLOMATIQUES
      NT    AMBASSADOR AT LARGE
               AMBASSADEUR ITINERANT
               AMBASSADOR DESIGNATE
                  AMBASSADEUR DESIGNE
      RT    AMBASSADORS WHEREABOUTS
               DEPLACEMENTS D'AMBASSADEURS
               DIPLOMATIC MISSION CHIEFS
                  CHEFS DE MISSION DIPLOMATIQUE
               PERSONAL REPRESENTATIVE
                  REPRESENTANT PERSONNEL
```

Exhibit 54 English/French thesaurus format. Reproduced by permission of Infodata Systems Inc.

translation and remarkable improvements in this technology. Rolling (1981) describes ongoing efforts in this area within the Commission of the European Communities. SYSTRAN, a system developed by the World Translation Center, is said to have a translation speed of 300,000 words per hour (Toma, 1977) and an "intelligibility rate" of 78 percent (Van Slype, 1979). Rolling implies that this can be

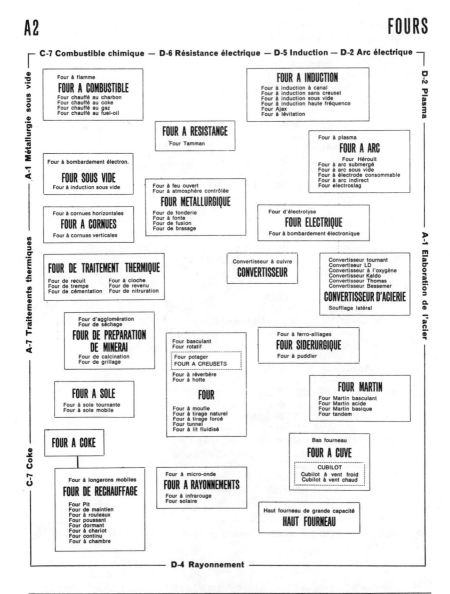

Exhibit 55   Graphic display of multilingual thesaurus. This page, on a transparent overlay, can be superimposed on Exhibit 21. Reproduced from the *Metallurgy Thesaurus* (1974) by permission of the Commission of the European Communities.

pushed to greater than 90 percent and refers to a new system, EURO-TRA, being developed by the Commission, which has as its goal an intelligibility rate of 99 percent. The system will be designed to handle all languages of the Commission countries (King and Perschke, 1982). Rolling points out that, within an international network such as the Euronet DIANE, it is not necessary to translate for input purposes. Instead, machine translation (e.g., of abstracts) can be achieved at the time of output from the system. The Commission also has developed a software package, Astute, for the compilation, maintenance, and printing of multilingual thesauri, as well as a multilingual terminology data bank, Eurodicautom, which is accessible on-line.

Multilingual processing is not necessarily infeasible in a natural-language environment. For example, Salton (1970) has reported on the use of his SMART system in the processing of English and German texts. By building an internal "thesaurus" (not a conventional structured tool but one including synonym tables and tables of conceptually related words) in the two languages, he achieved cross-language processing. German documents could be searched using English-language queries in sentence form, and vice versa. Salton claims that the results were almost as effective as processing with a single language. An approach to constructing a German/English thesaurus automatically, using bilingual and monolingual dictionaries as input, has been described by Bollmann and Konrad (1977).

Controlled vocabularies, coupled with automatic translation (or, alternatively, multilingual thesauri), make it increasingly possible to contemplate the production of printed indexes in various language editions. Gibb and Phillips (1977), quoting d'Olier, have referred to the possibility of producing an abstracts journal in two separate language editions at a cost of approximately 50 percent more than a single-language edition. Additional economies would be possible as further language editions were added.

In a multilingual community, however, it may be more expedient to abandon multilingualism (on economic grounds if no other) in favor of the adoption of a single language for indexing and searching. Thus, Russian is the working language in many of the information systems within the CMEA countries, especially systems having an element of internationalism (Sorokin, 1975). The same is true of various systems within the United Nations. For example, in AGRIS, English has been adopted as the carrier language, thereby facilitating consistency throughout the network. On the other hand, it also means that the indexers and searchers at each national center must have a good command of English and of the technical terminology of agriculture in particular. Wellisch (1973) claims that the ability to read English, or even to speak it, does not guarantee that one can effectively index or search an English-language data base. Moreover, as Wolff-Terroine (1976) has pointed out, "International cooperation requires a political and psychological consensus which is difficult to achieve if there is only one working language."

Bilingual or multilingual vocabularies can improve this situation. If a bilingual thesaurus exists in machine-readable form, a national center can index and search in its own language and still prepare input that is completely compatible with the needs of the parent system. The thesaurus of the International Nuclear Information System, for example, exists in French and Russian (Semenov et al., 1975), as well as in English.

For international operations, a strong case can be made for the adoption of a "neutral" language. Classification schemes, such as the *UDC*, satisfy this requirement since the class numbers in such a vocabulary are not dependent on language. The *UDC* has great advantages; namely, it exists in several languages and is used in many countries. Nevertheless, its use within the United States, still the world's largest producer of scientific and technical information, is insignificant.

Lloyd (1969, 1972), recognizing that information services in an international network would be reluctant to abandon vocabularies already in use, once urged that the *UDC* be adopted as a standard switching language (in effect, an intermediate lexicon) with which each existing vocabulary could be reconciled. Use of the *UDC* for this purpose has not found favor, partly because of wide dissatisfaction with the somewhat uncontrolled procedures by which this tool is updated. In fact, the development of the Broad System of Ordering can be considered a deliberate rejection of the *UDC* as an international switching device.

Classification schemes can provide multilingual pointers to the subject matter of documents. Of course, they do not provide a detailed level of access to the content of these documents. A different type of neutral language is the "constructed language," such as Esperanto. If adopted worldwide as the language of primary and secondary scientific publishing, there is no doubt that a constructed language could greatly simplify the international exchange of information. There has been some recent evidence of renewed interest in such artificial languages, and Frank et al. (1977) have presented cogent arguments in favor of their use in international documentation activities. Nevertheless, worldwide interest in this approach seems, at best, lukewarm, partly because an artificial language will tend to be biased toward a particular group of languages (e.g., those derived primarily from Latin) rather than being truly universal.

It must be reemphasized that the intermediate lexicon approach, if it works at all, is equally applicable in a multilingual environment. To reconcile six controlled vocabularies with an intermediate switching language may be only marginally more difficult if these vocabularies involve the use of, say, four national languages than if all six use a single language.

21 *Automatic Approaches to Thesaurus Construction*

A considerable amount of research has been performed over the past 25 years on fully automatic approaches to the operation of information systems. Presumably, the long-term objective is the implementation of large systems in which human intellectual processing is virtually eliminated and both documents and queries are processed by the computer. Queries can be posed to the system in phrase or sentence form (e.g., "irrigation using very hot water pumped from subterranean sources"), and the search procedures will identify those documents that match the query above some predetermined level. Such systems would retrieve items in ranked order, those matching the query most closely being displayed first. Research has been performed in several related areas, including

1. *Automatic extraction (or derivative) indexing.* Given a document in machine-readable form, computer programs can be used to identify words or phrases likely to be good indicators of content. These are stored in the form of a searchable representation of the document.

Extraction criteria are generally "statistical," that is, words or phrases that occur most frequently in the document (or, alternatively, occur more frequently than "expected" probabilistically) are selected. Other criteria (e.g., word position) can be used to supplement word frequency.

2. *Automatic assignment indexing.* This is similar to extraction indexing, but the words/phrases extracted are matched against word/phrase "profiles" associated with a limited set of index terms. An index term is assigned to the document when its profile matches the extracted terms above some threshold.

3. *Automatic abstracting.* Sentences containing a concentration of good content-indicating words (as defined in item 1 above) are extracted and printed out in sequence to form an abstract (strictly speaking, an "extract").

4. *Document/query pattern matching.* Full or partial document text is stored and processed in various ways to optimize subsequent search procedures. The query, in phrase or sentence form, is processed in the same way and matched against the document file. Each document receives a numerical score that reflects the extent to which it matches the query. The major system of this type is SMART, described by Salton (1971).

5. *Automatic "elaboration" of search terms.* Terms entered by a searcher, or derived from a sentence or phrase entered, are expanded on through various statistical procedures to give an enlarged set of terms that may yield better search results.

Experiments performed in these various areas, although important to the field of information retrieval, are somewhat tangential to the subject of vocabulary control. Much of the research has already been well reviewed, most notably by Stevens (1980) and Sparck Jones (1974).

There is one aspect, however, that is more highly relevant to the subject of vocabulary control: namely, automatic approaches to thesaurus construction. Systems such as SMART, which operate on the natural language of documents and requests, should achieve improved performance if equipped with an internal thesaurus consisting of groups of "related" words or phrases. Computer processing can be used to derive such a tool. The thesaurus produced in this way is quite unlike those constructed by humans; it more closely resembles a thesaurus of the Roget type. Nevertheless, however unlike the human product, the computer-generated thesaurus is justifiable if it can significantly improve performance in fully automatic systems.

Groups of related terms can be formed automatically on the basis of term co-occurrence in documents. The assumption is that the more frequently terms occur together in documents within a particular subject field, the more likely it is that their meanings are related. From a word/word matrix showing co-occurrence strengths for each word pair derived from a corpus of text, various types of word clusters can be derived (Salton, 1975):

1. *Clique.* A group of words in which each member co-occurs strongly with all others:

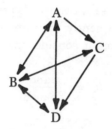

2. *String.* A chain of words in which each link is formed by a pair of highly associated words:

$$A \rightarrow D \rightarrow G \rightarrow L \rightarrow P \rightarrow Y$$

3. *Star formation.* A group of words that all tend to co-occur with a particular word ("star"):

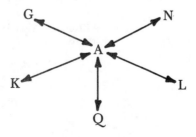

4. *Clump*. A group of words that tend to "adhere":

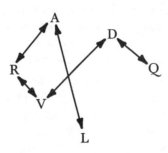

Various criteria can be used to define the boundaries of a clump. In general, however, each word is associated with the others as a group above some given threshold.

The formation of word classes is likely to be based on more than simple co-occurrence. Instead, two words are considered to be related if they co-occur more frequently than one expects them to co-occur probabilistically. For example, consider the equation

$$R \ = \ \frac{a \text{ and } b}{a \text{ or } b}$$

where R is a numerical value for "relatedness" of word a and word b, "a and b" is the number of documents in which a and b co-occur, and "a or b" is the number of documents in which either a or b or both occur. When R exceeds some preset value, the two words are considered to be related.

The classes formed by statistical procedures will be much less pure than those of a conventional thesaurus. A group of words that strongly co-occur may include genus/species, part/whole, and syntagmatic relationships, as in the following example:

WING	AERODYNAMICS
AIRFOIL	FLOW
DELTA	
TAIL	
FLUTTER	

The purity of the class is not the main issue. What is important is whether the class is potentially useful in retrieval. For example, is it likely that the hypothetical class of words identified above, if automatically substituted for any one of its members, would improve search results? Depending on the particular query, it seems likely that this type of substitution might improve recall. At the same time, it might cause a severe decline in precision, especially if the class (as in the example) is a very heterogeneous ensemble of terms.

Salton and McGill (1983) give examples of thesaurus entries automatically derived from a document collection in engineering (Exhibit 56). With such a thesaurus, the query "cryogenic properties of *x*" could be expanded to "*x* in relation to concept 415." As a result, items on the superconductivity of *x* might be retrieved.

Relationships among terms can be established on the basis of criteria other than direct co-occurrence. For example, two words may each co-occur strongly with a third but almost never with each other:

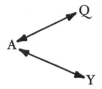

In this case, it is highly likely that Q and Y are synonymous since synonyms tend not to co-occur. If A is "wing," Q might be "triangular" and Y might be "delta." Work has been done on the automatic recognition of synonyms by word co-occurrence (see, e.g., Libove, 1968).

Thus far it has been assumed that thesaurus entries (of the type illustrated in Exhibit 56) are derived from a corpus of text, are stored, and can be pulled into a strategy when a searcher elects this course of action. A somewhat different approach has been described by Doszkocs (1978) and Doszkocs and Rapp (1979): Terms related to those used in a query are identified only when the query has been processed against the data base. The raw material worked with is the set of words (terms) associated with the documents retrieved. Thus,

408	DISLOCATION	413	CAPACITANCE
	JUNCTION		IMPEDANCE-MATCHING
	MINORITY-CARRIER		IMPEDANCE
	N-P-N		INDUCTANCE
	P-N-P		MUTUAL-IMPEDANCE
	POINT-CONTACT		MUTUAL-INDUCTANCE
	RECOMBINE		MUTUAL
	TRANSITION		NEGATIVE-RESISTANCE
	UNIJUNCTION		POSITIVE-GAP
			REACTANCE
409	BLAST-COOLED		RESIST
	HEAT-FLOW		SELF-IMPEDANCE
	HEAT-TRANSFER		SELF-INDUCTANCE
			SELF
410	ANNEAL		
	STRAIN	414	ANTENNA
			KLYSTRON
411	COERCIVE		PULSES-PER-BEAM
	DEMAGNETIZE		RECEIVER
	FLUX-LEAKAGE		SIGNAL-TO-RECEIVER
	HYSTERESIS		TRANSMITTER
	INDUCT		WAVEGUIDE
	INSENSITIVE		
	MAGNETORESISTANCE	415	CRYOGENIC
	SQUARE-LOOP		CRYOTRON
	THRESHOLD		PERSISTENT-CURRENT
			SUPERCONDUCT
412	LONGITUDINAL		SUPER-CONDUCT
	TRANSVERSE		
		416	RELAY

Exhibit 56   Example of thesaurus entries derived by automatic methods. Reprinted from Salton and McGill, *Introduction to Modern Information Retrieval,* 1983, by permission of the McGraw-Hill Book Company.

in items retrieved on terms A, B, and C, terms R and T may also occur frequently and may be useful in the expansion of the search. Terms R and T are not considered significant, however, unless they occur in the retrieved set more frequently than expected. Thus, frequency of occurrence of a term in the data base as a whole is also taken into account. For example, a library science data base may yield 85 abstracts on the query "collection" *and* "evaluation." The word "library" occurs in 59 of these but is not considered significant because its rate of occurrence in the retrieved set (59/85) does not exceed its occurrence rate in the data base as a whole. On the other hand, the word "delivery" might be judged to be significantly associated with "collection" and "evaluation": Even though it occurs in only 8 of the 85 abstracts, its rate of occurrence (8/85) greatly exceeds its rate of occurrence in the data base as a whole.

A major advantage of the Doszkocs approach is that it does not require the a priori calculation of term associations, a daunting proposition for a very large data base. The ability to derive useful term associations a posteriori (after the query has been processed against the data base), which requires much less machine processing, promises to make automatic search optimization procedures viable within very large operating information systems.

22 *Some Cost-effectiveness Aspects of Vocabulary Control*

It can be costly to construct and maintain a large controlled vocabulary. This makes it necessary to consider the cost-effectiveness of vocabulary control in information retrieval and dissemination systems.

Cost-effectiveness analysis is applicable to the design and application of index languages, but it is difficult to apply and the results are more difficult to express in tangible terms than they are in many other applications. One can improve the cost-effectiveness of an index language by altering the language in such a way that system costs are reduced while the present level of search effectiveness is maintained or by making changes that improve search effectiveness with no measurable increase in overall system costs.

The more sophisticated the vocabulary, the more expensive its application and maintenance. An important economic consideration is vocabulary size. Generally speaking, the more terms in the vocabulary, the greater the number of document classes that can be uniquely defined, the greater the specificity of the vocabulary, and the greater the precision capabilities of the system. A large, highly specific controlled vocabulary, however, will tend to be costly to develop, costly to apply, and costly to update. A highly specific vocabulary will change much more frequently than one with relatively broad terms. Most changes will occur at relatively low levels in term hierarchies, particularly to accommodate new concepts. The specificity of the vocabulary must be related directly to the specificity of the requests made to the system. It is certainly uneconomical and inefficient to develop and use a vocabulary considerably more specific than the level of specificity required by the demands placed on the system. Thus, there is a strong economic necessity for conducting a careful analysis of representative requests at the stage of system design. In considering vocabulary specificity, one must, of course, make allowances for data base growth and its effect on the average number of citations retrieved per search. A precision of 20 percent may be tolerable when the average search output is 12 citations, but it may be completely intolerable when the average output is 125 citations.

A related consideration is the need for additional precision devices such as links, role indicators, subheadings, and term weighting. These devices are intended to improve system precision by reducing the number of unwanted items retrieved in a search as a result of false coordinations, incorrect term relationships, or highly exhaustive indexing. They are usually costly to apply. Role indicators, in particular, are likely to add substantially to indexing costs and search formulating costs, and they may add to actual search processing costs. The productivity of indexers (i.e., the average number of items indexed per day) is likely to be reduced considerably in a system using links and roles.

Because they increase the specificity of the vocabulary, such syntactic devices as role indicators almost invariably cause reduced consistency of indexing and frequently have a devastating effect on recall. Subheadings, which may function simultaneously as links and roles, also add to indexing costs and reduce indexer consistency, although they tend to have a less-drastic effect than the use of role indicators. From a cost-effectiveness standpoint, it may be preferable to use an indexing scheme without syntax (thereby saving indexing and searching time), to allow some incorrect term relations to occur, and to put up with the extra irrelevant citations thus retrieved.

A very important but usually neglected component of an index language is the entry vocabulary (i.e., a vocabulary of natural-language expressions, occurring in documents or requests, that map onto the controlled vocabulary of the system). Generally, the entry vocabulary will consist of terms that, for indexing and retrieval purposes, are either considered synonymous with controlled-vocabulary terms or are more specific than controlled-vocabulary terms (e.g., HELIARC WELDING *use* SHIELDED ARC WELDING). Although an extensive entry vocabulary may be relatively expensive to construct and update, it can significantly improve performance (by reducing recall failures), particularly of large retrieval systems. It can also have considerable long-term benefits to the cost-effectiveness of the system by reducing the intellectual burden on indexers and searchers. An entry vocabulary is really a collection of records of intellectual decisions made by indexers. Unless a decision (topic X index under term Y) is recorded, it will have to be made again (not necessarily with the same mapping results—hence, inconsistency) by other indexers or by the same indexer at a later date. Moreover, the system searchers will also have to make intellectual decisions (not necessarily agreeing with those of the indexers) when they come to search for literature on topic X. The larger the entry vocabulary, the fewer current intellectual decisions need to be made by indexers and searchers (thus reducing indexing and search time), the greater the consistency in indexing, the better the recall of the system, and (possibly) the lower the professional level of the staff needed in the indexing operation.

Index language factors are as relevant to the cost-effectiveness of published indexes as they are to the cost-effectiveness of machine-readable data bases. Again, specificity of the vocabulary must be related to the types of demands placed on the system (i.e., the specificity of searches conducted in the index). Index terms should not be so broad that they accumulate a large heterogeneous collection of citations in each issue of the index, thus making the manual search a tedious, time-consuming process. Because most published indexes do not use post-coordinate principles, it is important that there be sufficient pre-coordination to allow the conduct of reasonably specific, high-precision searches. This can be achieved by pre-coordinate subject headings with subheadings (as in *Index Medicus*); by an index term (entry point) supplemented by a modifying phrase (an articulated index of the *Chemical Abstracts* type); or by specific, tailor-made headings constructed by adherence to a strict citation order (as in the *British Technology Index*). In a printed index, the specificity required in headings is partly determined by the type of document surrogate provided, because, with certain types of indexes, the heading itself acts as a specific content indicator for the document. An index using highly specific headings (such as the *British Technology Index*) may have less need to include abstracts than an index using broader headings. If the heading is broad, the document surrogate must indicate specific content. Without abstracts the user is entirely dependent on the quality of a document title for determining its probable relevance, although some indexes include tracings (i.e., a record of all the index terms assigned to a document) in place of the document abstract.

INPUT VERSUS OUTPUT COSTS

As with other aspects of information retrieval systems, in considering the cost-effectiveness of a controlled vocabulary one must balance input costs against output costs as well as against retrieval effectiveness. Economies in input procedures will almost invariably result in an increased burden on output processes and thus increased output costs. Conversely, greater care in input processing (which usually implies increased input costs) can be expected to improve output efficiency and reduce output costs. Two possible trade-offs relating to vocabulary control are

1. *A carefully controlled and structured index language versus free use of uncontrolled keywords.* The controlled vocabulary requires effort in construction and maintenance and is more expensive to apply in indexing. It takes longer, on the whole, to select terms from a con-

trolled vocabulary, which may involve a lookup operation, than it does to assign keywords freely; moreover, keyword indexing may be done by less-qualified personnel than indexing involving a more sophisticated controlled vocabulary. The controlled vocabulary, however, saves time and effort at output. Natural-language or keyword searching, without the benefit of a controlled vocabulary with classificatory structure, puts increased burden on the searcher, who is virtually obliged to construct a segment of a controlled vocabulary each time he prepares a search strategy (e.g., he must think of all possible ways in which "petrochemical" or "textile industry" could be expressed by keywords or in natural-language text). Likewise, the uncontrolled use of keywords may lead to reduced average search precision and thus may require additional effort and cost in output screening.

2. *A highly specific controlled vocabulary versus a relatively broader controlled vocabulary.* The former is generally more expensive to create, maintain, and apply. The more specific the vocabulary, the more difficult it becomes to achieve indexing consistency and the higher the level of professional personnel needed to apply it. On the other hand, a highly specific vocabulary may allow high search precision and thus save on output screening time. A particular form of specificity is achieved by role or relational indicators, and these comments apply equally to the use of such devices.

These are merely obvious examples of possible trade-offs between input effort and output effort. Other possibilities exist. Exhibit 57 presents a trade-off comparison of two hypothetical information systems. In System A, great care and expense is put into the input operation, with a resulting economy in output effort and costs. In System B, on the other hand, deliberate policies designed to economize on input costs are in effect, with the inevitable result that output effort and costs are increased. System A is not necessarily more efficient than System B or vice versa. The approach taken in System B may be more cost-effective than that taken in System A, if one can show that it achieves an acceptable level of performance for the end user with overall costs less than the costs associated with System A.

System A	System B
Input characteristics	*Input characteristics*
A large, carefully controlled vocabulary.	A small controlled vocabulary supplemented by the free use of keywords.
Indexing of medium exhaustivity (an average of 10 terms per document).	Low exhaustivity of indexing (5 terms per document).
Highly trained indexers at a high salary level.	Less highly trained indexers without college degrees.
An indexing revision process.	No indexing revision.
Average indexer productivity of 40 items per day.	Average indexer productivity of 100–125 items per day.
High input costs.	Low input costs.
Relatively long delay between publication and actual input to system.	Fast throughput.
Output characteristics	*Output characteristics*
Reduced burden on the searcher in preparation of strategies.	Greater burden on the searcher in the preparation of strategies.
High precision of raw output.	Low precision of raw output.
Tolerable recall.	Tolerable recall.
No screening needed.	Screening of raw output needed to raise precision to tolerable level for end user.
Fast response time.	Delayed response.
Relatively low search costs.	Relatively high search costs.

Exhibit 57   Trade-off comparison of two hypothetical information systems.

Many different factors enter into the decision to emphasize the input processes or the output processes of an information system. The most important considerations are probably the following:

1. *Volume of documents indexed and volume of requests processed annually.* In the extreme situation of many documents indexed but comparatively few requests handled, it would be reasonable (all other things being equal) to economize on input costs and place an additional load on output. In the reverse situation—comparatively few documents input but many requests handled—the opposite would be true, and savings would be best effected at the output stage.

2. *Required input speed.* In certain situations it is imperative that documents get into the system as rapidly as possible. This is certainly true, for example, when the information system serves a dissemination (current awareness) function, as in certain intelligence situations. Under these circumstances, it is likely that required speed of input would outweigh other considerations and that indexing economies would be adopted.

3. *Required output speed.* In other situations, rapid and accurate response may be vital (e.g., the case of a poison information center), and no economies at input will be justified if these are likely to result in delayed response or reduced accuracy of output.

4. *By-products.* Under certain conditions, it may be possible to obtain a searchable data base very inexpensively. For example, one may be able to acquire a machine-readable data base, perhaps in natural-language form, that is a by-product of some other operation (e.g., publishing or report preparation) or that has been made available by some other information center. Even though the input format and quality may not be ideally suited to the requirements, if the data base is available at nominal cost, it might be desirable, in terms of cost-effectiveness, to make use of it (possibly with some slight modifications) and to expend greater effort on the searching operation.

Cost-effectiveness analysis may be applied to any of the various subsystems of a complete information system: indexing, index language, searching, and user-system interaction. In the analysis of cost-effectiveness, just as in the evaluation of effectiveness, it is unrealistic and dangerous to consider any one of the subsystems in isolation. All of these components are very closely interrelated, and a significant change in one will almost certainly cause repercussions throughout the system as a whole. One must be aware of this and, in any cost-effectiveness analysis, consider the long-term, indirect effects of any system changes as well as the immediate direct effects. For example, suppose one decides to move away from a carefully controlled, sophisticated index language to something much simpler. One can expect the immediate effects to be

1. A reduction in vocabulary control and maintenance costs
2. A reduction in indexing time
3. Improved throughput time

There will also be some long-term, less-direct effects:

1. The time required to prepare search strategies may increase, resulting in a rise in searching costs.
2. Search precision may be reduced, and an output screening operation may become necessary.
3. If output screening is now needed, the quality of the document surrogates may need to be increased. Perhaps abstracts will be needed where previously unnecessary.

An information system is a complex organism, and one must not expect any change to have only local effects.

There are many possible ways to implement a successful retrieval system. Aesthetically, one may prefer to use a very carefully controlled vocabulary to allow greater search precision and to economize on output screening time and costs. This approach, however, is not necessarily the most cost-effective. It may be possible to operate an effective system much more economically through less-stringent vocabulary control, spending less time on indexing and more effort on the output stages of searching and screening. The Central Intelligence Agency, in a very large intelligence retrieval system, deliberately abandoned careful, complete vocabulary control in favor of uncontrolled keyword indexing (expanded titles) with a very broad subject code and a geographic code superimposed. This approach was much more satisfactory in terms of cost-effectiveness. Although different situations dictate different procedures, there is at present a clear trend toward simplification in information systems.

THE FUTURE

As discussed in Chapter 17, there is an evident move away from conventional controlled vocabularies and toward increasing reliance on natural language in the implementation and exploitation of machine-readable data bases. The main barrier to further abandonment of controlled vocabularies may well be the continued production of printed indexes. It seems virtually impossible to produce a large printed index in a form useful to subscribers without careful control of the headings used. Thus, an organization generating a data base in both printed and machine-readable form may be forced to continue to maintain a thesaurus applied by human indexers. Were the printed product discontinued, both the thesaurus and the indexing could also be jettisoned, since a machine-readable data base in the form of searchable abstracts could be supplemented by a much less-expensive level of indexing, based on a small vocabulary of rather broad terms (see Chapter 18).

Considering the cost-effectiveness of information services as a whole, the development of post-controlled vocabularies (see Chapter 17), independent of particular data bases, has much to commend it. This approach can potentially improve the overall quality of data base searching, as well as reduce the overall costs. For reasons discussed in Lancaster (1982), the next 20 years may bring the gradual replacement of print on paper by electronic access. This could mean the disappearance of data bases that index and abstract the primary literature (Lancaster and Neway [1982]) and the emergence of "filtering" networks that allow current awareness and retrospective searching activities to be performed on the full text of primary literature. Post-controlled vocabularies, of the type discussed in Chapter 17, may be essential components of this type of information-processing environment.

Bibliography

Agricultural Terms. 2nd Edition. Phoenix, Ariz., Oryx, 1978.

Aitchison, J., A. Gomersall, and R. Ireland. *Thesaurofacet: A Thesaurus and Faceted Classification for Engineering and Related Subjects.* Whetstone, England, English Electric Co., 1969.

Aitchison, T. M., A. M. Hall, K. H. Lavelle, and J. M. Tracy. *Comparative Evaluation of Index Languages. Part II. Results.* London, Institution of Electrical Engineers, 1970. (Report R 70/2)

American National Standards Institute. *Guidelines for Thesaurus Structure, Construction and Use.* New York, 1974. (ANSI Z39.19)

American Petroleum Institute. *Thesaurus.* 19th Edition. Washington, D.C., 1982.

Barhydt, G. H., and C. T. Schmidt. *Information Retrieval Thesaurus of Education Terms.* Cleveland, Ohio, Case Western Reserve University, 1968.

Bauer, G. "Zur Methodik des Aufbaus 'Koordinierfahiger' Fachthesauri im Rahmen des Thesaurussystems Chemie." In: *Thesauri fur Mechanisierte Informations Recherchesysteme.* Berlin, Zentralinstitut fur Information und Dokumentation, 1967, pp. 207–209.

Beling, G. "The Use of EDP in Terminological Work." In: *Overcoming the Language Barrier.* [Proceedings of the] Third European Congress on Information Systems and Networks, Luxembourg, 3–6 May 1977. Vol. 1. Munich, Verlag Dokumentation, 1977, pp. 101–121.

Beling, G., and G. Wersig. "The New Concept of an Intermediary Language System for Information Networks." In: *EURIM II: A European Conference on the Application of Research in Information Services and Libraries.* Edited by W. E. Batten. London, Aslib, 1977, pp. 117–121.

Bernier, C. L. "Correlative Indexes, 1. Alphabetical Correlative Indexes." *American Documentation,* 7(4):283–288, October 1956.

Bollman, P., and E. Konrad. "Automatic Association Methods in the Construction of Interlingual Thesauri." In: *EURIM II: A European Conference on the Application of Research in Information Services and Libraries.* Edited by W. E. Batten. London, Aslib, 1977, pp. 152–155.

Bourne, C. P. "Frequency and Impact of Spelling Errors in Bibliographic Data Bases." *Information Processing and Management, 13*(1):1–12, 1977.

British Standards Institution. *Guidelines for the Establishment and Development of Monolingual Thesauri.* London, 1979. (BS 5723)

BSO—Broad System of Ordering: Schedule and Index. The Hague, International Federation for Documentation, 1978.

Bureau Marcel Van Dijk. *Definition of Thesauri Essential Characteristics.* 2 vols. Brussels, 1976.

Butler, M., and T. Brandhorst. "Construction of a Tertiary Data Base: The Case of the Women's Educational Equity Communications Network." *Proceedings of the American Society for Information Science, 17*:174–176, 1980.

Bykova, L. N., and N. B. Muzrukov. "Experience Gained in Establishing a Bilingual Thesaurus for Indexing Documents Relating to Atomic Science and Technology." In: *Handling of Nuclear Information: Proceedings of a Symposium.* Vienna, International Atomic Energy Agency, 1970, pp. 545–555.

Cahn, D. F., and J. J. Herr. *Automatic Database Mapping and Translation Methods.* Berkeley, University of California, Lawrence Berkeley Laboratory, 1978. (LBL-6782)

Caless, T. W. "Subject Analysis Matrices for Classification with UDC." In: *Proceedings of the First Seminar on UDC in a Mechanized Retrieval System.* Copenhagen, Danish Centre for Documentation, 1969. (FID/CR Report No. 9)

Chepkasov, A. *INIS: Thesaurus Maintenance System.* Vienna, International Atomic Energy Agency, 1977.

Chernyi, A. I. "Information Retrieval Languages: Types, Design Principles, Compatibility." *Automatic Documentation and Mathematical Linguis-*

tics, *12*(1):1–13, 1978. [Translation of *Nauchno-tekhnicheskaya informa-tsiya, Seriya 2, 12*(1):1–10, 1978.]

Cleverdon, C. W. *A Comparative Evaluation of Searching by Controlled Language and Natural Language in an Experimental NASA Data Base.* Frascati, Italy, European Space Agency, 1977.

Cleverdon C. W., J. Mills, and M. Keen. *Factors Determining the Performance of Index Languages.* 3 vols. Cranfield, England, College of Aeronautics, 1966.

Coates, E. J. *Subject Catalogues: Headings and Structure.* London, Library Assn., 1960.

――――. "Switching Languages for Indexing." *Journal of Documentation, 26*(2):102–110, June 1970.

――――. "The Broad System of Ordering." *International Forum on Information and Documentation, 4*(3):3–6, July 1979.

――――. "The Broad System of Ordering." *International Forum on Information and Documentation, 6*(1):24–30, January 1981.

Colbach, R. "Thesaurus Structure and Generic Posting." In: *Handling of Nuclear Information: Proceedings of a Symposium.* Vienna, International Atomic Energy Agency, 1970, pp. 585–595.

Cook, K. H., et al. *Large Scale Information Processing Systems.* 6 vols. Syracuse, N.Y., Syracuse University, School of Library Science, 1971. (Final Report to the Rome Air Development Center)

Dahlberg, I. "The Broad System of Ordering (BSO) as a Basis for an Integrated Social Sciences Thesaurus?" *International Classification, 7*(2):66–72, 1980.

――――. "Conceptual Definitions for INTERCONCEPT." *International Classification, 8*(1):16–22, 1981a.

――――. "Toward Establishment of Compatibility Between Indexing Languages." *International Classification, 8*(2):86–91, 1981b.

Datatrol Corporation. *Common Vocabulary Approaches for Government Scientific and Technical Information Systems.* Silver Spring, Md., 1963.

De Besse, B. "Multilingual Terminology." In: *Overcoming the Language Barrier.* [Proceedings of the] Third European Congress on Information Systems and Networks, Luxembourg, 3–6 May 1977. Vol. 2. Munich, Verlag Dokumentation, 1977, pp. 129–134.

Dextre, S. G., and T. M. Clarke. "A System for Machine-Aided Thesaurus Construction." *Aslib Proceedings, 33*(3):102–112, March 1981.

Diener, R. A. V., and M. L. Tsuffis. "A Method for Evaluating the Feasibility of the Intermediate Lexicon Concept for Existing Information Retrieval Systems." *Proceedings of the American Society for Information Science,*

14:28, 1977. (Full paper on microfiche.)

Doszkocs, T. E. "AID, an Associative Interactive Dictionary for Online Searching." *Online Review, 2*(2):163–173, June 1978.

Doszkocs, T. E., and B. A. Rapp. "Searching MEDLINE in English: A Prototype User Interface with Natural Language Query, Ranked Output, and Relevance Feedback." *Proceedings of the American Society for Information Science, 15*:131–139, 1979.

Ducrot, J. M. "The TITUS II System." *NEWSIDIC*, April 1974, pp. 4–6.

Dym, E. D. "A New Approach to the Development of a Technical Thesaurus." *Proceedings of the American Documentation Institute, 4*:126–131, 1967.

Engineers Joint Council. *Rules for Preparing and Updating Engineering Thesauri.* New York, 1965.

EURATOM Thesaurus. 2nd Edition. Brussels, European Atomic Energy Community, 1966–1967.

Fangmeyer, H. *Semi-Automatic Indexing: State of the Art.* Neuilly sur Seine, North Atlantic Treaty Organization, Advisory Group for Research and Development, 1974.

Felber, H. "International Efforts to Overcome Difficulties in Technical Communication." In: *Overcoming the Language Barrier.* [Proceedings of the] Third European Congress on Information Systems and Networks, Luxembourg, 3–6 May 1977. Vol. 1. Munich, Verlag Dokumentation, 1977, pp. 86–99.

―――. "A Plan for Data Management Within Termnet." In: *Terminological Data Banks.* Munich, K. G. Saur, 1980, pp. 190–196. (Infoterm series 5)

―――. *A Study of Terminological Data Elements on the Basis of the General Theory of Terminology and a Comparative Study of Those Data Elements Used in Terminological Data Banks All Over the World.* Vienna, Infoterm, 1981. (Draft)

Felber, H., C. Galinski, and W. Nedofity. "Ten Years of Infoterm, a Report on Activities and Achievements." In: *Terminologies for the Eighties.* Munich, K. G. Saur, 1982, pp. 19–95. (Infoterm series 7)

Foskett, A. C. "The Broad System of Ordering: Old Wine into New Bottles?" *International Forum on Information and Documentation, 4*(3):7–12, July 1979.

―――. *The Subject Approach to Information.* 4th Edition. London, Bingley, 1982.

Frank, H., R. Hilgers, and I. Meyer. "Documentation in a Constructed Language and Man-Machine Communication." In: *Overcoming the Language Barrier.* [Proceedings of the] Third European Congress on Information

Systems and Networks, Luxembourg, 3–6 May 1977. Vol. 1. Munich, Verlag Dokumentation, 1977, pp. 33–37.

Gaaze-Rapoport, M. G. "A Unified System of Information Languages: Dreams and Some Problems." *Automatic Documentation and Mathematical Linguistics, 12*(1):5–48, 1978. [Translation of *Nauchno-tekhnicheskaya informatsiya, Seriya 2, 12*(1):32–34, 1978.]

Gardin, N. "Intermediate Lexicon: A New Step Toward International Cooperation in Scientific and Technical Information." *UNESCO Bulletin for Libraries, 23*(2):58–63, April 1969.

Gerd, A. S. "Associative Relations in an Information Retrieval Thesaurus and Ways to Identify Them." *Automatic Documentation and Mathematical Linguistics, 14*(3):25–30, 1980. [Translation of *Nauchno-tekhnicheskaya informatsiya, Seriya 2, 14*(5):14–16, 1980.]

Gibb, J. M., and E. Phillips. "Scientific and Technical Publishing in a Multilingual Society." In: *Overcoming the Language Barrier.* [Proceedings of the] Third European Congress on Information Systems and Networks, Luxembourg, 3–6 May 1977. Vol. 1. Munich, Verlag Dokumentation, 1977, pp. 13–27.

Giertz, L. M. "The SFB System: Case Study on an Information System for Global Cooperation in the Field of Buildings Construction." In: *Ordering Systems for Global Information Networks.* Edited by A. Neelameghan. Bangalore, India, International Federation for Documentation, 1979, pp. 349–355.

Glushkov, V. M., E. F. Skorokhod'ko, and A. A. Strognii. "Evaluation of the Degree of Compatibility of Information Retrieval Languages of Document Retrieval Systems." *Automatic Documentation and Mathematical Linguistics, 12*(1):18–26, 1978. [Translation of *Nauchno-tekhnicheskaya informatsiya, Seriya 2, 12*(1):14–19, 1978.]

Goetschalckx, J. "Terminological Activities in the European Institutions with Special Reference to Eurodicautom." In: *Overcoming the Language Barrier.* [Proceedings of the] Third European Congress on Information Systems and Networks, Luxembourg, 3–6 May 1977. Vol. 1. Munich, Verlag Dokumentation, 1977a, pp. 123–152.

————. "Automatic Translation." In: *Overcoming the Language Barrier.* [Proceedings of the] Third European Congress on Information Systems and Networks, Luxembourg, 3–6 May 1977. Vol. 2. Munich, Verlag Dokumentation, 1977b, pp. 142–146.

Gopinath, M. A., and K. N. Prasad. "Compatibility of the Principles for Design of Thesaurus and Classification Scheme." *Library Science with a Slant to Documentation, 13*(2):56–66, June 1976.

Hammond, W. "Satellite Thesaurus Construction." In: *The Thesaurus in Action: Background Information for a Thesaurus Workshop at the 32nd Annual Convention of the American Society for Information Science.* San Francisco, Calif., American Society for Information Science, 1969, pp. 14–20. (AD 694 590)

———. "Statistical Association Methods for Simultaneous Searching of Multiple Document Collections." In: *Statistical Association Methods for Mechanized Documentation: Symposium Proceedings.* Edited by M. E. Stevens, V. E. Giuliano, and L. B. Heilprin. Washington, D.C., National Bureau of Standards, 1965, pp. 237–243. (NBS Miscellaneous Publication 269)

Hammond, W., and S. Rosenborg. *Experimental Study of Convertibility Between Large Technical Indexing Vocabularies.* Silver Spring, Md., Datatrol Corp., 1962.

———. *Indexing Terms of Announcement Publications for Government Scientific and Technical Research Reports: A Composite Vocabulary.* 2 vols. Silver Spring, Md., Datatrol Corp., 1964.

Holm, B. E., and L. E. Rasmussen. "Development of a Technical Thesaurus." *American Documentation,* 12(3):184–190, July 1961.

Holst, W. "Problemer ved Strukturering og Bruk av den Polytekniske Tesaurus." *Tidskrift för Dokumentation,* 22(5):69–74, 1966.

Horsnell, V. "The Intermediate Lexicon: An Aid to International Cooperation." *Aslib Proceedings,* 27(2):57–66, February 1975.

———. *Intermediate Lexicon for Information Science: A Feasibility Study.* London, Polytechnic of North London, School of Librarianship, 1974.

Horsnell, V., and A. Merrett. *Intermediate Lexicon Research Project. Phase 2.* London, Polytechnic of North London, School of Librarianship, 1978.

Hulme, E. W. "Principles of Book Classification." *Library Association Record,* 13:354–358, October 1911; 389–394, November 1911; 444–449, December 1911.

———. *Statistical Bibliography in Relation to the Growth of Modern Civilization.* London, Grafton, 1923.

Iljon, A. "Creation of Thesauri for EURONET." In: *Overcoming the Language Barrier.* [Proceedings of the] Third European Congress on Information Systems and Networks, Luxembourg, 3–6 May 1977, Vol. 1. Munich, Verlag Dokumentation, 1977a, pp. 417–437.

———. "Scientific and Technical Data Bases in a Multilingual Society." In: *Overcoming the Language Barrier.* [Proceedings of the] Third European Congress on Information Systems and Networks, Luxembourg, 3–6 May 1977. Vol. 1. Munich, Verlag Dokumentation, 1977b, pp. 28–32.

International Organization for Standardization. *Guidelines for the Establish-*

ment and Development of Monolingual Thesauri. Geneva, 1974. (ISO 2788)

International Organization for Standardization. *Guidelines for the Establishment and Development of Multilingual Thesauri.* Geneva, 1985. (ISO 5964)

Jaster, J. *Subsumption Scheme for Dictionary of Indexing Equivalents.* Silver Spring, Md., Datatrol Corp., 1963.

Jones, K. P. "Problems Associated With the Use of Gompound Words in Thesauri With Special Reference to BS 5723: 1979." *Journal of Documentation, 37*(2):53–68, June 1981.

Juhasz, S., et al. "AKWAS." *Mechanical Engineering, 102*(7):34–39, July 1980.

King, M., and S. Perschke. "EUROTRA and Its Objectives." *Multilingua, 1*(1):27–32, 1982.

Kirtland, M., P. Atherton, and S. Harper. "Integrating Borrowed Records Into a Data Base: Impact on Thesaurus Development and Retrieval." *Database, 3*(4):26–33, December 1980.

Knapp, S. D. "BRS/TERM, a Database for Searchers." *Online '83 Conference Proceedings.* Weston, Conn., ONLINE, Inc., 1983, pp. 162–166.

Kochen, M., and R. Tagliacozzo. "A Study of Cross-Referencing." *Journal of Documentation, 24*(3):173–191, September 1968.

Lancaster, F. W. *Evaluation of the MEDLARS Demand Search Service.* Bethesda, Md., National Library of Medicine, 1968.

———. *Information Retrieval Systems: Characteristics, Testing and Evaluation.* 2nd Edition. New York, Wiley, 1979.

———. *Libraries and Librarians in an Age of Electronics.* Arlington, Va., Information Resources Press, 1982.

Lancaster, F. W., and J. M. Neway. "The Future of Indexing and Abstracting Services." *Journal of the American Society for Information Science, 33*(3):183–189, May 1982.

Lancaster, F. W., R. L. Rapport, and J. K. Penry. "Evaluating the Effectiveness of an On-Line Natural Language Retrieval System." *Information Storage and Retrieval, 8*(5):223–245, October 1972.

Lefever, M., B. Freedman, and L. Schultz. "Managing an Uncontrolled Vocabulary Ex Post Facto." *Journal of the American Society for Information Science, 23*(6):339–342, November/December 1972.

Levy, F. "Compatibility Between Classifications and Thesauri: Evaluation of a First Study in the Field of Information Storage and Retrieval." Paper presented at the conference of the International Federation for Documentation, Tokyo, 1967.

Libove, G. A. *Automatic Generation of Synonyms.* Philadelphia, University of Pennsylvania, Moore School of Electrical Engineering, 1968.

Lloyd, G. A. "The UDC in Its International Aspects." *Aslib Proceedings, 21*(5):204–208, May 1969.

———— . "The *Universal Decimal Classification* as an International Switching Language." In: *Subject Retrieval in the Seventies: New Directions.* Edited by H. H. Wellisch and T. D. Wilson. Westport, Conn., Greenwood, 1972, pp. 116–125.

Louzada, V. L. D. "Construção de Thesauri: Experimento Empírico para a Coleta de Termos em Formação Profissional." Master's dissertation. Rio de Janeiro, Instituto Brasileiro de Informação em Ciência e Tecnologia, 1979.

Mandersloot, W. G. B., E. M. B. Douglas, and N. Spicer. "Thesaurus Control—The Selection, Grouping and Cross-Referencing of Terms for Inclusion in a Coordinate Index Word List." *Journal of the American Society for Information Science, 21*(1):49–57, January/February 1970.

Markey, K., and P. Atherton. *ONTAP: Online Training and Practice Manual for ERIC Data Base Searchers.* Syracuse, N.Y., Syracuse University, ERIC Clearinghouse on Information Resources, 1978. (ED 160 109)

Metallurgy Thesaurus. Luxembourg, System of Documentation and Information for Metallurgy of the European Communities, 1974.

Michel, J. Personal communication. Paris, May 1982.

Morton, S. E. "Designing a Multilingual Terminology Data Bank for United States Translators." *Journal of the American Society for Information Science, 29*(6):297–303, November 1978.

Muench, E. V. "A Computerized English Correlation Index to Five Biomedical Library Classification Schemes Based on *MeSH.*" *Bulletin of the Medical Library Association, 59*(3):404–411, July 1971.

Narin, F., and M. P. Carpenter. "National Publication and Citation Comparisons." *Journal of the American Society for Information Science, 26*(2):80–93, March/April 1975.

Neelameghan, A. "Absolute Syntax and Structure of an Indexing and Switching Language." In: *Ordering Systems for Global Information Networks.* Edited by A. Neelameghan. Bangalore, India, International Federation for Documentation, 1979, pp. 165–176.

Neicu, S. D. "Languages, Thesauri, Standardization." *Probleme de Informare şi Documentare, 9*(6):348–364, 1975.

Neville, H. H. "Feasibility Study of a Scheme for Reconciling Thesauri Covering a Common Subject." *Journal of Documentation, 26*(4):313–336, December 1970.

Niehoff, R. T. "Development of an Integrated Energy Vocabulary and the Possibility for On-line Subject Switching." *Journal of the American Society for Information Science, 27*(1):3–17, January/February 1976.

———— . "The Optimization and Use of Automated Subject Switching for

Better Retrieval." *Proceedings of the American Society for Information Science,* *17*:397–400, 1980.

Niehoff, R. T., et al. *The Design and Evaluation of a Vocabulary Switching System for Use in Multi-base Search Environments.* Columbus, Ohio, Battelle Columbus Laboratories, 1980.

Niehoff, R. T., S. Kwasny, and M. Wessells. "Overcoming the Data Base Vocabulary Barrier—A Solution." *Online, 3*(4):43–54, October 1979.

Niehoff, R. T., and G. Mack. *Final Report on Evaluation of the Vocabulary Switching System.* Columbus, Ohio, Battelle Columbus Laboratories, 1984.

Overcoming the Language Barrier. [Proceedings of the] Third European Congress on Information Systems and Networks, Luxembourg, 3–6 May 1977. Munich, Verlag Dokumentation, 1977. 2 vols.

Painter, A. F. *An Analysis of Duplication and Consistency of Subject Indexing Involved in Report Handling at the Office of Technical Services, U.S. Department of Commerce.* New Brunswick, N.J., Rutgers—The State University, 1963. (PB 181501)

Papier, L. S., and E. H. Cortelyou. "Use of a Technical Word Association Test in the Preparation of a Thesaurus." *Journal of Documentation, 18*(4):183–187, December 1962.

Paré, M. "Les Banques Automatisées de Terminologies Multilingues et les Organismes de Normalisation." In: *International Cooperation in Technology: First Infoterm Symposium.* Munich, Verlag Dokumentation, 1976, pp. 224–233.

Perez, E. "Text Enhancement: Controlled Vocabulary vs. Free Text." *Special Libraries, 73*(3):183–192, July 1982.

Perreault, J. M. "Some Problems in the BSO." *International Forum on Information and Documentation, 4*(3):16–20, July 1979.

Perry, J. W., and A. Kent. *Tools for Machine Literature Searching.* New York, Interscience Publishers, 1958.

Pershikov, V. F. "The Facet-Block Principle in Designing an IRL for an Automated IRS." *Automatic Documentation and Mathematical Linguistics, 11*(4):20–27, 1977. [Translation of *Nauchno-tekhnicheskaya informatsiya, Seriya 2, 11*(10):15–20, 1977.]

Pickford, A. G. A. "An Objective Method for the Generation of an Information Retrieval Language." *Information Scientist, 2*(1):17–37, March 1968.

Pigur, V. A. "The Linguistic Basis for the Construction of Multilingual Thesauruses: Selecting Equivalents." *Automatic Documentation and Mathematical Linguistics, 13*(6):19–31, 1979. [Translation of *Nauchno-tekhnicheskaya informatsiya, Seriya 2, 13*(11):11–18, 1979.]

Plante, S., C. Gruson, and M. Wolff-Terroine. "Le Macrothesaurus des Sciences et Techniques." *Documentaliste, 14*(1):20–26, 1977.

Price, D. J. de Solla. *Little Science, Big Science.* New York, Columbia University Press, 1963.

Reisner, P. *Evaluation of a "Growing" Thesaurus.* Yorktown Heights, N.Y., IBM, Thomas Watson Research Center, 1966.

Riggs, F. W. "A New Paradigm for Social Science Terminology." *International Classification, 6*(3):150–158, 1979.

Rolling, L. "Graphic Display Devices in Thesaurus Construction and Use." *Aslib Proceedings, 23*(11):591–594, November 1971.

———. "Computer Management of Multi-lingual Thesauri." In: *Ordering Systems for Global Information Networks.* Edited by A. Neelameghan. Bangalore, India, International Federation for Documentation, 1979, pp. 382–388.

———. "The Second Birth of Machine Translation: A Timely Event for Data Base Suppliers and Users." *Electronic Publishing Review, 1*(3):211–216, September 1981.

ROOT Thesaurus. London, British Standards Institution, 1981.

Sager, J. C., H. L. Somers, and J. McNaught. "Thesaurus Integration in the Social Sciences. Part 1. Comparison of Thesauri." *International Classification, 8*(3):133–138, 1981.

Salisbury, B. A., Jr., and H. E. Stiles. "The Use of the β-Coefficient in Information Retrieval." *Proceedings of the American Society for Information Science, 6*:265–268, 1969.

Salton, G. "Automatic Processing of Foreign Language Documents." *Journal of the American Society for Information Science, 21*(3):187–194, May/June 1970.

———. *Dynamic Information and Library Processing.* Englewood Cliffs, N.J., Prentice-Hall, 1975.

——— (ed). *The SMART Retrieval System: Experiments in Automatic Document Processing.* Englewood Cliffs, N.J., Prentice Hall, 1971.

Salton, G., and M. J. McGill. *Introduction to Modern Information Retrieval.* New York, McGraw-Hill, 1983.

Schuck, H. J. "Linguistic Aspects in the Translation of Thesauri." In: *Overcoming the Language Barrier.* [Proceedings of the] Third European Congress on Information Systems and Networks, Luxembourg, 3–6 May 1977. Vol. 1. Munich, Verlag Dokumentation, 1977, pp. 447–462.

Schulz, J. "A Terminology Data Bank for Translators: Methods of Interrogation in the TEAM System." In: *Overcoming the Language Barrier.* [Proceedings of the] Third European Congress on Information Systems and

Networks, Luxembourg, 3–6 May 1977. Vol. 1. Munich, Verlag Doku-mentation, 1977, pp. 153–188.

Semenov, V. F., et al. "Creation of a Bilingual Thesaurus for Indexing Documents and Inquiries in the Field of Nuclear Science and Technolo-gy." In: *Information Systems: Their Interconnection and Compatibility.* Vienna, International Atomic Energy Agency, 1975, pp. 167–174.

Semturs, F. "STAIRS/TLS—A System for 'Free Text' and 'Descriptor' Searching." *Proceedings of the American Society for Information Science. 15*:295–298, 1978.

Sharp, J. R. "The SLIC Index." *American Documentation, 17*(1):41–44, Janu-ary 1966.

Shemakin, Yu. I., and A. N. Kulik. "Compatibility of Information Retrieval Systems and the Function of a Polytechnical Thesaurus in a Unified In-formation Network." *Automatic Documentation and Mathematical Linguis-tics, 4*(3):35–41, 1970. [Translation of *Nauchno-tekhnicheskaya informa-tsiya, Seriya 2, 8*:30–34, 1970.]

Shumway, R. H. "Some Estimation Problems Associated with Evaluating Information Retrieval Systems." In: *Evaluation of Document Retrieval Sys-tems: Literature Perspective, Measurement, Technical Papers.* Bethesda, Md., Westat Research, Inc., 1968, pp. 78–96.

Smith, L. C. "Systematic Searching of Abstracts and Indexes in Interdis-ciplinary Areas." *Journal of the American Society for Information Science, 25*(6):343–353, November/December 1974.

Snow, D. C. "Development and Monitoring of Indexing Systems: Evalua-tion of Term Lists by Comparison with a Sample of Claims in New Patent Applications." Paper presented at the Annual Meeting of ICIRE-PAT (International Cooperation in Information Retrieval Among Exam-ining Patent Offices), London, September 1965.

Soergel, D. "A General Model for Indexing Languages: The Basis for Com-patibility and Integration." In: *Subject Retrieval in the Seventies: New Di-rections.* Edited by H. Wellisch and T. D. Wilson. Westport, Conn., Greenwood, 1972, pp. 36–61.

———. *Indexing Languages and Thesauri: Construction and Maintenance.* Los Angeles, Calif., Melville, 1974.

———. "The Broad System of Ordering: A Critique." *International Forum on Information and Documentation, 4*(3):21–24, July 1979.

Sokolov, A. V. "A Way to Ensure Thesaurus Compatibility." *Automatic Documentation and Mathematical Linguistics, 11*(1):22–30, 1977. [Transla-tion of *Nauchno-tekhnicheskaya informatsiya, Seriya 2, 11*(1):19–24, 1977.]

Sokolov, A. V., I. A. Mankevich, and A. P. Fedotova. "An Experiment in

the Development of Compatible Specialized Information-Retrieval Thesauri." *Automatic Documentation and Mathematical Linguistics, 12*(4):8–19,
1978. [Translation of *Nauchno-tekhnicheskaya informatsiya, Seriya 2,
12*(10):5–12, 1978.]

Somers, H. L. "Observations on Standards and Guidelines Concerning Thesaurus Construction." *International Classification, 8*(2):69–74, 1981.

Sorokin, Yu. N. "Principles Involved in Creating an International Scientific
and Technical Information System for the Member States of the Council
of Mutual Economic Assistance (CMEA)." In: *Information Systems: Their
Interconnection and Compatibility.* Vienna, International Atomic Energy
Agency, 1975, pp. 257–264.

Sparck Jones, K. *Automatic Indexing 1974; A State of the Art Review.* Cambridge, England, University of Cambridge, 1974.

SPINES Thesaurus. Paris, Unesco, 1976.

Stevens, M. E. *Automatic Indexing: A State-of-the-Art Report.* Washington,
D.C., National Bureau of Standards, 1980.

Stiles, H. E. "Machine Retrieval Using the Association Factor." In: *Machine Indexing: Progress and Problems.* Washington, D.C., American University, 1961.

Tancredi, S. A., and O. D. Nichols. "Air Pollution Technical Information
Processing—the Microthesaurus Approach." *American Documentation,
19*(1):66–70, January 1968.

TDCK Circular Thesaurus System. The Hague, Wetenschappelijk en Technisch Documentatie- en Informatiecentrum voor de Krijgsmacht, 1963.

Terminological Data Banks. Munich, K. G. Saur, 1980. (Infoterm Series 5)

Terminologies for the Eighties. Munich, K. G. Saur, 1982. (Infoterm Series 7)

Theoretical and Methodological Problems of Terminology. Munich, K. G. Saur,
1981. (Infoterm Series 6)

Toma, P. P. "SYSTRAN as a Multilingual Machine Translation System." In:
Overcoming the Language Barrier. [Proceedings of the] Third European
Congress on Information Systems and Networks, Luxembourg, 3–6 May
1977. Vol. 1. Munich, Verlag Dokumentation, 1977, pp. 569–581.

Toman, J., and G. A. Lloyd. "Introduction to the Subject-Field Reference
Code (SRC) or Broad System of Ordering (BSO) for UNISIST Purposes."
In: *Ordering Systems for Global Information Networks.* Edited by A. Neelameghan. Bangalore, India. International Federation for Documentation,
1979, pp. 321–324.

Uhlmann, W. "A Thesaurus *Nuclear Science and Technology:* Principles of
Design." *Teknisk-Vetenskaplig Forskning (TVF), 38*:46–52, 1967.

UNBIS Thesaurus. New York, United Nations, Dag Hammarskjöld Library,

1981. (Publication Sales No. E.81.I.17)

Unesco Thesaurus. Paris, Unesco, 1977.

UNISIST Guidelines for the Establishment and Development of Multilingual Thesauri. Revised Edition. Paris, Unesco, 1980. (PGI-80/WS/12)

UNISIST Guidelines for the Establishment and Development of Monolingual Thesauri. 2nd Edition. Paris, Unesco, 1981. (PGI-81/WS/15)

Union of Soviet Socialist Republics, State Committee for Science and Technology, Interdepartmental Commission on Classification. "Comments on the Broad System of Ordering." *International Forum on Information and Documentation,* 4(3):25–27, July 1979.

Urban Thesaurus. Kent, Ohio, Kent State University, Center for Urban Regionalism, 1968.

Urbandoc Thesaurus. New York, City University of New York, Project URBANDOC, 1967.

U.S. Federal Council for Science and Technology. *COSATI Subject Category List.* Washington, D.C., 1964. (AD 612200)

Van Dijk, M. "Un Thesaurus Multilingue au Service de la Coopération Internationale." *Bulletin de l'Association Internationale des Documentalistes et Techniciens de l'Information,* 5(4):85–87, 1966.

Van Slype, G. "The Qualitative and Quantitative Characteristics of Monolingual and Multilingual Thesauri." In: *Overcoming the Language Barrier.* [Proceedings of the] Third European Congress on Information Systems and Networks, Luxembourg, 3–6 May 1977. Vol. 1. Munich, Verlag Dokumentation, 1977, pp. 403–415.

––––––. "SYSTRAN: Evaluation of the 1978 Version of the SYSTRAN English-French Automatic System of the Commission of the European Communities." *The Incorporated Linguist,* 18(3):86–89, 1979.

Vasarhelyi, P. "The Relevance of INTERCONCEPT for Classification and Indexing." *International Classification,* 7(1):6–9, 1980.

Vickery, B. C., and I. C. McIlwaine. "Structuring and Switching: A Discussion of the Broad System of Ordering." *International Forum on Information and Documentation,* 4(3):13–15, July 1979.

Viet, J. *Thesaurus: Mass Communication.* Paris, Unesco, 1975.

Vilenskaya, S. K. "Information Retrieval Language Compatibility (the Intermediary Language and the Switching Language)." *Automatic Documentation and Mathematical Linguistics,* 11(2):54–62, 1977. [Translation of *Nauchno-tekhnicheskaya informatsiya, Seriya 2,* 11(5):16–21, 1977.]

Vitukhnovskaya, A. A. "K teorii sovmestimosti informatsionno-poiskovykh tezaurusov." *Nauchnye i tekhnicheskie biblioteki SSSR,* 11:6–14, 1976.

Wadington, J. P. "Unit Concept Coordinate Indexing." *American Documen-*

tation, 9(2):107–113, April 1958.

Wall, E. *Information Retrieval Thesauri.* New York, Engineers Joint Council, 1962.

Wall, E., and J. M. Barnes. *Intersystem Compatibility and Convertibility of Subject Vocabularies.* Philadelphia, Pa., Auerbach, 1969. (Technical Report 1582-100-TR-5)

Wellisch, H. H. "Linguistic and Semantic Problems in the Use of English-Language Information Services in Non-English-Speaking Countries." *International Library Review, 5*(2):147–162, April 1973.

————. "The Broad System of Ordering, or Bishop Wilkins Redivivus: A Review Article." *Library Quarterly, 49*(4):444–452, October 1979.

Wersig, G. "Experiences in Compatibility Research in Documentary Languages." In: *Ordering Systems for Global Information Networks.* Edited by A. Neelameghan. Bangalore, India, International Federation for Documentation, 1979, pp. 423–430.

Willetts, M. "An Investigation of the Nature of the Relation Between Terms in Thesauri." *Journal of Documentation, 31*(3):158–184, September 1975.

Williams, M. E. "Experiences of IIT Research Institute in Operating a Computerized Retrieval System for Searching a Variety of Data Bases." *Information Storage and Retrieval, 8*(2):57–75, April 1972.

Williams, M. E., and S. E. Preece. "Automatic Data Base Selector for Network Use." *Proceedings of the American Society for Information Science, 14*:34, 1977. (Full paper on microfiche.)

Wilson, T. D. *An Introduction to Chain Indexing.* London, Bingley, 1971.

Wolff-Terroine, M. "Multilingual Systems." In: *Second European Congress on Information Systems and Networks.* Munich, Verlag Dokumentation, 1976, pp. 149–158.

————. "A Macrothesaurus. Why? How?" In: *Ordering Systems for Global Information Networks.* Edited by A. Neelameghan. Bangalore, India, International Federation for Documentation, 1979, pp. 431–436.

Zamora, A. "Automatic Detection and Correction of Spelling Errors in a Large Data Base." *Journal of the American Society for Information Science, 31*(1):51–57, 1980.

Index